The Reality Game

A guide to humanistic counselling and psychotherapy

3rd edition

John Rowan

Routledge
Taylor & Francis Group

LONDON AND NEW YORK

Third edition published 2016
by Routledge
2 Park Square, Milton Park, Abingdon, Oxon OX14 4RN

and by Routledge
711 Third Avenue, New York, NY 10017

Routledge is an imprint of the Taylor & Francis Group, an informa business

First published by Routledge, 1983

Second edition published by Routledge, 1998

British Library Cataloguing in Publication Data
A catalogue record for this book is available from the British Library

Library of Congress Cataloging in Publication Data
A catalog record for this book has been requested

ISBN: 978-1-138-85011-8 (hbk)
ISBN: 978-1-138-85012-5 (pbk)
ISBN: 978-1-315-66642-6 (ebk)

Typeset in Times New Roman
by Florence Production Ltd, Stoodleigh, Devon, UK

The Reality Game

In the years since it was first published, *The Reality Game* has become a classic text. For all those training and practising in humanistic and integrative psychotherapy it is an essential guide to good practice, and an excellent introduction to the skills used in individual and group therapy. This new edition has been updated to take into account changes in the field and John Rowan's own work, while still providing guidance on establishing and developing the relationship between counsellor and client, and covering: assessment; the initial interview; the opening session; aims; transference; resistance and supervision.

With the student's needs always at the forefront, this extensively revised new edition responds to the questions most often asked by trainees in these disciplines, and includes discussions of ethics and new chapters on transpersonal psychology, and on dialogical self theory. It will be a must read for psychotherapists and counsellors in practice and training, especially those involved in humanistic and integrative psychotherapy.

John Rowan is a counsellor and psychotherapist, working with both individuals and couples, in private practice in north-east London. He is a Fellow of the British Association for Counselling and Psychotherapy and has an Honorary Fellowship from the UKCP. He is also a Fellow of the British Psychological Society and a founder member of the UK Association of Humanistic Psychology Practitioners. He has written a number of books including *Ordinary Ecstasy*, *Healing the Male Psyche* and *Personification*.

'This incitement to work from the heart is much more than merely a newly packaged edition of Rowan's seminal work. What you have here is a comprehensive and comprehensible integration of many of the most important lines in today's psychotherapy and counselling: the humanistic, the existential, the authentic, the relational and the transpersonal. It will captivate students and trainees as well as more experienced therapists – and, I really think this time, will send out ripples way beyond the humanistic/ existential communities, reaching psychodynamic psychotherapists and counsellors, psychoanalysts and Jungians in many countries.'

– Andrew Samuels, Professor of Analytical Psychology,
University of Essex

'This erudite work, by one of the most senior veterans of the British therapy world, is a must read for all students and practitioners of counselling and psychotherapy. John Rowan presents complex ideas and debates in a straightforward, no-nonsense way that is sophisticated yet accessible. This book will help get new practitioners started on their professional journey and will be a useful refresher for those with many years of experience. Although many of the sometimes problematic issues that Rowan discusses have been around for a couple of generations, he has managed to update much of his thinking, based on a long lifetime of teaching and practice, to give this latest edition a contemporary and vital feel.'

– Keith Silvester, psychosynthesis psychotherapist,
supervisor and trainer based in London,
currently Chair of Training Standards of the
Humanistic & Integrative College of UKCP

Contents

Introduction

This is the third edition of a professional handbook for psychotherapists, counsellors, therapeutic counsellors, counselling psychologists and coaches. As before, it will be particularly useful for those involved in training courses in these areas, both lecturers and students. It tries to do justice to five complementary streams in the field: the Humanistic, the Existential, the Authentic, the Relational and the Transpersonal. So some people have called it a HEART approach. Thus it complements the more common psychoanalytic and cognitive-behavioural texts. It shows that this combined approach is both deeper and broader than most others. It has been completely updated, doing justice to the recent research on the dialogical self, which takes the place of the old idea of subpersonalities, and a new chapter on the transpersonal has been added, since this is an area of greater concern today.

The first thing was that I discovered the theory of the Dialogical Self. This had two effects on me. First, it made me give up the notion of subpersonalities, and adopt instead the notion of I-positions. Second, it clarified once and for all that the notion of the Freudian unconscious was much too clumsy for therapeutic use. As a result I brought out a new book, published in 2010, entitled *Personification: using the dialogical self in psychotherapy and counselling*, which put all this material together. My chapter on using this view of therapy also appeared in the *Handbook of dialogical self theory* (Hermans and Gieser 2012).

Next, Ken Wilber's book *Integral psychology* came out in 2000, and provided all the evidence from research to confirm his theory of psychospiritual development. This was not only useful in itself, but it also confirmed Maslow's hierarchy of needs once and for all, thus making links not only with therapy but also with management theory.

Then I went much further along the path of spiritual development, and became familiar with the Causal and the Nondual realms. I also became much more familiar with using the spiritual realms in the therapeutic field. I started to use this material in psychotherapy, starting in my workshop in the year

2000. My chapter on transpersonal psychotherapy appeared in *The handbook of individual therapy* (Rowan 2014).

Somewhere along the way – no particular event – I became much more aware of the relational movement in psychotherapy, and wrote an article called 'Linking', which was published in 1998. This interest grew and grew, and ended up with a chapter which appeared in the book edited by Rosanne Knox and others, emerging in 2013, on the idea of relational depth. One of the great phenomena of recent years, in many forms of therapy, has been the increased understanding and appreciation of the depth and importance of the therapeutic relationship.

My involvement with the Society for Existential Analysis also grew during this time, and I became very critical of my earlier hero, Sartre. He now seemed to me out of tune with the new relational discoveries, being far too much devoted to the naked individual, self-aware and self-sufficient. People such as Emmy van Deurzen, Ernesto Spinelli and their colleagues were now very much into the relational sphere. The existential position is now much better understood, and Kirk Schneider has shown us how closely connected the humanistic and the existential positions actually are.

These developments meant that I was now seeing connections where no connections had been before. Not only that, these developments ran into and illuminated the original focus of the book – humanistic psychology. A moment of illumination revealed that these things belonged together – the humanistic, the existential, the authentic, the relational and the transpersonal. So now, instead of the naked and self-sufficient individual who might be found lurking in the pages of *The reality game*, we had the fully integrated individual who brought together all of these five threads and wove a much more exciting and adequate pattern. This person now seemed to represent to me a new kind of therapist – the **HEART** therapist.

Many students have said how much they appreciated the original edition of this work, and this new edition will perhaps also be welcomed for what has been described as its deep and humane approach. This field has recently seemed in danger of succumbing to pressures from funding bodies for cheaper and quicker forms of therapy. This book shows how this pressure can be resisted in the interests of a therapy which aims at liberation rather than adjustment.

Some people have expressed an interest in the title of this book – where does it come from? The explanation is to be found in the original introduction to the first edition, where I said:

> One other thing: the word 'humanistic' is often misunderstood. Some people misunderstand it by thinking it means that we are humanists, in the sense of members of the British Humanist Association; this is far

from the truth, because we value spirituality and feeling and intuition in a way which would offend the average humanist very much. Others misunderstand it by thinking it means that we are soft and mushy and want to spread peace and love all the time; but we are not in the peace and love business, we are in the reality business. Or better still, since there is always some element of play in good therapy, the reality game.

John Rowan, PhD

1 Psychotherapy, counselling, coaching and personal growth

This is a book intended for the practitioner in psychotherapy, counselling, coaching or personal growth who wants to adopt an integrated approach. It is also intended for courses that train people in this approach, or something close to it. While mainly devoted to one-to-one work, nearly everything in this book also applies to groupwork, because this is also an active field for the integrative practitioner.

What is this approach? It comprises Humanistic, Existential, Authentic, Relational and Transpersonal elements, woven into a fabric which shows how they fit together to form a truly human challenge to many of the fashions of the day. We might perhaps call it a HEART approach.

Humanistic psychology was first named when Abraham Maslow, Anthony Sutich and a few others were trying to find a name for a new journal. The *Journal of Humanistic Psychology* started to come out in 1961. It defined itself as differing from psychoanalysis on the one side and the cognitive or behavioural approach on the other. Humanistic psychology is particularly concerned with self-actualization and with body–mind unity, and has a great deal to say about that, as we shall be seeing later. People in this orientation are very concerned about human diminution, and the way in which social roles can diminish people. It has a good deal to say about liberation from the shackles of compulsion, whether they be internal or external.

It is quite diverse within itself, and includes some people, such as Abraham Maslow (1987) and Carl Rogers (1978), who are optimistic about human nature, and other people, such as Rollo May (1983), Jim Bugental (1999) and Alvin Mahrer (1989), who are not particularly optimistic at all. One of the standard misunderstandings about humanistic psychology is to think that it is all about Maslow and Rogers.

One of the most important ideas is self-actualization. This refers to the theory of Abraham Maslow (1908–1970) that there is a hierarchy of needs, ranging from lower needs such as food and security up to higher needs such as self-esteem and self-actualization. It used to be said that Maslow's theory was weak because of lack of good research, but in recent years huge amounts of research have come out backing up the Maslow theory in a remarkable way. The work of Kohlberg (on men and boys), Loevinger (on women and girls), Torbert (on managers), Kegan (also in industry and commerce), and particularly Cook-Greuter (1999), all bear witness to this. Ernesto Spinelli (1989) from the existential school has said that 'The notion of authenticity bears striking similarity to Maslow's ideas concerning self-actualization' (p.116). Self-actualization is all about being that self which I truly am, and the notion of the real self is central to humanistic psychology (DeCarvalho 1991). In recent years, it has become clear from the work of Ken Wilber (2000) and others that self-actualization is not the end of the line, so to speak, but simply a way-station on a longer journey, which extends all the way to the heights of mysticism. If we take Wilber as a useful guide, we can distinguish four levels of consciousness useful in therapy, and see more clearly how they are differentiated.

Carl Rogers (1902–1987) believed that people were capable of growing and developing into what he called 'the fully-functioning person', and used counselling, psychotherapy and groupwork to achieve this. His ideas are highly compatible with those of Maslow. In his work he laid great stress on empathy, non-possessive warmth and genuineness. This emphasis on genuineness reminds us of the great philosopher Martin Buber, and Rogers and Buber had a famous dialogue which helps us to see the similarities and differences between them rather clearly (Kirschenbaum and Henderson 1990). The person-centred approach is one of the central disciplines within humanistic psychology, and is still being developed today (Mearns and Thorne 2000), even after the death of its founder. It has become clear that Rogers' thinking is very much in line with the later idea of Constructivist psychotherapy (Neimeyer 2009), and in that sense anticipated much later thinking in a remarkable way.

Humanistic psychotherapy owes to Wilhelm Reich (1897–1957) a strong emphasis on the importance of the body. Alexander Lowen was one of Reich's students, and introduced an approach to psychotherapy which he called Bioenergetics. Later on, David Boadella (1988) in Britain developed a further extension of this which he called Biosynthesis.

Because all the pioneers of humanistic psychology were very individual people, there is no one single accepted theory that we can lay out and say – this is it. But there are some very consistent themes running through all the material put forward by these people.

The first is that, deep down underneath it all where it really counts, you are OK. This goes against many other and much older theories which say that people are fundamentally bad, selfish, narrow and nasty. By saying that people are fundamentally OK, we do not at all mean that people are not sometimes destructive, or that there is no evil in the world (see for example Goldberg 1995). What we mean is that if someone will agree to work with us on his or her destructive actions or evil wishes, in an atmosphere of trust and acceptance, that person will discover that the evil and destructiveness are just as phoney and just as forgettable as the false niceness of other people, which apparently causes no problems.

In other words, we believe that personal nastiness and personal niceness are most often, in both cases, masks and illusions, put on for reasons which seemed good at the time, but which have now become stuck and rigid, and out of our control. In that sense, if you want to use labels, we are all neurotic. By working on ourselves to unstick the rigidities and loosen the mask, we can eventually learn how to live without needing masks at all – though it may still be useful to put one on occasionally, as we might have a dress suit or an evening gown.

Existentialism is also very varied, and when Mick Cooper (2003) came to write his useful work on such an approach, he too had to make it clear that there was not just one version to consider.

The phenomenological tradition, coming from Edmund Husserl (1859–1938) originally, says that it is possible to cleanse our perceptions and see things as they are. But we can only do this by a rigorous examination of our assumptions, first of all becoming aware of them and then learning how to set them aside or bracket them (Jennings 1992). This requires a degree of self-knowledge, because otherwise our unaware beliefs can trip us up all the time. This lays great stress on our responsibility for not taking for granted anything about the ground on which we stand when we make any general statement. We have to put everything in doubt, and assume that nothing is absolutely true.

Husserl took from Franz Brentano (1838–1917) the notion of intentionality. This says that consciousness is always directed towards the real world in order to interpret it in a meaningful manner. Consciousness is always consciousness of some thing. So we do not talk about behaviour, we talk about action – a very important difference. The difference is that action is always intentional. Gestalt therapy in particular lays great stress on its phenomenological roots. 'Phenomenology . . . is the philosophical approach which is at the very heart of Gestalt' (Clarkson 1989, p.13).

Ronald Laing (1965) pointed to the close connection between phenomenology and existentialism, and so did Merleau-Ponty (1908–61), who said – 'The world is not what I think, but that which I live'. Phenomenology is one of the most important influences in the new study of consciousness which is arousing so much interest in philosophical circles. A special issue of the journal *Self & Society* (2014) was devoted to a full discussion of the work of Maurice Merleau-Ponty. People such as Shaun Gallagher (1997) and

Francisco Varela (1997) are arguing that we cannot understand the nature of consciousness until we fully bring phenomenology into the argument.

This tradition lays stress on the inescapable dilemmas of the human condition – death, the inner struggle over anxiety, the need for authentic living. Rollo May (1909–94) is one of those within humanistic psychology who has written a great deal about existentialism, and has claimed that William James (1842–1910) was an existential thinker, who in fact influenced Husserl. May wrote one of the best books (1983) on the existentialist approach to psychology and psychotherapy.

From Heidegger (1889–1976) comes the central idea of authenticity. He says that we are thrown into the world, and that our existence in the world is simply a matter of being-there (*Dasein*). Authenticity is a combination of self-respect (we are not just part of an undifferentiated world) and self-enactment – we express our care in the world in a visible way. Jim Bugental puts it well when he says:

> By authenticity I mean a central genuineness and awareness of being. Authenticity is that presence of an individual in his living in which he is fully aware in the present moment, in the present situation. Authenticity is difficult to convey in words, but experientially it is readily perceived in ourselves or in others.
>
> (Bugental 1981, p.102)

Again, it is Gestalt therapy which has stayed most strictly close to this existentialist position. Fritz Perls claimed that Gestalt therapy was one of three existential therapies, the other two being Frankl's logotherapy and Binswanger's *dasein* therapy (Perls 1969).

But Moreno too (who we shall return to in a moment) thought of himself as an existentialist, and David Brazier says – 'Psychodrama evolved from the existential approach to psychotherapy of Jacob Levi Moreno. Although it is possible to graft psychodramatic methods on to other philosophical approaches, the method is primarily attuned to an existential outlook' (Brazier 1991, p.1).

Martin Buber (1878–1965) is another representative of the existential position who has had much influence upon humanistic psychology. He says – 'There is genuine relation only between genuine persons . . . Men need, and it is granted to them, to confirm one another in their individual being by means of genuine meetings'. The encounter group, one of the innovations of humanistic psychology, is founded on this idea of genuine meetings (Rowan 1992a).

Another humanistic psychotherapist strongly influenced by existentialism is the late James Bugental (first president of the Association for Humanistic

Psychology), who actually calls his approach 'Existential-Humanistic Psychotherapy'. He has written a number of books, including *The search for existential identity* (all about patient–therapist dialogue), *Psychotherapy and process* (his main theoretical book), *The search for authenticity* and *The art of psychotherapy*. In the latter book he lists his own set of 'givens': Embodiedness (implying change), Finitude (implying contingency), Ability to act or not act (implying responsibility), Choicefulness (implying relinquishment) and Separate-but-related-ness (implying being at once a part of and apart from another person). Bugental says this:

> For me, the truest existentialism is humanistic and the soundest humanism is existential. The two are not the same, but their overlap is rich in potential for greater understanding of human experience and for greater effectiveness in the effort to enrich that experience.
>
> (Bugental 1981, p.10)

Bugental is one of the most important voices in the humanistic and existential fields.

Much influenced by existentialism is the late Alvin Mahrer, another theorist we shall be referring to in this book. He has reworked the whole humanistic-existential connection in a very exciting way. He continually quotes Binswanger, and to a lesser extent Boss, and also Laing and May. But he is not a slavish follower: he disagrees with the Sartrean position, for example, that one person can never really know another. He shows that it is indeed possible for one person to get inside another person's skin, to know from the inside what it is like to be that other person (Mahrer 1996).

Possibly the best-known existential therapist is Irvin Yalom (1980), who has written a number of short books which are entertaining and insightful. But I find that his big basic book is too heavy – he has four or five chapters on death anxiety, which I think is too much: very few of my clients are bothered by death anxiety, and to be so insistent seems to me rather dogmatic and not very useful.

In England, a school of existentialism has grown up under the tutelage of Emmy van Deurzen, who has created what almost amounts to a sort of cottage industry, with book after book appearing. She has added to the usual three realms of life – the Umwelt, the Mitwelt and the Eigenwelt – the Uberwelt, thus including the transpersonal aspect. It has to be said, however, that she has herself not done much with the idea, setting, as it were, a place for a guest who never actually turns up. A useful compendium is Barnett and Madison (2012).

But the central issue in it, I would say, is self-responsibility. For the first time in human history, people such as Kierkegaard and Nietzsche urged that we are totally responsible for our own lives, and cannot blame our parents, our teachers, our media or our governors for our faults and failings. Of course, existentialism can be traced back into various historical antecedents (Friedman 1991), but basically it is a recent form of philosophy. It is not to be found in classical philosophy, or in Eastern texts. A recent compendium (Cooper 2003) of existential therapies has made it clear that it represents a wide field, highly compatible with the other elements within this book. More recently, Kirk Schneider (Schneider and Krug 2010) has been arguing that it is much closer to humanistic psychology than most existential writers are willing to admit. Perhaps the best recent account of existential therapy is to be found in the book by Ernesto Spinelli (2015), which argues in a rigorous way that the three basic essentials are relatedness, uncertainty and anxiety.

One of the key concepts in the humanistic and in the existential approach is *Authenticity*. One of the great authorities on authenticity, James Bugental (1981), had the unique honour of serving on the editorial boards of the Society for Existential Analysis and of the Association for Humanistic Psychology. So when we talk about authenticity, about getting in touch with what is the deepest truth within us, and allowing that to come out, we are not saying something fearful or dangerous. People often say – 'How do I know I won't hate my deepest self when I come across it?' But this is an unrealistic fear, and we may sometimes suspect that it is really designed to enable the person to avoid the necessary effort. A more recent researcher and writer is Jenny Wade (1996), who has shown that human development has, at a certain point, to be divided into male and female types of authenticity – a useful innovation. We shall be examining this point in detail later.

The authentic therapist is naturally creative, and may use ideas or techniques taken from other specialities, such as the Winnicott Squiggle method, or the Narrative Therapy approach (Freedman and Combs 1996), or the Farrelly Provocative Therapy (Farrelly and Brandsma 1989), without specific training in such things. In my experience, a Gestalt therapist can happily use Gestalt Art Therapy with a client, without having had specific training in such a speciality.

Relational approaches are now central to our conception of therapy. One of the most remarkable things that has happened in the field of psychotherapy over the past 20 years is the spread of relational thinking. We used to think of therapy in all its forms as a client encountering a professional. The client had a fixed role, and so did the professional: the professional was there to help the client, using various means. But about 20 years ago – the exact date is disputed – the magic word *intersubjectivity* started to be used. The idea of intersubjectivity is that the relationship between client and professional is primary, rather than the separate individuals. Language is now seen as an 'intersubjective dynamics of co-construction of meaning' (Salvatore and

Venuleo 2008). This implies an openness that is quite radical. We now see the whole therapy as a two-person event, in which both parties are equally involved and equally responsible (Sparks 2009). This does not mean (and this was the great struggle of the 1990s) that there is just a social field, and that the individuals disappear: it simply means that equality begins to be respected in quite a new way. We now see that *communication is only possible between equals*. Many of the most interesting ideas about this now come from the constructivist position (Neimeyer 2009). 'Constructivism sees meaning making as relational, social and cultural to the core' (p.ix). There is a good discussion of this in Greenberg, Watson and Lietaer (1998), and it is clear that their excellent description of experiential psychotherapy makes them necessary to the argument of this book. Another good account is to be found in the chapter by Bott and Howard (2014), where they say –

> in the drama of the therapeutic encounter this becomes the 'therapeutic dance', where the client brings to therapy the steps of existing 'dances' with an invitation for the therapist to join in . . . for productive therapy to take place, the therapist is required to introduce new possibilities. This is achieved by introducing some new steps while ensuring that both partners remain on their feet.
>
> (p.67)

Narrative therapy (Freedman and Combs 1996) is also a brilliant source of ideas in this area.

A good discussion of the relational approach is to be found in the book edited by Loewenthal and Samuels (2014), and it is clear that the dust has not yet settled on this disputed territory.

And the fifth element is the *Transpersonal*. This is the field of spirituality, seen as a universal birthright, common to all, containing such features as creativity, vision, openness to non-rational phenomena, compassion, intuition, a deeper and fuller type of empathy and mystical insights. This is the area where we admit that we are spiritual beings and that there might be such things as dreams, signs, images, symbols, archetypes, angels, previous lives and so forth, which might at some point become relevant to us. Not everyone needs to go into this area, or spend much time in it, but to admit to its existence, and own up to our own experiences in the dream world, is great wisdom and gives us a depth which is valuable to all therapists, counsellors and coaches. It is here that we have to admit the existence of different levels of consciousness, and we shall be looking at this issue in Chapter 14.

The four Eastern philosophies (which always include some psychology as well) that have had the most influence in this field have been: Zen

Buddhism, with its emphasis on letting go; Taoism, particularly in its ideas of centring and the yin-yang polar unity of opposites; Sufism, particularly with its emphasis on regaining one's naturalness and acquiring creative vision; and Tantra, particularly in its emphasis on the importance of the body as a spiritual energy system. Particularly influential in the field of therapy have been the books of Shunru Suzuki, Alan Watts, Sogyal Rinpoche, Ramana Maharshi, Jiddu Krishnamurti, Paul Reps, Daisetz Suzuki and Thich Nhat Hanh.

Transpersonal psychology has been called the 'fourth force', and it clearly comes after the 'third force': in fact, the same man – Anthony Sutich – who edited the *Journal of Humanistic Psychology* later became the first editor of the *Journal of Transpersonal Psychology*. It is not easy to produce a definition of transpersonal psychology, but the most succinct version I have seen is that of Stan Grof (1975) where he says it is concerned essentially with 'experiences involving an expansion or extension of consciousness beyond the usual ego boundaries and beyond the limitation of time and/or space' (p.155).

We already know that psychosynthesis prefers to work back and forth between the humanistic and the transpersonal (Ferrucci 1982) and would be unhappy about making too big a division between the two. One of the pioneers of the transpersonal was Carl Jung, and he has made a huge contribution, as have his followers and successors. In fact, it seems to me that in years to come we may have to keep saying that transpersonal psychotherapy is not just Jung and Grof, just as we have to keep saying that humanistic psychology is not just Maslow and Rogers.

In recent years there has been a huge increase in the worldwide interest in the transpersonal, and in 2013 there came out the magnificent *Handbook of transpersonal psychology* edited by Friedman and Hartelius. Its 38 chapters and 700-odd pages cover a huge area of ground, including some good material on transpersonal psychotherapy. Other interesting books are coming out all the time, and two recent star items are Sperry (2012) and Matteson (2008).

But the essence of the transpersonal is that it is an entire realm of experience different from the everyday. It is another world, rich in entrancing and challenging experiences, and full of insights, visions, challenges and inspirations, in which the normal order of things is irrelevant and even handicapping. So we are now talking about an approach of great expansiveness and openness, which can do real justice to every aspect of the person. We shall be seeing much more about this in Chapter 14.

This means that we are interested in integration. By integration we mean that the splits in the person can be healed, and that the holes in the personality can be filled. The various parts of the person can get to know each other better, accept each other more, and change in that process. This is not a process of subordinating all the various tendencies in the person to one overall control, like some kind of totalitarian ego – it is more like a harmony of contrasts. We shall have more to say on this later.

The thread we can follow all through our new approach is the emphasis on change and development. Human beings are seen not as static victims or villains, but as people in a natural process of growth. This process can continue, if we let it, in adulthood, too. We have all seen people we recognize as being further ahead than us, more complete, more evolved, more themselves. What this new psychology says is that we could all continue to grow if we did not limit ourselves and sell ourselves short.

Most of us normally think that if we have enough worldly goods, then we can do what we want to do, and then we can be happy. The sequence is HAVE – DO – BE. But what we are saying here is that it is exactly the other way round. If we can be who we really are, we will find ourselves doing things which genuinely satisfy us and give us enjoyment, and then we shall have all we really want. The sequence for us is BE – DO – HAVE.

For a full diagrammatic representation of the characteristics of four levels of consciousness and how they relate to specific psychotherapies, see Appendix 1.

Some negatives

Now we come to some of the things we don't do. Unlike some other schools, we do not adopt a medical model. This idea of a medical model is all-pervasive in our Western culture, and hard to get away from. It is a mechanistic view, holding that the client is a kind of machine, which only has to be treated in the right way to get invariable results. We think the client has choices, and that the object of therapy is to increase the range of choices, and encourage and enable the client to handle successfully this increased range of choices. And we think the medical approach tends to reduce choice, even though this is what the medical practitioner does not intend. Wheelis (1975) has the basic argument on this – that if you treat a person like a machine they lose freedom (see Chapter 5). But even in medicine itself, there is nowadays much more interest in holistic medicine – forms of medical practice where the patient is seen as a whole human being who is responsible for their own process. Perhaps the best discussion of this whole question is to be found in the book by Ken Wilber and his wife, entitled *Grace and grit* (1991). Much more so in psychotherapy and counselling, which have always taken the view that the responsibility for change lies with the client. We do not believe that there is a disease or illness which with suitable treatment will be cured (see Chapter 2). Rather do we believe that the client needs to own up to what they are doing: that awareness in itself, together with its empathic reception by a therapist, is productive of change.

Unlike psychoanalysis, we do not try to build up a transference neurosis between therapist and client. There is a good discussion of this from our point of view in Clarkson (2003). We do not use transference very much in therapy, because we have an alternative, called the theory of the dialogical self (see Chapter 7).

Most psychotherapy and counselling argues, or tries to assume in some way, that theory should guide action. Our view is that theory is important and worth pursuing, both in preparing for work as a therapist, and in talking to a supervisor or other professionals. But it should be left outside the consulting room. It should not intrude into the relationship between therapist and client. Hence our objection to manualization – that is, the belief that therapy should be conducted strictly in accordance with a manual, thus enabling scoring and assessment to be carried out more easily. We differ from the other schools in having a place for spirituality. We shall consider this more fully in the next section. All we need to say here is that this is a most important aspect of the work, which I have described in full detail elsewhere (Rowan 2005a).

And finally, the other schools, because of their external orientation, go in for styles of research that do not permit any of the important things that happen in therapy to be expressed. This old paradigm research, as it is now called, measures variables instead of finding out what is going on inside people. We are more in favour of qualitative research (Reason and Rowan 1981) which sees people from the inside – see Chapter 11 for much more detail and argument on this.

Having covered this much ground very briefly, we can now say that the HEART practitioner is concerned with psychotherapy, with counselling, with coaching and with personal growth. Not, however, with psychiatry, psychoanalysis, cognitive behaviour therapy, behaviour therapy or behaviour modification. We do not use drugs or shock therapy, completely reinterpret transference (the main mechanism of psychoanalytic therapy), and do not make more than incidental use of the principles of reciprocal inhibition or systematic desensitization (behaviour therapy) or of the principle of reinforcement (behaviour modification). Our kind of practitioner seldom uses tests, but can be a clinical psychologist so long as a reasonably free hand is allowed.

Further, we can say that we see psychotherapy, counselling, coaching and personal growth as all using the same methods and the same approach. For the rest of this book, then, we will refer only to therapy (mainly because it is the shortest, as well as the most general, of the four words) on the under-standing that everything we say will be applicable to counselling, coaching and personal growth too. Of course there are differences of practice, with psychotherapists generally having the most reserved attitude to therapy. Counselling is much more likely to be a front-line activity, as is coaching, and personal growth is available to all, though a preliminary interview may be required for new people embarking upon certain particularly demanding types of work. Coaching is usually conducted with people who have no overt pathology, although deeper problems do sometimes appear when coaching is continued for longer periods.

The reader who is familiar with the standard literature in this field (most of it written by psychoanalysts) may be horrified at this seemingly cavalier treatment. What about the important distinction between the normal and the neurotic, between the neurotic and the borderline case, between the borderline and the psychotic? What about the importance of selecting the right patient for the right treatment? This brings us to the whole question of diagnosis, or assessment as it is now more often called, and it is to this that we must now turn.

Useful websites

Association for Humanistic Psychology Practitioners: http://ahpp.org
Guide to Humanistic Psychology: www.ahpweb.org/rowan_bibliography
Society for Existential Analysis: www.existentialanalysis.org.uk
Association for Transpersonal Psychology: http://atpweb.org
Transpersonal Psychology section of the British Psychological Society: www.trans personalpsychology.org.uk/index.html
General guide to psychotherapy in the UK: www.allaboutpsychotherapy.com/ home/
British Association for Counselling and Psychotherapy: www.bacp.co.uk. The BACP issues a complete list of all the counsellors in Britain, together with some details about them, such as their usual fees.
The United Kingdom Association for Psychotherapy Integration: www.ukapi.com
The Association for Humanistic Psychology in Britain: www.ahpb.org.uk
The International Primal Association: www.primals.org/links.html#top

2 Assessment or not

The question of assessment is one of the most striking areas in which we differ from the older orthodoxies. It seems at first sight, and certainly it must be so if one adopts a medical model, that there is no way out of some responsibility for assessment. Surely we must find out what problem a person has before we can put it right? A doctor has to find out the disease before he knows what drug to prescribe; a motor mechanic has to find out what is wrong before fitting a spare part; a plumber has to find out the cause of the trouble before he can put it right. Isn't mental illness like this?

The problem

Certainly the vast majority of people working in the field of psychotherapy would argue in this way. And yet, after a hundred years or more of research in this area, we still find the authors of an encyclopaedic handbook of research (Garfield and Bergin 1978) saying this:

> Ideally, one would like to be able to say that, given Problem X, the optimal approach is Technique Y. In practice, as the reader will discover, things are rarely so simple or straightforward; on the contrary, since human problems are extraordinarily complex, so are the issues facing the therapist who attempts to deal with these difficulties in therapeutic ways. For the same reason it is unlikely that there will ever be a single optimal approach to the solution of a psychological problem.
>
> (p. 4)

In other words, they don't have the answer. It seems that assessment is more problematic than we might have thought. This is worrying, because more and more courses nowadays are teaching people about the American Diagnostic and Statistical Manual (DSM-V), the fifth edition of which came out in 2013. Many agencies in the United States, though not very much in Britain as yet, ask for formal diagnostic classification of a client before they will pay insurance or other costs. But just as more and more people are taking it on, more and more criticisms are appearing too. For example, Mary Boyle (2002) has urged that there are real conceptual complications about accepting schizophrenia as a disease entity in medical terms. And in a later article, she has made a most important point. She says that the assessment of mental illness often states or implies that the labels used are the names of diseases.

> The problem with this language is that it confers on these concepts a permanence and solidity which is quite unwarranted, and suggests that they are entities possessed by people.
>
> (Boyle 1996, p.7)

This is very dangerous, because the human mind is fluid rather than solid. It flows, rather than being broken up into chunks. If assessment suggests that things are fixed, it lies. And it suggests that once someone has been classified, they have been identified in a fixed way.

> Calling individuals phobic, obsessive-compulsive, histrionic or dependent personalities holds at least the suggestion that they are in a class by themselves, that is, that they are a different kind of human being.
>
> (Costello *et al.* 1995, p.71)

Another objection is that assessment hides everything it takes for granted. The famous DSM-V diagnostic manual hides the fact that it was designed by psychiatrists, with their particular base of experience and knowledge coming from mental hospitals. The book essentially helps them to decide what drug to prescribe. This is very different from the experience and knowledge established in the counselling field. As Peter Ross says:

> It is difficult to draw up a list of diagnostic categories. The most glaring difficulty is that different theoretical orientations can persuade one to see problems in a very different light. A second problem is that a typical young person's counselling service sees large numbers of developmental problems rather than clinical ones. There is even less agreement among experts on how to categorise developmental problems than there is on how to categorise clinical ones. A third problem is that a counselling service of any size will have to face the necessity of getting all its counsellors to agree definitions so that when counsellor A records a client as 'mild reactive depression' and counsellor B records the same for a different client a month later, they mean the same thing. If they do not, the computer will be producing very hollow information.
>
> (Ross 1996, p.478)

In this particular case, Ross and his co-workers went on for six years trying to make a system work, but up to the moment of writing there is no success-ful result. Well, if assessment is no good for classifying people, perhaps it is good for predicting their treatment and its outcome? For example, we might well feel that at least assessment could tell us one important thing – which patients were going to go crazy if they start into psychotherapy. This is sometimes referred to as 'precipitating a psychotic episode', sometimes as 'provoking a breakdown' and sometimes as 'inducing decompensation', but it's all the same problem, and a fairly obvious one, at that. Surely assessment can at least get us this far? Well, apparently not. In a book (Malan 1979) on the science of psychodynamics by one of the best-established therapists at one of the most reputable clinics, the author has this to say:

> During many years at the Tavistock Clinic, I have accumulated a long list of patients in whom this question arises [relief vs increased disturb-ance]; and, even being wise after the event, I have found myself quite unable to distinguish between these two possibilities. I am constantly being surprised by patients whom I would not expect to break down, who do break down, and those whom I would expect to break down, who don't. This remains an area where systematic research is badly needed.
> (p.223)

But we don't want to do this systematic research, because of severe doubts not only about the efficacy, but also about the morality, of this process of assessment. Because to diagnose someone is to label them. And labelling does harm to people, even when the labels are correct. As Irvin Yalom says: 'The standard diagnostic formulation tells the therapist nothing about the unique person he or she is encountering; and there is substantial evidence that diagnostic labels impede or distort listening' (Yalom 1980, p.410).

Human beings do have problems, but when it comes to psychotherapy, they are not isolable separate problems that can be treated like a disease or a faulty component or a blocked pipe. They are problems connected with being that person. This is why one label can never be enough to tell us what to do about a person. One of the main characteristics of our approach is a refusal to label people in any firm or final way. Of course we have tentative ideas as to what is basically wrong with any client, but as George Kelly once said: 'The client does not ordinarily sit cooped up in a nosological pigeonhole, he proceeds along his way' (Kelly 1955, p.773). Accordingly, he advocated making a 'transitive assessment' which gives us a lead for action, but which is open to change as the interaction goes on.

Possibly the best discussion to be found of this whole area is that to be found in the book by Walkenstein (1975). She tells of giving patients labels – 'Your assessment is Excessive Politeness ... the only cure for you is to practise some excessive rudeness.' 'You're a Zombie.' 'You're a marshmallow.' These are all temporary labels – they don't have the certainty or the permanence of science – they just represent a moment of insight, a moment of seeing the obvious in a flash of clarity. They have implications for something to do about changing them.

To someone such as Walkenstein, the symptoms represent a shield; they don't represent the personality. The assessment then becomes not a life sentence but rather something to be put aside when the person is ready to do so. She looks on the symptoms as a message, a plea for attention, and the assessment as a method of giving that attention, in a temporary and non-hurtful way. And by the way, Jung agrees with this: 'Jung pointed out, somewhat ironically, that the really correct diagnosis is to be made only at the end of treatment' (McCurdy 1985, p.48).

Labelling

Much of what we have been saying comes under the heading of what is often called 'social constructivism' (Neimeyer 2009). Social constructivism says that social situations tend to be ordered in accordance with social meanings and intentions of various kinds. That is, a whole series of expectations are created just by the way the set-up is arranged. Whatever then happens within the boundaries of that set-up will be in terms of those specific expectations, and no others. That behaviour which fits in with the expectations will be seen as normal, and any behaviour which does not fit in will be seen as deviant. And this opens up the whole question of assessment. How is it constructed, and who has the contract for the construction process?

Who, then, are the people who are most likely to be labelled? They are the most powerless. Just as those criminals are most likely to be caught who go most against the norms of a top-down society, so those other deviants are most likely to be put inside who go most against the norms of such a society. As Brown (1974) reports, most prisoners in state psychiatric hospitals (sorry, most patients in state psychiatric hospitals) are working class, most are women, and Third World people make up a disproportionate percentage of the patient population in relation to the general population. As he says: 'The social context of present-day America is of class, sex and race oppression, and those oppressed by these social relations are the prime candidates for the brain police'. This is no less true of Britain or any other country. It appears, then, that psychiatric assessment offers an acceptable 'scientific' story to justify taking a person out of his or her home and putting them in an institution.

But having seen some examples of how the theory works, it seems in order to examine the theory itself: what does it actually say? One application of social constructivism is labelling theory. Labelling theory starts with a simple distinction – that between explicit norms (rules whose breaking can be punished) and residual rules. The residual rules are not stated anywhere, and it may not be legitimate to punish infringements of them, yet they may on occasion be important to specific people. These much more vague and variable infringements tend, in each age, to drift into a catch-all category. Once it was witchcraft (and still is in a number of countries), once it was possession by spirits, sometimes it was possession by the Devil, and so on: today, in our culture, it is 'mental illness'. The magazine *Asylum* comes out regularly and discusses these issues in a very thorough way (see website at end of chapter).

When someone in our family is doing something unacceptable and inconvenient, which cannot be condemned under any existing law, but which makes us nervous or excited, we are liable to see that person as a candidate for the mental hospital. The case histories by Laing and Esterson (1970) give a rather clear picture of this process in action. So labelling theory says that the symptoms of 'mental illness' can be seen as the violations of residual rules.

The implication of this is that if we refused to label people, they would drift into and out of mental states often regarded as 'neurotic' or 'psychotic' without ever losing their status as citizen, friend, child, human being or whatever.

Assessment for therapy

Let us look at what each of our five traditions says about assessment. Assessment, which is done at the beginning, before therapy starts, is often carried out by professionals who are aiming at objectivity. The idea is to hand over the potential client with enough information to enable decisions to be made as to which therapist is suitable to treat this person. The argument is that it is more efficient to do this than to pass on potential clients willy-nilly, with no hints as who is the best person to deal with them.

Humanistic

The humanistic view is that since it is the client who does the work, and since most of the effective influences on outcomes come from the client, it is ridiculous for the therapist to be the one who makes the decisions, or is supposed to. The magisterial book on this is Miller, Duncan and Hubble (1997). They say that no matter what the therapist may think, the client actually knows better what the problem is. And 'the responsibility for cure is the patient's business', as they quote from Adler (p.68). One of the humanistic heroes, Alvin Mahrer, told me that at one time there was pressure from the Canadian Psychotherapy Association to make a rule that all psychotherapists had to start by taking a history from the patient. He managed to muster up enough opposition to this so that it never happened. His own practice was quite against this – in fact he was quite extreme in his refusal to do any kind of assessment, so much so that on one occasion when a man came to his place he suggested that he lie back on his big black client chair, only for the man to explain that he had come to fix the TV! This is perhaps extreme, but it does show an appreciation for the fact that it is the client who has to decide, not the therapist.

Existential

The existential view is well expressed in the classic book by Hans Cohn (1997), which says: '1. The client you meet as the therapist is the client who meets you. There is no client *as such*. If two therapists meet the same client, it is not the same client. 2. What the client tells you as the therapist, she or he tells only you. She or he may tell another therapist something quite different. 3. There is no "history" to be taken for that is no history *as such*. A client's history is disclosed in the process of interaction between therapist and client. 4. This means that there cannot be an "assessment" as this would imply an objective situation independent of time, place and the contribution of the assessing therapist' (p.34).

Also this chimes in with dialogical self theory (Rowan 2010), which says that not only is there not just one client in the room, but also there is not just one therapist in the room. The self of the client and the self of the therapist are both brought out by the situation, and may well be unique to that situation. The idea that there is just one fixed client to be assessed is just an idea, convenient for anyone who wants to make the client conform to a pre-existing template. Objectivity is not to be had.

Authentic

The authentic view says that what we are aiming at in therapy is a real meeting between two real people. This may not be possible at the beginning, because of fears about openness and self-revelation. It is something that tends to grow over time, based on trust and acceptance. The idea that this can normally be achieved in the first session is quite ridiculous. Martin Buber (1963) says:

> The abyss does not call to his confidently functioning security of action, but to the abyss, that is to the self of the doctor, that selfhood that is

hidden under the structures erected through training and practice, that is itself encompassed by chaos, itself familiar with demons, but is graced with the humble power of wrestling and overcoming, and is ready to wrestle and overcome thus ever anew.

(p.94)

This kind of meeting is precious and unusual, and requires commitment from both parties. An authentic meeting requires openness on the part of both parties, and this takes time to achieve. What is at stake is not objectivity, but a disciplined subjectivity on the part of the therapist.

Relational

The relational view says that reality is co-constructed by therapist and client in the process of meeting. It is not just simply present at the start, as if it did not have to be fought for and committed to. How could it be known in full at the beginning? And if not, what meaning can be attributed to any assessment? 'Intersubjectivity entails reciprocal causal relationships of all parts of the human universe with all other parts. All human events are co-created by the participants. Everyone changes, and is changed by, everyone else' (Natterson and Friedman 1995, p.xiii). And just because this is a continuous and never-ending process, there is obviously no way of setting out the whole story at the beginning.

Ullman (2014) says:

The relational perspective, on the other hand, locates the authority in the dyad, assuming that the knowledge is not there to be applied, but to be constructed in the dialogue. The knowledge is not there in the therapist and does not exist *a priori*, but is constructed in the dyadic process.

(p.112)

Again, this means that prior assessment is not possible.

Transpersonal

The transpersonal view is that both therapist and client are part of something larger, a mystery which can never be fully known. How, then, could the client be known in advance? The whole idea is quite ridiculous. This is really the most radical rejection of all. In this tradition, therapy has been called 'a dance of soul-making', and this clearly is something very different from many conceptions of what therapy is all about. It seems clear that the HEART therapist cannot use diagnosis or assessment at all.

Alternative models

It is clear that we must reject the medical model. In doing so we are on common ground with most psychologists, and the overwhelming majority of social psychologists. The *Handbook of social psychology* has an article by Freeman and Giovannoni (1969) describing the medical model of mental distress as 'entirely irrelevant and handicapping' and as 'unreliable or meaningless'. We have seen above how true this is. By contrast, Watson and Bohart in the *Handbook of humanistic psychology* (2015) say: 'The basic purpose of existential-integrative therapy is to maximise clients' freedom' (p.592).

What we say is that people have problems. Where they attribute these problems to outside forces or other people, we can't help them much; we probably can't do a lot to change the people around them or the world in which they find themselves. (There are important exceptions to this, which we shall look at in the chapter entitled 'Listening with the fourth ear'.) But where they attribute their problems to themselves, or to what is going on inside them, then we have an opportunity to work with them on solving those problems.

One of the most interesting books to come out on this topic is by Lucy Johnstone and Rudi Dallos (2014). The final chapter is quite brilliant. It is headed 'Controversies and debates about formulation', and is the best account I have seen of the whole question of categorizing clients. They say: 'Formulation should be an ongoing process rather than a one-off expert pronouncement, and therefore one would hope that reformulation based on the client's feedback would ensure that unhelpful formulations are revised or abandoned. Unfortunately this does not always happen' (p.215). They are clear that formulations can easily go wrong in the eyes of the client, and quote Butler to the effect that 'Being on the receiving end of a formulation can feel like being weighed up, evaluated or judged – like being "seen through" or "rumbled" rather than understood' (p.216). In their summary they say: 'The potential criticisms and limitations of formulation echo the potential criticisms and limitations of therapy itself' (p.230).

This is a very worthwhile book, and could be a revelation to anyone reading it. On the other hand, the recent book by van Rijn (2014) should have a health warning, as it tries to square the circle in quite a hopeless way, and ultimately pleasing no one. The book by Mary Jo Peebles (2012) tries to get round the problem by using the metaphor of a map, but this seems to me still too left-brained an approach.

From this point of view the standard psychiatric diagnoses are of no use. If you work in an organization such as a counselling agency there may be rules that have to be followed about assessment. But it is not an ethical requirement and if there is any possibility of changing such rules this would be highly desirable. There is only one distinction which does seem to be useful and to be of practical import to a humanistic practitioner: can the person benefit from a 'session' (the usual 1-hour session or an extended session) or do they need some form of residential care?

A quite different approach is followed by Barbara Ingram (2012), who has created a questioning procedure, over a period of 20 years or more, which is oriented towards psychotherapy rather than psychiatry. Her procedure consists in covering the following areas:

- Crisis, stressful situations and transitions
- Biological hypotheses (biological causes, medical interventions, mind/body connections)
- Cognitive models (Utopian expectations, faulty cognitive maps, faulty information processing, dysfunctional self-talk)
- Behavioural and learning models (antecedents and consequences, conditioned emotional responses, skill deficits, lack of competence)
- Existential and spiritual models (existential issues, avoiding responsibility, spiritual issues)
- Psychodynamic models (internal parts and I-positions, re-enactment of early childhood experiences, immature sense of self and conception of others, unconscious dynamics)
- Social, cultural and environmental factors (family system, cultural context, social support, social role performance, social problem, social role of mental patient, environmental factors)

By probing these seven areas, the therapist can make sure of not omitting any of the factors that may be uppermost for any individual at any time or in any context. And she goes into some detail as to how this information can be used in the therapeutic work. I personally have found this framework very useful, and invaluable when talking to fee payers and such people.

It has to be said at this point that in recent years there has been a rise in the numbers of referrals from agencies such as EAPs, health insurance specialists, solicitors, doctors and so forth. These used to be quite good sources of clients, but more lately there has been a lowering of fees, which makes such contacts much more problematic. In addition to this, the amount of detail required from the practitioner has increased, often requiring specific completion of lengthy forms at diminishing intervals. Some of these require the use of DSM categories, which is very constraining, and in our view quite inappropriate.

It is also important, of course, to make a judgement as to how well the client can stand up to the stresses of therapy itself. Not everyone is ready for the systematic deep probing that may be necessary. (See Appendix 4: Should I take on this client?)

Useful websites

Asylum – the magazine for democratic psychiatry: www.pccs-books.co.uk

3   The initial interview

The previous chapters have been of a more objective character, where it seemed important to give chapter and verse for each of the points made, and to justify each of the arguments put forward. In most of this chapter, however, I think it is more appropriate to adopt a more subjective posture, where I talk about what I do. By talking about what I do I am therefore putting myself forward as one practitioner who has thought a good deal about what he is doing, and has had to observe students making a great many mistakes and asking many awkward questions.

First contact

Very often, the first contact is through an email or text message. I always suggest a telephone call to fix up a first meeting, because text exchanges are clumsier and slower, and in any case less 'human'. To admit that one needs the services of a psychotherapist is often very difficult. The reception one gets from the selected practitioner is keenly observed and deeply felt. 'Am I acceptable?' is the unspoken question. There is a lot of research now to show that inclusion is the first issue to arise in any group situation (Schutz 1983), and this group of two people is no exception.

If this is so, then with the first phone call the therapy has started. The therapist may be busy or tired, may have no free places for new clients, nevertheless the therapy has already started, and anything the therapist does is going to be therapeutic, non-therapeutic or anti-therapeutic. It is therapeutic to show concern and be of some help, so as to achieve rapport with the client. This concept of rapport is so important that we may as well spend some moments with it.

Rapport means being connected to the other person, relating well to the other person, being on the same wavelength, being able to communicate well, and so on. Where rapport exists, the client feels accepted, welcomed and included. The client may soon begin to feel – 'Here is someone who understands me' – and this makes the whole task of therapy very much easier. The essential basic trust has been set up. So how do we achieve rapport? Bandler and Grinder (1979) have given this point a lot of thought and conclude that the best way to achieve rapport is to take your cue from the other person: not by responding to them in your own way, but by copying them in their own way. So if the person speaks slowly, I speak slowly; if they use visual images, I use visual images; if they talk quietly, I talk quietly. At this stage I feel that rapport is virtually the only thing I can achieve, so I may as well achieve it well. And I do it by mirroring the client.

Now all that refers not to what the client says, but to how the client says it. We must now consider what is said. It is important that the client should see somebody fast. They may or may not have an emergency, but they are at a point where they are ready for action, and I like to give them some. It may be that I have no appointments vacant for some days, but even so I like to see the person, if only for a short time, rather than to let them wait around. But I always make it clear as to what I am offering. If there is no prospect of my taking this person on at all, I refer him or her on to a colleague with available time.

I feel that a client is entitled to goodwill and sympathy at least from any therapist, and that it is important that someone who rings a therapist for the first time should feel these qualities coming across. If I can't feel reasonably warm and concerned about someone who rings me up with a problem, I wonder whether I should be a therapist at all.

If I listen well to what the client has to say during the first phone call, I can begin to collect impressions, information and data from the first moment. These can be useful in later work, so I make notes either during the phone call or after it; this in itself reminds me that the therapy has already started.

If the person making the call is not the client, but simply a relative, a receptionist or secretary or assistant or colleague, I insist on talking to the actual client before making a decision. I personally would be reluctant to work in a situation where the person who does the initial interview is different from the person who continues to work with the client. This sometimes has to happen in training situations where the trainee is seen as not capable of assessing a prospective client in a professionally adequate way. And really much the same considerations apply to the first phone call. I would hate anyone else to take this call.

The reason is that any process which separates the entry to therapy from the therapy itself entails the medical model which we have have just abandoned. If, as we have seen in Chapter 2, there is no such thing as legitimate diagnosis or assessment, there is no place for someone who does diagnosis and nothing else. The therapeutic process is inevitably begun during any initial interview which is going to be useful, and to pretend that this is not going to happen is to close one's eyes to reality. If we want to treat people as persons rather than as things – and all psychotherapy depends on this assumption – we should not hand their intimate openness on from one expert to another as if it were a car on an assembly line. It does harm both to the client and to the practitioner; the therapist who is faced with a client who has been handed on from someone else really has to start from scratch – for there is no way of taking a set of notes at face value and simply accepting what they say, and no way of going back to pretend that they do not exist. It seems illogical and self-contradictory to start a process designed specifically to restore someone to personhood by reducing them to nothing more than a machine with faults to be corrected. Jim Bugental (1978) says:

> I am aware that many settings call for the client to be seen by an intake worker who makes the assignment to the therapist. This may be administratively efficient, but I believe very strongly that the assignment should only be a recommendation, subject to the outcome of the first encounter of client and therapist and thus to their deeper reading of how they come together.
>
> (p.28)

Wilson (1996) suggests that there are three types of client; those in crisis, those who are 'visiting' and those who are willing to engage in a serious attempt at working on themselves. The 'visiting' category is an interesting one: here the person is just not ready for therapy, but thinks for some reason that they should be doing it. This is sometimes difficult to discern, but one clue is that such a person very often views their problems as caused and owned by another person or organization. This seems to me a useful thought.

The initial interview

Let us now assume that the contact has been made, by whatever means, and that the client now turns up for the first appointment. The first thing to be considered is the room in which the interview is to take place. My room has a number of cushions of different shapes and sizes and colours, including some very large ones; it has a clock that I make sure is always correct. I have several boxes of tissues, a supply of paper to draw on and many felt pens and crayons of different colours. The light has a dimmer on it, and the curtains are heavy, so that the room can be made dim even on a sunny day. I have facilities for recording sessions on tape, and for playing music. I have a tennis racquet and a baby's feeding bottle. There is a bowl available for being sick into, and a towel for strangling, using as a poisonous snake, etc.

If I were more body-oriented than I am, I would probably have a massage table, and I might well have a bioenergetic stool or a mini-trampoline. The first sight of this room is not usually strange for my clients, because many of them hear of me through groups where these things are regularly used. If I get a client who has never been to a group, I sometimes explain that in therapy we often find it a good idea to change the actual body position, and this sort of arrangement makes it easier to do that.

When the client arrives, I go to the door and greet him or her warmly. Psychoanalysts worry a great deal about whether to shake hands or not, but with me handshakes, hugs, kisses or other marks of affection are not particularly unusual and do not give cause for concern: although of course they are noted as much as any other piece of body language. Whatever is thoroughly genuine and personally felt is probably going to be all right. In the initial stage, of course, the greeting is likely to be more tentative than it will be later, since both parties are sizing the other up and sounding them out.

I always like to leave it to the client where to sit. I used to use chairs, and there are good arguments in favour of that, but nowadays I don't use them any more. Emmy van Deurzen says very wisely:

> I personally favour an arrangement where clients have several choices of position, for different clients prefer different arrangements. Some like the closeness of facing confrontation, some like the armchair-to-armchair fireside talk, while others like to be able to stretch out in different directions by taking a position on the couch. Fixed positions are unhelpful; one-sided recommendations need to be viewed with suspicion. The client needs room to explore what comes naturally to them, whilst reflecting on the significance of such a preference.
>
> (Van Deurzen-Smith 1997, p.193)

This whole question of the furniture and layout of the consulting room is of course an enormous one, and I have written elsewhere of the complex ins and outs of the appearance of the room where the client is seen (Rowan 1996).

Once the client is sitting down, I get him or her to talk. This is usually easy, because that is exactly what the client has come for. It just needs starting off, with one of those meaningless phrases like 'What seems to be the trouble?' or 'What brings you here?' or 'Why have you come to see me?' or 'How can I help you?'

There are some exceptions, however. It may be that this client has been sent by someone else – her husband, his mother, her superior, his doctor, or whoever – and that there is no real commitment of a personal kind. Or it may be that this client has had to wait a long time, due to some mistake having been made somewhere along the line, and therefore comes in angry or resigned or with a problem which has changed considerably. Or it may be that the client has a secret motive for coming which is not obvious – to get up the courage for a divorce, to get help with an insurance claim, to gain support in changing jobs or moving house, or something like this. In such cases, I may have to work much harder to find out whether work with this client is going to be mutually satisfying.

For this is the task of the initial interview – to establish whether there is or is not a basis for working together. Incidentally, I always refuse to set a fixed number of sessions, and would avoid any such restriction if humanly possible. How can we possibly know whether a fixed number of sessions is adequate for a client or not? The very idea is ridiculous as soon as stated. Judging what to offer a client is a very ticklish task, because it essentially involves foreseeing the future, which is impossible. Experience shows that it is best to solve this impossible problem by treating the initial interview as therapy, rather than as history taking, or as a diagnostic test, or as a questionnaire interview. The objection to this is that we may stir up sensitive material and then decide not to take this client on. The client is then left high and dry, it is said, feeling worse than at the beginning. This objection applies even more to the idea sometimes suggested, and which in fact I used to adopt, of a trial period with the therapist, of five or six sessions, before deciding whether it is good to work together on a more long-term basis. I gave this up on the grounds that it was unrealistic: the relationship is quite often formed in the first five minutes (Hobson 1985). The fifth or sixth session is very rarely a suitable point to consider the continuation of the relationship, and if the therapist insists on raising the point, many clients experience this as a rejection. What I do nowadays is to say that we should continue for at least a year before starting to worry about whether the therapy is working or not. That gets over the 'how long is a piece of string?' question, and give a realistic sense of the work involved.

The answer to this objection (about stirring up sensitive material) is that there is nothing particularly fatal about someone having sensitive material stirred up. People have immense numbers of defences, and if they don't want stuff stirred up, not all the efforts of the most skilled therapist can persuade them to stir it up. If, on the other hand, they are good and ready to face that material at the moment, it may only take a word from any therapist to open the floodgates. It is not so much the therapist stirring as the client opening. It is the client doing it and not the therapist doing it, and this applies to everything in therapy. There is a good example in Malan's (1979) book – he is a psychoanalyst but it could have happened to anyone – where he picked up a clue from something a client said in an initial interview, and asked her whether she had ever been seriously depressed. She then came up with a very depressing story about how she had had a very bad experience with another therapist, as a result of which she had almost committed suicide and had been committed to a mental hospital. He then decided, for various reasons, not to take her on as a client. As he says, this was 'traumatic enough' for the client; but in spite of this, a good relationship continued afterwards between him and her, keeping in touch over quite a period of time, while she went to another therapist.

What we are saying here, then, runs very much in line with the recommendations of the classic book by Gill *et al.* (1954) where they come out in favour of a spontaneous unfolding of the client's problems in the initial interview. I personally do not charge for a first interview, on the grounds that this encourages clients to shop around, to see several therapists and make a good choice. This makes it much easier to maintain rapport and hence to encourage the client to come back for more, so that information which does not come out in the initial interview has a chance to come out later instead. It is the client who has the power in therapy, as brilliantly argued by Scott Miller and his colleagues (1997). This is also in line with the views of William Console (Console *et al.* 1978) as exemplified in the five initial interviews that he gives in full with a running commentary. So, we are to conduct the initial interview like a therapy session (which indeed it is). But how do we do this?

Rapport

Rapport again comes in here. We have already mentioned it in connection with the first phone call. But now, in this face-to-face situation, we have far more to go on, and far more possible responses. Bandler and Grinder (1979) point out that we can mirror the client in a three-dimensional way, always taking care not to mimic or ape the client in a way that is noticed and is interpreted as mocking. We can also now do cross-over mirroring. Instead of, for example, just breathing in the same way as the client, the therapist can use hand movements to copy the chest movements of the client. Or you can match the tempo of your voice to the rate of the client's breathing. This makes for great flexibility in the means of gaining rapport. The effect of all this is to put me in tune with the client, so as to make communication that much easier. I can feel the weight, as it were, of the client, by feeling my own responses. And this puts me in touch with the client in a very special way, because this is something that the client can experience at a body level, quite independently of what may be going on mentally.

One time I saw a film of Ronnie Laing doing a first interview with a client. He did exactly what I have been talking about, echoing the movements and positions of the client. I asked him afterwards whether it had been just intuitive or whether he had done it deliberately as a matter of policy. He said the latter, adding that he always did this nowadays. It felt strange and artificial when I did this for the first time, but it had such good results that I persevered with it, and now it comes naturally. All the way through this first interview, we are trying to gain rapport, because this is first base, so to speak. Unless this is achieved, the client will not come back for more. There are many cases of clients who come for one interview and are never seen again, and this is wasteful all round. Inexperienced therapists often think they can gain rapport by smiling a lot and being nice to the client, but this is not it at all.

The second thing we are trying to do in the initial interview is to get information. At the end of the interview we are going to have to say something to the client about coming back for more meetings. So the decision has to be made: do I take this client on for regular therapy, do I refer this person on to someone else, do I lay down certain conditions before I agree to take the person on, do I tell the person that what they need is not therapy but something else, or what?

Since we have already established that I am not interested in diagnosis, what is to stop me taking on every client who comes? As we said in the last chapter, the key issue is whether the person needs residential treatment or not. And there are certain key things that would point to this: if the person is very out of touch with reality, so that they do not respond to my suggestions or questions, but seem to spend a good deal of the time in a world of their own; if the person very easily gets into suicidal states as soon as certain subjects are mentioned; if the person gets very physically aggressive as soon as certain issues are raised – these and other obvious indications of deep disturbance show the need for residential treatment. So we certainly need information on such subjects as: Has the person ever been in a mental hospital? Is the person on a course of psychiatric drugs at the moment? Does the person have hallucinations? Does the person have violent and long-lasting mood swings? Has the person tried to commit suicide? (and when, and how). All these things are highly relevant to our most basic decisions about this person as a potential client. (See Appendix 4: Should I take on this client?).

The question is, then, how do we get this information without doing or saying things to the client that could be anti-therapeutic? We do it simply by making the initial interview the first therapy session. In therapy, we are all the time inviting the client to open up to what is really important and central for them: we are continually asking the question in some way – 'Where does it hurt most?' And if we keep on probing in the normal way during the initial interview, all these points will come up spontaneously and of their own accord.

Going wrong

So what is this 'normal way' we have just referred to? It is slightly different for each therapist, but it essentially consists in paying attention to what the client is saying and doing, and responding in such a way that the client becomes more aware of what he or she is saying and doing. We shall be going into this in detail in the next chapter. What we can look at now are some of the typical ways in which the inexperienced therapist may get off on the wrong foot, and be unable to get back on to the right track again very easily. These are the main things that can get in the way of good communication in the therapy session.

Getting angry with the client

It is surprising how often the unskilled therapist will try to put the client down, score points off the client, punish the client and so on. It is easy to feel that the client is getting it wrong, not really trying, covering up, running away, avoiding the real issue, acting dumb, etc., and to express this in some form implying blame. But this is what is known as blaming the victim, and it doesn't help.

Being scared of the client

Some clients come out with statements that frighten the therapist – they may be about violence, or about craziness, or about sex, or about death, or whatever – and from that point on the therapist keeps a noticeable distance from the client. There is also the question of professional narcissism, as described in my paper on that subject (Rowan 2008), which also deals with general defensiveness on the part of the therapist.

Seducing the client

It is also possible for the therapist to be so keen on getting rapport going, being nice and approachable, achieving good contact and so forth, that he or she can quite overwhelm the client with warmth and smiles. This can be smothering and confusing for the client, who can be so sucked in as to lose all track of their inner processes.

Getting confused by the client

Sometimes the client is so vague or scattered that it is hard to pin down the real problem. A good basic question to ask yourself is – 'Who is doing what to whom, and how is this a problem?' Another good question is – 'How did you get to contact me at the particular time you did, rather than some other time?' Another question that can help in several different ways is – 'What can you think of that would be a good sign that something was beginning to change?' This is sometimes called 'The Miracle Question', phrased in the form – 'If you woke up next morning and your problem had disappeared by some miracle, what is the first thing you would notice that would tell you that had happened?'

Getting intimidated by the client

Oftentimes, when a therapist is still in training, clients will come along who have more experience of therapy than the therapist has. If the client asks questions such as 'How old are you?' – 'What are your qualifications?' – 'How can you understand my problems when you're so different?' – 'How come you work in a dump like this?' – and so on, it is important not to be put on the defensive. It usually makes sense to say 'Can you make the statement behind that question?' In other words, without avoiding the question, probe for its meaning, what lies behind it. This is not an ordinary conversation, and the client does not really expect the normal rules of polite conversation to apply. Much more likely is that the client is testing the therapist in some way.

After this digression, let us get back to the question of what information we are trying to get in the initial interview. One key issue is the question of relationships – past, present and future. Relationships in the early home environment up to school age, and then relationships at school, are certainly worth getting. How many siblings, and where in the sequence the client was born, can often be significant. How the client left home, and first job and marriage details, can be of value, and also relationships with the client's own children if any.

Why this is important is that there may be some very obvious indications there of what problems there are, and what the answers to them may be. It helps us to see which of the client's reactions to events are exaggerated, neurotic, inappropriate, etc., and which are thoroughly justified and healthy and appropriate. It is often helpful to the client, too, in clarifying issues and making connections.

There are even some more basic reasons for getting this information. Supposing that we see a client, and have what we think is a very good meeting, where everything went well, and then we meet someone who says – 'I hear you're seeing Charlie. Did he mention that all his three brothers committed suicide?' It seems that one would feel a little foolish if this had not come out. It is something we ought to know about, because how our client feels concerning this may be one of the things we should tackle first, just to check that he is not going to do the same thing. And of course in doing this, it is very important to listen properly. And this issue of listening is so important that we need to examine it in detail.

Listening

Why listening is so difficult for the new therapist is because there is a lot of unlearning to be done. In most conversations, we are formulating a reply when the other person is talking, so as to be ready when he or she finishes; we are going back and forth between what is being said and our reply, so that we never really hear properly all that is said. The therapeutic meeting is very different from that:

Ordinary listening	Therapeutic listening
Interest in the content of the statement – what it is intended to convey.	Interest in the statement itself as a symptom of things the client did not intend to say.
Trying to relate the other person's experience to your own.	Not paying attention to your own previous experiences.
Thinking of interesting replies to carry on the conversation and keep one's end up.	Not being concerned with replies or conversations, only with the client's efforts at self-exploration.

It would be tedious to enumerate all the ways in which therapeutic listening differs from ordinary listening; all that is intended here is to underline the point that there is a good deal of unlearning to be done. But the other important thing to realize about listening is that there are a number of different levels involved (Rowan 1992b).

Content

The thing with what is being said is continually to push the client into being more specific. If the statement is 'People don't like me', the next question is – 'Which people? Name one'. If the statement is – 'I know you have to make allowances', the client might be asked to change it to – 'I know I have to make allowances', or asked the question – 'Who exactly says you have to make allowances?' This gentle urging in the direction of being more specific and more personal is one of the most basic moves of the therapist, as Bandler and Grinder (1975) have pointed out. It always has the effect of moving the client into deeper levels of experience.

Feelings

The feelings behind what is being said come out most prominently in the way things are said. If the whole tone of voice is flat and depressed, for example, that may be more important than anything the client is saying. Sometimes you can hear a kind of suppressed panic in the voice which is very characteristic once you can spot it; in such a case I would want to get the person to relax more before doing anything else. Feelings of anger (resentment, irritation, antagonism, rage, etc.) and feelings of hurt (pain, suffering, injury, etc.) can be very important, because either one can cover up for the other: in men I have noticed that it is more common for anger to cover up for hurt, while in women it is more common for hurt to cover up for anger, but it can happen either way in either sex.

It is impossible really to listen for feelings without having feelings yourself. Hence this kind of listening can be hard on the therapist unless the therapist has fully worked through the same level of feelings in themselves. This is one of the main reasons why we need to go through the whole process of psychotherapy ourselves. Another reason is that therapists tend to stop clients from going into a level of feelings deeper than those they have experienced and worked through themselves. Thus clients can be cheated of part of their own experience, if the therapist has blocks still remaining. This is sometimes phrased as the therapist needing to have worked through their own Shadow material. The Shadow is a useful concept from Jungian therapy, which should be more widely known and used, in my opinion. This is a terribly important issue.

The body

It is possible to listen also to body language. The way that a person is sitting may be all screwed up even when what they are saying sounds perfectly reasonable. Persistent gestures can be very revealing. Expressions of the face may tell you something, but the hands and feet are much harder to keep under control: the actual movement may be disguised, but the moment when it starts can say a lot. The breathing can be very important: often by breathing at the same rate and the same depth or shallowness as the client, you can pick up something worthwhile. How the person moves may be revealing – do they talk bold and act timid, or vice versa? Many clients have a stiffness or rigidity somewhere in their body. Where is it exactly, and how do they keep it stiff or rigid, and how come it is so important not to let go of it? The book by Smith, Clance and Imes (1998) has a lot of useful ideas about all this.

Sexuality

A lot can be going on at a sexual level between therapist and client.The therapist may seduce the client, the client may seduce the therapist, and spontaneous mutual falling in love cannot be ruled out. All these things are harder to sort out if the therapist is not clear in this area, so again it is important for the therapist to have worked through his or her own sexual material first. A therapist who is still engaged in a personal 'search for the beloved' can be a menace to all and sundry (Russell 1993). This is made doubly difficult by the fact that we often touch the client in some way. For these reasons it is even more important for us to have gone through the full process of psychotherapy than it is for the psychoanalyst. Otherwise there is likely to be a trail of broken hearts rather than a trail of real meetings.

Spirituality

A client is a spiritual being on a spiritual path (even though they may not be aware of it yet) and some of the material they bring up may be at that level (Boorstein 1996). Jung showed long ago how dreams might reveal spiritual directions and spiritual longings which could be quite surprising to the person at a conscious level: and James Hillman (1989) notably followed up this insight. Unless we are listening for these things, we are quite likely to miss them. We can in fact help the client to get into this area by using symbols. It is often possible to ask the person to put forth their problems in the form of a drawing, or by the use of a sand-box, or through a guided fantasy, or by just asking for an image or symbol of their problem.

Again it cannot be overemphasized that the therapist who has not worked through this material in the course of their own development is likely to stop the client going through it. As always, the therapist needs to be at least a few steps ahead of the client in order to work effectively (Rowan 2005a). And this spiritual area is likely to be particularly important for creative people, or those who want to be creative or more creative. It can open a whole new way of being creative, which the person did not have access to before.

The great clarifier in this area has been Ken Wilber, who has written with enormous clarity about the exact way in which psychology and psychotherapy relate to spirituality. Anyone who wants to sort out this area of listening would do well to read Wilber (1981). See also Chapter 14.

The political

Sometimes the things that are bothering people are just as much political as personal. In such cases it may be advisable to suggest action other than therapy, such as joining a women's group, doing some community organizing, blowing the whistle on an employer, going on a demonstration, duplicating a leaflet or whatever. It may also at times be desirable to join with the client in changing a situation that is politically oppressive (Freedman and Combs 1996). So it is necessary to be able to listen at this level, and to be able to hear the political element in what is being said (we shall be looking at this further in Chapter 10).

Of all the levels of listening, it is the emotional level which is the most important. It links, in a unique way, the earliest and the latest experience, the deepest and the shallowest, the most refined and the most earthy. If there is one thing the therapist has to learn, it is how to listen, and how to encourage the client to relate, at this level. And it is in the initial interview that this listening needs to start. In recent years, there has been much more interest in the relationship between therapist and client (Hycner 1993, 1991).

Of course, there may be more than one 'initial interview', because not all the essential groundwork will have come out in one session. In the next chapter we shall see how the opening moves in therapy are made over a number of sessions. But in the initial interview some structural decisions must be made, and it is to these that we must now turn.

Structure

This is an extremely important area, because it sets the scene for the whole of the rest of the therapy. It raises the whole question of what is often called the 'contract'.

The first and most important element in this is to get it clear as to what the meetings are about. Freud always used to explain his basic rule to people straight away – 'Say whatever goes through your mind'. He would embroider on this, and explain it further, but this was the basic contract.

Nowadays we tend to be a bit more aware that the client may have quite limited aims; the idea of an open-ended time-period extending into the dim future may not appeal very much. Also the therapist may not think in the long-term way that Freud did. These issues are problematic and are not to be taken for granted. Wilson (1996) has a good discussion of these issues, saying that there are several choice points where decisions have to be made about whether to continue, and how to continue.

In terms of the actual content of the sessions, I usually give the client a handout which says, among other things:

In these sessions you will be exploring your own experience. I am just here to help you to do that, by offering the time and space you need. I can offer certain skills which may enable you to do it better or quicker than you could on your own, but basically it is you doing it, not me doing it. And unless you really treat it in that way, nothing much is going to change.

This seems to me a statement of obvious fact rather than of therapeutic policy, but it certainly is a question of policy as to whether you say that, or say something else. What can be fatal here is to make this statement too late. If, at a certain point, once the therapy has started, you say – 'What do you think this therapy is about?' or 'What do you think you are doing here?', this will come across as angry and blaming, and probably will be angry and blaming.

It is very important to raise this issue early, because it immediately opens up the crucial area of what the relationship is going to be. If therapy is going to work, the relationship must be one where the client is being honest with the therapist, not censoring, not holding back, not lying. And for this to happen the client must trust the therapist. Surprisingly often, this does not happen. A survey once showed that of all the people to whom one would admit one's deepest secrets, therapists came about tenth on the list! Now it is not possible to deal with this issue completely in the first interview – trust often takes time to build up – but it would be irresponsible not to raise it at all.

Another aspect of this is the question of what relationship I am going to have with the client. There is a lot of new thinking in this area now, which says that the relationship is the most important thing in therapy, and that both parties are deeply involved at a personal level: this makes it sound as if the relationship is much more equal than has previously been conceived, and that in fact therapist and client are co-constructing reality together (Paul and Charura 2015).

Nevertheless, the relationship with the client is going to be an unequal one, and it can only do harm to pretend otherwise. This is clear from the practice of co-counselling, a system dear to all democrats, which has a very clear distinction between what belongs to one role and what to the other (Kauffman and New 2004). It is also clear from co-counselling that this inequality does not depend on mystification or expertise or money – it simply depends on the fact that the client is the one who is working on problems, and the therapist is the one assisting the process. This means that the client is putting forward the least adequate, the sickest, the most needy aspects of self; while the therapist is putting forward the most adequate, the healthiest, the most nurturing aspects of self.

It is important to be clear that you are not necessarily any healthier than the client, mentally or in any other way. You may even be less healthy, in some absolute overall sense, and yet be able to do a good job for the client. During the session, you are laying aside your various hang-ups and inadequacies, or using them constructively, but you are not exploring them or abandoning yourself to them: this is the task of the client. This can actually be quite a reassuring point, because many people who want to be therapists put it off in the belief that they have to be perfect before they start. You don't. In fact, there is evidence to show that untrained people are just as effective as trained psychotherapists in getting good outcomes for clients (Durlack 1979; Hattie *et al.* 1984; Berman and Norton 1985). It is obviously a good thing to do plenty of personal work on yourself, but it does not necessarily make you a better therapist (Garfield 1979).

In fact, it is often advisable to deliberately adopt a posture of being one-down to the client, and to adopt what the Buddhists call 'beginners' mind'. This kind of flexibility enlarges my range of choices, and means that I am more manoeuvrable in what I do. It limits a therapist very much to adopt always a one-up position, though this is a great temptation for many.

There is, however, an enormous pitfall just here, which it is important not to fall into. Once we agree that the therapist/client relationship is a professional one, which is fundamentally unequal, it is all too easy to then assume that we are responsible for the client's feelings, and for the client getting better or worse. And it is in the first interview that this issue is most confusing and hard to sort out; yet if you get off on the wrong foot it can affect the whole subsequent course of the therapy.

The therapist is not a rescuer

Obviously in the initial interview the major responsibility for gaining rapport, for getting information, for starting off the therapeutic process and for setting the structures is mine. It is my space as a therapist that is being used, my time that is being paid for, and in general I own the situation – it is my set-up, in which I can call the shots in a great many ways. But the one thing I am never, and can never be, responsible for is the client getting better. As soon as I think thoughts such as – 'I am going to cure this client' or 'I really want this person to get better', I am getting tangled up in a different role altogether, the role of rescuer. And the point is that you can actually be a good therapist, but there is no way of being a good rescuer.

A rescuer wants to control the other person, and get them to be the way the rescuer wants them to be. Now the object of therapy is that the client should have more self-control (autonomy, self-determination, spontaneity, access to personal power, etc., as is explained in Chapter 5), and it is counterproductive to try to achieve this by exerting control over the client. More important even than this, as soon as I have a programme for the client, or a set of aims that the client is supposed to live up to, I am storing up frustration for myself when the client doesn't live up to it, and this frustration is likely to lead to aggression against the client. I will blame the client for not living up to my programme. James Bugental (1978) puts it very well when he says:

> One of the most fundamental characteristics of the ideal therapist is a conviction, born of experience as well as of theory, that the intrinsic healing/growth process of the client can be trusted. What this means is that such a therapist knows full well that no one can heal or cure or even directly 'therap' the client. At a gut level, one learns that the only force which can produce genuine and lasting change is the power and thrust of the client toward greater realization of what is potential within. The therapist who knows this deeply does not waste her or his own or the client's time and emotions trying to do what cannot be done: solve the client's problems, guide the client's life choices, or urge forth the client's latent capacities for living more fully. Instead such a therapist concentrates on aiding the client in recognizing and releasing the blocks that keep the *aliveness* uneasily imprisoned within.
>
> (pp.35–6)

This has to do with the whole theory of change. One of the classic statements on this came from Arnold Beisser (1972), who wrote from a Gestalt therapy standpoint about what he called the paradoxical theory of change. He stated it very succinctly: 'real change occurs when people become what they are, not when they try to become what they are not'. It can be seen immediately how well this fits in with the statement of Jim Bugental just quoted. And Beisser goes on to say that the same argument applies to social change too.

This has to do with the whole question of what therapy is about, a topic that we shall return to in Chapter 5. It is not about curing clients. As George A. Kelly beautifully puts it, the key to our destiny is our ability to reconstrue what we cannot deny. Joan was terribly abused in her own home as a child, and concluded that she was worthless. In order to keep her down, she was told over and over again that she was worthless. In therapy she learned that no matter what was done to her it didn't mean she was worthless. It was the change in meaning that did the trick. It was seeing the past differently. And it was something she had to do for herself, not something the therapist could possibly do for her. It is not the therapist's insight that does the work, but the client's readiness to reconstrue, redefine, re-experience, revise, re-decide, re-view what happened in the past. And at the end of the process, the client may emerge just ordinary, as in this example:

Tom started to college during the second year he was in therapy. This was the fourth time he'd entered college. Each time before he'd given up because his need to do exceptionally well had foundered on his fear of really trying (for if he really tried and then failed he'd be shown up so terribly; while if he wasn't really trying then of course there was no real test). Now he could say, 'It's a funny experience just to listen to a professor to hear what he's saying. It may sound crazy, but I've never really done that before. I always was listening to prove to myself I already knew what he was going to say or to find out the trick he was going to pull on the exam or with the expectation that any minute I'd discover I really didn't know what it was all about and that I had no business being there at all. Now I just listen, and, you know, it's really interesting, and I get most of it, but not all, and that's all right too'. 'Now I just listen', Tom says. This is the essence of authentic being. The changed concern of authentic being is that concern is directed toward that which one is intending, not dispersed on what one may be disclosing or other irrelevant matters.

(Bugental 1981, p.268)

The game of being a rescuer is well described in the TA Drama Triangle. The rescuer finds a victim who is suffering from a persecutor. But if the victim doesn't respond in the right way, the rescuer starts to experience the victim as a persecutor who is frustrating the whole enterprise, and starts to fight back against this. But to the victim, this seems as if the rescuer has turned into a new persecutor, so the victim has been victimized all over again. The gamelike quality of this set-up can be recognized by the fact that the rescuer is always doing a bit more than he or she really wants to, and the victim is always finding new ways of frustrating the rescuer. The only way out of a game such as this is to bring in a third party who can see things a bit more clearly, and sort out the rescuer's hidden desire for control, as well as the victim's hidden desire to avoid all responsibility.

So if you don't want this to develop, it is important to avoid ever trying to rescue a client. You are there to assist the client to do whatever the client is ready and willing to do, not to know better than the client what the client needs. Every time I do something for the client, I stop the client doing it. Every time I take responsibility for the client, I stop the client taking responsibility. Every time I try to help, I get in the client's way.

Whenever someone takes over for me and tells me what to do, I find myself back as a little boy, in a dependent state. When I went to San Francisco with a friend, she told me where to turn because she knew the streets better. I became very dependent on her, even asking for obvious directions. Actually, when she wasn't along, I got places quite well by myself.

(Schutz 1971, p.113)

And this means abandoning two very seductive traps for the therapist – being right and being successful. Every time I want to be right about a client I am limiting the client to my categories and my assumptions. I am setting limits to the client's own process of change, because once I think I am right I will defend my opinion and thus find it harder to change; I won't want to be proved wrong. But in reality I don't need to be right, and I don't want to be right – I just want to stay in contact with the client.

And every time I want to be successful I am secretly working for self-aggrandizement, striding to the far shores of my profession on the stepping stones of my clients. Success and failure are both largely illusion; people develop in quite a wavy and contradictory way, and what is success on one level may often be failure on another level. It is really a mistake to use the words 'good' and 'bad' at all: every failure is a success, and every advantage is a disadvantage. All a client really needs is someone who is prepared to stay with them while they explore the darkest and most difficult parts of their experience. There is an excellent discussion of experiences of success and failure in the book by Dave Mearns and Windy Dryden (1990).

These traps do not only exist in the initial interview – they apply right through the process of therapy. But if the relationship is to get off on the right foot, it is particularly important to keep them in mind during the initial interview.

Frequency and length of sessions

A simpler structural matter is the question of frequency of meeting. Even if a few trial meetings are set up, their frequency still needs to be thought about carefully. On the whole, experience has shown that it is much better to have high frequency at first, and then relax it, rather than to have low frequency at first, and then step it up. It is more encouraging to drop the frequency, more worrying to step it up. And it is a fact that the new client coming for therapy is usually impatient: now that they have taken the decision to do something like this, they want to get on with it as quickly as possible.

Three meetings a week is about the maximum for practitioners such as me, and this would usually be for relatively short periods of time. Obviously the question of money comes in here. Can the client afford three sessions a week? Some compromise may be necessary between what would be ideal and what the client can manage. So very often it seems that twice-weekly sessions are set up at first, which may drop down to once a week later on, when it seems right. Once a fortnight always seems too long for real therapy, though it may be all right for a 'ticking-over' stage where nothing much is happening, but contact needs to be kept for some reason or another – and the same applies to longer intervals. If the client asks for once-a-month meetings, or something like that, it is best to query it. If it is a question of money, it is better to have a batch of weekly meetings and then a break of two or three months.

One interesting issue about this is that the longer the interval, the more time the client will have to use to tell about all sorts of incidents which have happened in the interim. This will then leave less time for the deeper material to be worked on and resolved. So when deep work is required, it is usually best to have a higher frequency of meeting or a longer session, so that the right proportion can be kept between daily experience and deep work.

On the question of length of sessions, there is tremendous variety. Many techniques, particularly the heavier ones such as body work and regression, take the person very deeply into early material; it takes time to go down and time to come back up again. For this reason some practitioners favour a 2-hour or even a 3-hour session. I found one client worked best with a one-and-a-half hour session. Some people working in the primal area have even used anything up to a 10-hour session.

Even with the 1-hour session, which is usually most convenient for all concerned, I will always give the full hour, rather than the 50-minute hour favoured by analysts. (I once went to a lecture by an analyst who said that no one could concentrate for more than 50 minutes, but there is no research to support this idea). The reason for this is that I do not have clients coming as close together as the analyst. Freud used sometimes to have as many as ten patients a day, one after the other, and obviously if you are doing something like this, you need a break between each one to gather yourself together and maybe write up some notes. I read about some analysts in New York who see four clients for 45 minutes each back-to-back in the morning and another four in the afternoon. This sounds horrible to me. The much more intensive work of the therapist described in this book needs more in the way of a break than this, and usually I leave half an hour between clients. So here again it is often best to set up the longer sessions at first, and then move to the shorter ones as and when that seems possible or desirable.

Fees

The last structural matter we shall need to discuss is the question of fees. Obviously this may have been raised already, but it is material for the initial interview, and should be discussed here. At any given time, there is a 'going rate' which the therapist will have adopted on the basis of the current level of prosperity, the amount of his or her experience, the location of the practice, the acuteness of demand for his or her services, the practice of other therapists, and so on. But nearly always this is flexible, so that a well-off person can expect to pay more, and a poor person less, than this going rate. Some therapists, including me, simply charge twice the hourly rate for a 2-hour session, while others have a special rate for 2- or 3-hour sessions. Some therapists charge twice the hourly rate for two sessions a week, while others have a special rate for that. It is partly a matter of what kind of practice one wants, and partly a matter of what people can afford. I like to charge fees that are high enough so that I don't feel exploited, and low enough so that I don't feel like an exploiter. This is a matter that can only be settled by a sensitive discussion with the client.

Often the question arises here – 'How long does therapy take?' Evidently this has some bearing on the same fee issue, because a certain amount a week can be found for a short period, but not indefinitely, perhaps. I used to be very vague about this, suggesting that symptom relief might come relatively quickly, but that deeper and more far-reaching changes might take longer. Nowadays I say that for any therapy worth bothering about, we should think in terms of a year's work together, before we start to worry whether we are getting far enough. But by the end of the year, we should have dropped down to one hour once a week. This seems to me much more realistic. The psychoanalysts tell people to expect 2 years' work before starting to think about any change. This is less realistic, because most patients drop out of psychoanalytic psychotherapy after less than a year's work.

A number of research studies have been done on the length of therapy (for example, see Garfield 1978) which all seem to show that the drop-out rate is very high: it is quite common for a client to come for just one or two sessions and not come back, and in a long series of studies the average number of sessions actually achieved was about five. This was mostly in public outpatient clinics, rather than in private practice, but according to Wolberg (1977) ten to fifty sessions is usual in private practice. This makes it all the more important to have a good initial interview, where the client feels welcomed and understood, and where both parties see eye to eye on what needs to be done. It can be seen now why I lay so much stress on building rapport and starting therapy within the initial interview; it is on this foundation that the therapeutic enterprise is built.

Boundaries

There are certain issues that hover round the edges of the therapy which need to be addressed. A psychotherapist, in my understanding, takes no medical or legal responsibility for the client, and does not contact the client's GP unless there is some specific reason to do so. We do not advise on psychiatric drugs, either to take them or not to take them; though of course we may mention that such drugs (a) may interfere with the aware consciousness which is optimal for therapy, and (b) have to be taken indefinitely if relied on to the exclusion of all else, because they deal with symptoms rather than causes. In recent years some therapists have been agitating for access to psychiatric drugs, but in my opinion this is a mistake.

It is wise for the therapist to take out professional insurance, because clients have become much more litigious in recent years, and damages can be very high in some cases. Because so many therapists are taking out insurance now, the rates have come down from what they were a few years ago.

Anything which falls outside the set framework of the sessions needs to be taken up and dealt with as an issue, even if it is very small. Such things as lateness, attempts to extend the session, gifts to the therapist, visits to the lavatory, late or non-payment of fees, accidental meetings outside the sessions, phone calls, attempts to hug or kiss the therapist, accidental interruptions to the session – all these need to be brought into the session and dealt with as issues that may affect the relationship and may affect the course of the treatment. This can be done in such a way as not to seem like a criticism of the client, but rather an effort to understand.

The question of gifts depends rather on the value of the gift. A small bunch of flowers may be acceptable, though it should still be raised as an issue – what does it mean? A diamond necklace would be highly suspect, on the other hand. The essence of a gift is that it puts the other person in your debt. It is an attempt to extend the relationship in the sessions beyond the sessions themselves. I remember discussing the gift of a rather expensive pen to a therapist in supervision. We spent about half an hour going into all the pros and cons of accepting it. On raising the subject with the client, it turned out that he had obtained it quite cheaply, and this clarification enabled the therapist to accept it.

One key thing to remember in all these areas is that there is more than one thing going on at any time within the client. Take something as apparently minor as changing the time of a session to accommodate the client. On a conscious, overt, adult level there is no problem about this – the therapist agrees, the client is grateful. But at another level – and here we may talk in various vocabularies about the unconscious, the awareness level, the inner child, the alternate I-position, the alter ego or even the Shadow – the client may feel a deep sense of the boundaries not being safe, of being given too much power, of being indulged too much, of being chosen and special, or just a vague uneasiness. It is very important for a therapist to be aware of these other possibilities, and not to assume that what appears on the surface is all there is. Sometimes it is good to change the session time to accommodate the client, and sometimes it is important to say no. Only experience – or perhaps good supervision – can inform the therapist as to which is better.

4 The opening sessions

Once the initial interview is over, we start the therapy proper. We now know the main lines of the client's problem, and have set up the structures within which it can be tackled. I always start the session by keeping quiet. If nothing happens, I then ask – 'What is on your mind right now?'

Asking questions is an obvious way of getting some kind of response. But open-ended questions are much better for this purpose than questions which can be answered with a yes or no. Get into the habit of always asking questions such as – 'What happened then?' 'What was the worst thing about that?' 'How did you feel?' 'Tell me all you can about him' 'Can you tell me some more about that?' and so on. Of course, the traditional 'Mm-hm' is always good – some noise to indicate that you are listening with interest and expecting some more. But it is no good asking questions and then not listening to the answers. (This is one of the faults common to new therapists who are nervously trying to fill the silence.) The object of asking questions is simply to give you something to listen to, as explained in the last chapter. The answers should be followed up in such a way as to convey to the client that you are not only listening but also hearing and understanding the replies.

There is a warning to be given at this point, however, which is that it is usually best to avoid any question starting with the word 'Why?' There are several reasons for this: first, it is basically an aggressive question, suggesting that there must be an answer or explanation known to the client; second, it takes the client out of the level of feelings and into the level of abstract intellect; and third, it is asking the client to do something which is really the business of the whole interaction – namely to get insight into the pattern of the client's life choices. In other words, the question 'why?' usually represents an attempt to cut corners in therapy, and it very seldom works. And it usually turns out, in any case, that another approach is much more appropriate and useful. If someone says – 'I hate my mother!' we don't ask 'Why?', we say – 'Could you express that more fully?', or 'How do you experience that in your body?', or 'Can you bring to mind a time when you felt that strongly?', or 'Would you like to go further into that?', or 'Are there times when you don't feel like that?' All these responses keep the client on the feeling level, and invite the client to go deeper in self-exploration.

There are exceptions to this general rule, and no rule should be left unexamined and untested in any case, but on the whole it is worth keeping to it.

Offering choices is usually good. These are usually things which in a group we would call exercises. But in the individual session they can be strictly tailored to the person. So you might say – 'Try clenching your fists when you say that' or 'Could you say that louder?' or 'Say that again' or 'Would you like to stand up and say that?', 'How about lying down and saying that again?', 'Try hitting the cushion', 'What do your hands want to do?', and so on. There are hundreds of these ideas, and new ones can be made up as occasion demands. They all depend on the basic idea of noticing what is going on at a physical level, an idea which was first brought into therapy by Ferenczi in the early 1920s, and greatly developed by Moreno and the Gestalt therapists in their quite different tradition. It is most important for the therapist to be able to pick up and use these physical cues.

Feeding back impressions can be very useful. It should normally be done in a permissive manner, rather than in a dominant way. Thus – 'I wonder if there isn't some anger behind that depression?' or 'Is there perhaps someone you are being depressed at?' would be better than just – 'Tell me about the anger behind that'. It is both appropriately modest (you can never be certain, you are always guessing to some extent) and appropriately comradely.

The general approach of the therapist is to act as a comrade engaged with the client in a common search, a common concern. It is always a question of saying – 'You can do it'. You may add – 'Here is a hint, try this, use this', but always in a context of trying to increase the client's choices, the client's autonomy. This cannot be done by diagnosing the client, by telling the client what is wrong with him or her, by trying to know better than the client what is going on. The relationship can be a very intimate one as time goes on. This is usually good, but it can also be threatening to a nervous client, so it needs to be handled with great care.

Feeding back impressions can be done in ways that are imaginative, and these are often very effective. The therapist can say – 'I had this flash' – and then describe a symbol or image of the client, or the client's situation. The therapist can say 'My fantasy is . . .' and tell about a scene or picture that seems to express in some way what is going on for the client. The therapist may mimic the client's posture or gesture in a way that is funny without being intentionally hurtful.

All feedback can be felt as hurtful or disturbing to the client sometimes, but if it is accurate in the first place, this hurt can be worked through successfully and can add to the relationship rather than taking away from it. It is one form of self-disclosure, particularly when it takes the form – 'My feeling is . . .' and really does reveal the therapist's own feelings. Mistakes in therapy can be very useful if they are handled well, and the repair of misunderstandings has been shown to be healing if done well.

The issue of **self-disclosure** is an important one, and needs some attention in its own right, particularly in the first few meetings, where it is most likely to arise. There are two extreme views on self-disclosure. At one extreme there is the traditional psychoanalytic view that therapist self-disclosure is out, because the ideal therapist is a mirror, merely playing back the client's unconscious fantasies. On this account, attempts by the client to relate to the real person behind the therapeutic front are always suspect, as being merely attempts to get off the hook, and play some kind of power game instead of doing therapy. At the other extreme, there is the traditional existentialist view that the therapist is first and foremost a real person, and that the whole value of the therapeutic encounter lies in the real meeting of real people in a setting where it is made hard to evade these realities. There is a very good discussion of all this in the book edited by Andrea Bloomgarden and Rosemary Mennuti (2009).

If the request for information is basically hostile – 'I bet you have never had problems of poverty like mine; how much money do you earn in a year?' – it is usually best just to pick up on the hostility and say something like – 'It seems you are angry with me; could you say some more about that?' If it seems to be a request for reassurance, a question such as – 'How can you possibly understand childbirth, when you've never been through it?' – then it is often possible to emphasize the difference between form and content. It is possible to have the same depth of experience, and therefore to be able to go down to the same level of feeling or pain, without having had the same specific experience. But you as the therapist have to decide whether it is reassurance the client needs, or something else. You may feel that it is best to give straightforward reassurance first, and then, if the questioning goes on, to deal with the hostility, which by then will be more obvious. There is a good discussion of all this in the book by Barry Farber (2006).

Another type of information that the client may seek consists of personal details about you: are you married or single, how many children have you got, how old are you, what school did you go to, where have you lived, are you gay, etc. It is your choice whether to give these or not, but it is always best to probe the answer before giving it, by asking what difference it would make. This will tell you whether it was a casual question or a question heavily loaded with meaning and feelings for the client.

A further type of question may be something very immediate and direct, such as – 'What are you feeling about me right now?' Rather than giving an impulsive answer to this – the first thing that pops into your mind; rather than giving a highly controlled answer to this – a diplomatic reply; the best thing is to give a spontaneous answer – reach into your consciousness for all that is going on in you, at every level, and integrate all those feelings, all those considerations, all those values, into your answer. Some research evidence backing up this stand is to be found in Hill (1989). But all the new thinking on the relationship says that questions such as this are valuable and to be welcomed and used therapeutically. Of course, one possible answer may be silence – there is no compulsion on you to answer at all – but be aware that this can be perceived as a defensive and status-conscious way of dealing with such a question.

Opening up spaces for the client to move into is a very important activity for the therapist, and there are a number of ways of doing it. One of the most important is the use of metaphor, symbols and images. The best chapter I have come across on the use of metaphor is the one by Kate Maguire (2001). If the client seems to have some problem with heterosexual relationships, you can say – 'There are two large boxes on the ground, one with a man in it, and the other with a woman in it. Imagine that scene and tell me what happens next'. The answer must reveal actual attitudes, since there is no factual content.

Or if the client wants to escape and be somewhere else, you could say – 'Close your eyes and go in your imagination to the place you would most like to be right now. Tell me what happens when you get there'.

These are just examples. Absolutely anything the client says or does can be picked up in this way and a space opened up for him or her to move into. The most general way of all is just to say 'What would you most like to do right now?' Or this can be put more negatively by saying – 'Is there anything you are avoiding right now?' This all has to do with the important issue of **tracking the client**. This means staying in contact with the client, following what is going on, exploiting every opportunity to get deeper into the client's experience. This involves a moment-to-moment awareness which is actually a different state of consciousness from that which we use in ordinary conversation. It is not exactly a trance, but it is akin to certain states found in meditation, as Schuster (1979) has pointed out.

Awareness

A great deal has been said by various people about the importance of this kind of awareness. Perhaps John Enright (1972) puts it most clearly:

> I am quite serious in asserting that most of us, including those of us in the mental health professions, are much of the time, to a surprising

extent, not fully aware of our actual present. Much of the content of our consciousness is remembering, speculating, planning ('rehearsing' for our next interpersonal performance), or carrying on a busy inner dialogue (or monologue). More specifically, we professionals sitting with a patient may be diagnosing, 'prognosing', planning our next intervention, wondering what time it's getting to be, etc. – we are only too rarely being really open to our experience of self and other. Those of us who are not seriously mentally ill remain sufficiently in touch with the actual environment to move through it reasonably effectively. We respond to its salient characteristics, but miss so many nuances that our experience of the world and the other is often pale and our memories of it, therefore, weak. Engaged as we are with our own phantoms, we attend only sketchily to the other. Since he then seems rather pale and incomplete, we fill him out with our own projections and react vigorously to these. The resulting encounter often gives a convincing show of life and involvement where, in fact, there is little.

What should we be cultivating, then, instead of this? It is a state of consciousness where we are genuinely open to listen, on all the levels we mentioned earlier. Freud called it 'free-floating attention', and emphasized how it hovered evenly over the client and the therapist, being aware of what was going on in each, and between both. Reik (1948) called it 'listening with the third ear', and emphasized how important it was to stay in touch with the feelings involved, which might be beneath the surface. Rogers (1968) calls it 'intuitive sensing', and emphasizes that it is the opposite of having clear-cut constructs – it is a whole person awareness, not just an intellectual awareness. Torbert (1972) just calls it consciousness, as opposed to the mystery-mastery way of thinking that he sees as much more common in our culture. It is hard to describe, but it seems that the essence of it is openness to one's own experience as well as that of the other, in a context of action. It entails a deliberate effort, in the early stages, to switch off one's own usual state of consciousness, where one is trying to be sharp and accurate and focused. It is a kind of deliberate unfocusing, which is well described in the Taoist literature (see Rawson and Legeza 1973). As long as we stay focused and single-minded, we are limited by the categories that our intellect has set up; we are at the mercy of old knowledge which has become fixed and inflexible. When we unfocus, we let in the object, and we let out our other faculties – feeling, intuition, remote associations, creativity.

Schuster (1979) suggests that this kind of awareness can be cultivated by the practice of meditation, particularly those types which encourage mindfulness and witnessing. He says:

In this way one begins to train the mind to stay in the present moment. Likewise a 'directness of vision' develops as the meditator learns to bypass the intellectual-analytical screen of conditioned thought (Thera 1972). Reality is experienced directly and this results in a resurgence of spontaneity and freshness that has been likened to the unconditioned perception of a small child.

We must not be misled by this last phrase to imagine that this state of awareness is regressive in character, going back to some pristine state before the intellect started to do its work. We can never do that. We have to go beyond the intellect, not try to put the clock back. A small child is not aware of his or her own inner complexities to nearly the same extent that we can be. We have to bring all of ourselves into the present, not leave part of ourselves behind. The intellect is not ditched, it is transcended, taken up into a higher unity which includes it but is not dominated by it. I have explained this at more philosophical length elsewhere (Rowan 2005a). But for now it is enough to say that what you should be aiming for as a therapist is to suspend thinking and to stay aware of your experience in the ever-flowing present. If you find this difficult, Torbert (1972) has a sympathetic discussion of what happened in a group who tried this together, which may help to encourage you.

Empathy

How does this relate to the more traditional category of accurate empathy, so much emphasized by Rogers (1961) and his followers (Truax and Carkhuff 1967) and rivals (Egan 2009)? Truax and Mitchell (1971) define empathy as the moment-by-moment exploration of another human being by viewing that person's world from his or her perceptual and emotional perspective. In other words, we put ourselves into the other person's shoes. This is really a two-step process of acceptance followed by understanding:

> Acceptance does not mean much until it involves understanding. It is only as I understand the feelings and thoughts which seem so horrible to you, or so sentimental, or so bizarre – it is only as I see them as you see them, and accept them and you, that you feel really free to explore all the hidden nooks and frightening crannies of your inner and often buried experience.
>
> (Stevens and Rogers 1967)

In this sense empathy is one of the three conditions that Rogers says are necessary and sufficient for good therapy; the other two are therapist genuineness and non-possessive warmth. The research evidence (Parloff *et al*. 1978) doesn't support the view that this is all there is to therapy, but empathy has been generally accepted as an important non-specific factor (that is, it runs through all forms of therapy, including psychoanalysis and behaviour modification) which is ignored at the therapist's peril. In 1979 Daniel Hogan, a Harvard-based attorney-therapist, published four scholarly volumes called *The regulation of psychotherapists*. They constitute a comprehensive review of research on effective psychotherapy, as well as a history of legal disputes involving the regulation of psychotherapists. In this authoritative work Hogan identifies empathy as the most important ingredient in effective psychotherapy. The book edited by Haugh and Merry (2001) contains a very full discussion of this.

It seems that there are three levels of empathy, as described in detail in the Rowan and Jacobs book (2003). The first is the most basic and comes from the Mental Ego (otherwise known as First Tier thinking, or Blue/Orange thinking) and is largely based on visual cues. But it is important to remember that, even here, empathy is a quality rather than a skill. In other words, empathy cannot really be taught: it is more a question of recognizing it and allowing it to develop. The second type is deeper and is sometimes called Inclusion, or Imagining the Real (Kirschenbaum and Henderson 1989), and it comes from the Centaur level, the existential level, the authentic or real self. The third comes from the Subtle level, the soul, and it is sometimes called deep empathy (Hart 2000), Linking (Rowan 2005a), or transcendental empathy (Macecevic 2008). It is the main form used by Alvin Mahrer (1996), whose bold ventures into this area became so influential. Here the boundary between client and therapist may sometimes disappear altogether, creating a single or common consciousness. There is a good discussion of this in the book by Knox *et al*. (2013), and indeed the whole idea of working at relational depth has now become much more popular.

Empathy, then, has been studied a great deal and a lot is known about it. It is important to emphasize that empathy is acting 'as if' we were the other person, without ever losing sight of the fact that we have remained ourselves. It is therefore much less threatening than what we have earlier called full awareness, where we do run the risk of actually becoming one with the other person, and deliberately run that risk (see Chapter 14 for more on this).

Genuineness

What about the other conditions that Rogers recommends as being essential to the therapy process? Genuineness (which Rogers has also called 'congruence') is a quality of the therapist that consists in being aware of one's own feelings and one's own process, at the same time that one is in contact with the client. It is a question of doing justice to oneself in the same way that one tries to do justice to the client. The therapist is completely open to his or her own experience. It is important to note here the close connection between congruence in this sense and authenticity:

> It is my feeling that congruence is a part of existential authenticity, that the person who is genuinely authentic in his being-in-the-world is congruent within himself; and to the extent that one attains authentic being in his life, to that extent is he congruent.
>
> (Bugental 1981, p.108)

So congruence is a human quality, not a skill to be switched on and switched off. We cannot fake genuineness, and if we try we shall only produce a phoney performance that fools no one.

Note that Rogers is not advocating that the therapist should blurt out feelings at all times but simply that the therapist should be aware of them, and allow the whole situation to determine whether they are uttered or not, and if so, how. The important thing, Rogers says, is to be real.

Warmth

It has often been pointed out that this demand of Rogers can conflict with his other requirement, that the therapist demonstrate non-possessive warmth (which he first used to call 'unconditional positive regard'). If I am supposed to be real, and what I am really feeling is cold or hostile, doesn't that conflict with the warmth I am supposed to show? Let us see what Rogers says:

> It involves . . . genuine willingness for the client to be whatever feeling is going on in him at that moment – fear, confusion, pain, pride, anger, hatred, love, courage or awe. It means that the therapist cares for the client, in a non-possessive way. . . . By this I mean that he does not simply accept the client when he is behaving in certain ways, and disapprove of him when he behaves in other ways (1961).

This attitude of the therapist was phrased by someone else as, 'I care, but I don't mind'. That is, I care about you, but when you do something bad, wrong or stupid, it doesn't hurt me, it doesn't make me suffer – I won't add my evaluations to your burdens. And this comes out of the basic outlook that each human being, deep down underneath it all, is all right. There is a basic lively health and intelligence there that we can believe in, and rely on. So we may as therapists have all sorts of negative feelings of our own, but these do not contradict our basic respect for the wholeness of the other person.

It is important to emphasize, however, the word non-possessive in this. There is a kind of warmth which comes across as very possessive – a kind of seduction, where the therapist is making emotional demands on the client to respond in a warm way. There is a big difference between being warm yourself, and expecting the client to be warm in return. Rogers says: It involves an acceptance of and a caring for the client as a separate person, with permission for him to have his own feelings and experiences, and to find his own meanings in them (1961).

This seems clear enough, and perfectly non-seductive, but in practice it seems that quite often the therapist can go much too far, in the eyes of the client. Frankland (1981) suggests that there are many parallels between courtship and the gaining of rapport in therapy. In both cases there is an initial nervousness which develops gradually into trust; in both cases there is an increase in the giving of more and more intimate information about oneself; in both cases there are body signals of high arousal, such as pupil dilation and colour in the face. If the client is misled by such reactions into thinking that there is a sexual element coming to the fore – a sexual relationship in the making – then this may put the client off, even to the extent of making them withdraw from therapy. Frankland also suggests that there are many parallels between the early stages of therapy and what Argyle (1967) calls 'affiliation' – that is, making friends. In other words, the client may pick up the cues given by the therapist as meaning that the therapist wants to be friends; but this is not so, and quite inappropriate expectations may result from this. Friendship is a much more two-way thing than therapy, and also a much more informal thing. Friends spend time with each other for the company and for relaxation, rather than for concentration on some task, and so this model again would not be helpful for the pursuit of good therapy. Third, and finally, Frankland suggests that even more than sex or friendship, the warm approach of the therapist may set up expectations of dependency:

> Analysis of this part of the pattern of non-verbal cues in the therapeutic interaction leads to the quite unoriginal conclusion that many clients will perceive their relationship to the worker in terms of a dependent pattern of caring, modelled on parent–child transactions (1981).

So what he is saying is that the perception of the therapist's behaviour, both verbal and non-verbal, may very easily be diverted in these three ways: into a sexual pattern, into an affiliative pattern, into a dependency pattern. If 'warmth' is taken in the proper Rogerian sense, as prizing the client's separateness and individuality, this is not so likely to arise as if the new (or old) therapist acts in a seductive manner, trying to extract warm responses from the client.

But there is really no way of totally preventing such misconceptions and such misperceptions. Certainly we can become more aware, as therapists, of the implications of our body language, and more aware of our secret desires for intimacy or domination or indeed for sex; but ultimately we cannot stop the client getting the wrong message completely. This is just one of the many issues that can arise between therapist and client, and that all have to be dealt with in the same way – by bringing them to the surface and enabling them to be worked through.

Frankland would no doubt reply to this that he is seeking for relationship styles that are living and potent but are not essentially friendly, dominating or seductive. And he would emphasize that his main concern is for the new client who does not come back for a second or third interview, rather than for the client who is already coming regularly. Here we must leave the point, but it can be seen that it can be a very important one. The interested reader can read more about these issues in Rowan and Jacobs (2003).

Depth and surface

These three variables – empathy, genuineness and non-possessive warmth – are the established and so-called traditional non-specific elements in any therapy; in other words it does not matter what approach you adopt, these will be important in any case. But there is a newer one, pointed out most clearly and succinctly by Bandler and Grinder (1975). This is based on a distinction between depth and surface structures in grammar and communication. If we assume that the sentences actually spoken by the client represent the surface structure, and that the deep structure underlying that represents what the client really meant to say, we can look at all the client's sentences as symptoms. Each sentence will reveal in some way the client's own way of distorting his or her own experience when communicating it. But in order for it to be possible for the therapist to detect these distortions, it is obviously necessary for the therapist to be able to compare the surface structure with the deep structure. This the therapist does by looking for gaps in the communication – words that appear to fill the necessary spot in the sentence, but which actually say nothing.

For example, suppose the client says – 'I can't relate to people' the therapist immediately notices that the word 'people' actually represents a gap. It is a way of not saying who the client can't relate to – a way of covering up feelings that may be painful. But it is precisely these painful feelings that need to be brought out into the open if the therapy is to proceed; they are the main material that needs to be worked with. So the therapist says 'Which people?' or 'Who in particular?' or 'For example, who?' or 'Who is the person you would most like to relate to?' This then takes the client down to a more emotional level, and puts the client in touch more with his or her deep structures – the real meaning of what is being said.

Another example is the case where the client says – 'When you come into a room full of people you feel nervous'. Here there is a gap where the word 'you' is used. It can't mean the therapist; it can't mean humanity in general; it presumably means the client. But it is a way of avoiding the feelings that are personal about this, by spreading them around in an indeterminate way – a kind of mental fog hides the gap. So the therapist would say – 'Do you mean that you personally feel nervous?' or 'Who feels nervous?' or 'Could you say that again, this time using the word "I" instead of "YOU"?' or 'See what it feels like to say the word "I" in that sentence'.

This is a very simple technique to use, and it does not contradict the tenets of any form of therapy known to me. It is particularly useful in the early sessions, when you as the therapist may be quite reluctant to use any techniques that seem out of the way or odd.

One of the most important things in therapy, however, is something so simple that it is easy to overlook. It is the therapist being there. If the therapist can be there, then the client can more easily be there too. Jim Bugental (1978) puts it like this:

> A therapist facilitates the client's fullest use of the capacity for inward searching through (a) identifying the resistances which block the search process; (b) through insisting on the necessity for the client's being as fully and genuinely present as possible; and (c) through persistently taking the client and what the client says with complete seriousness.
>
> (p.55)

We shall be seeing more about this in later chapters, but let us just focus for the moment on presence. Ronnie Laing often used to speak about the importance of the therapist being truly present with and for the client. Bugental (1981) again clarifies the matter:

> Presence is immensely more than just being there physically, it is obvious. It's being totally in the situation . . . Presence is being there in body, in emotions, in relating, in thoughts, in every way . . . Although fundamentally presence is a unitary process or characteristic of a person in a situation, accessibility and expressiveness may be identified as its two chief aspects.
>
> (pp.36–7)

Accessibility and expressiveness – how important these are, and yet how rarely they are referred to or properly given their due weight. Primarily it is for the therapist to be accessible, and for the client to be expressive; but it is equally important in our eyes for the client to be accessible and for the therapist to be expressive. We have no place for the passive or mirror-like therapist.

Intersubjectivity

This has become one of the key features of recent psychotherapy, affecting many different modalities, closely tied in with the notion of relationality. We are all relational now, and this is one of the key sources of such ideas. Petruska Clarkson (2003) wrote the classic book on the therapeutic relationship, urging that there are five relationships going on at the same time in all therapy, whether we recognize them or not. But we must also take account of the recent work on intersubjectivity.

> First, intersubjectivity maintains that psychotherapy is mutual, that is, it is an interaction, an exchange occurring between two people and about two people. Much of this interaction is unconscious. Second, it emphasizes that each individual is constructed both by himself and by the other during the process of interaction.
>
> (Natterson and Friedman 1995, p.19)

More recent work has much expanded these ideas. One of the best writers on the open relationship that the more recent thinking prefers is Richard Hycner (1993, 1991), who has made it very clear that the two people in the room are sharing in a kind of consciousness which is created in that very room. One succinct statement of this is to say that what goes on in the therapy room is the co-creation of reality. And this agrees with the view of Kirk Schneider (2015), another powerful and recent writer in this area.

This is, of course, a very central idea in the existentialist approach, as has been very thoroughly described and explained in the recent book by Ernesto Spinelli (2015). See Appendix 4: Should I take on this client?

5   Aims

As we have seen earlier (Chapter 3) it is important for the therapist not to get attached to the notions of success and cure. These are not things that the therapist can ever be responsible for, and it only leads to frustration and disappointment for the therapist who sets these things at the forefront of his consciousness. It is the client doing it, not the therapist doing it.

Nevertheless, it is inevitable that the therapist always has some idea of where the therapy is going. In the moments when teaching is going on, the therapist actually tells the client something about this direction and rationale. But even if this never happens, the therapist does already have some background of theory and knowledge which suggests a certain set of aims.

Background contrasts

Psychoanalysis has quite limited aims. The remark of Freud about exchanging hysterical misery for ordinary unhappiness has often been quoted, as also has his dictum about the eventual outcome for the client being the ability to love and to work. Other phrases used include 'Where Id was, there shall Ego be', and 'making the unconscious conscious'. All this suggests that the ultimate goal of psychoanalysis is adjustment to the current social order.

Behaviour therapy and behaviour modification also have limited aims. They too see the individual as in need of being put back on the track of normality. The individual has somehow engaged in faulty learning. But what has been learned can be unlearned; new ways of behaving can be induced which will be more adaptive and more adequate to the world which exists. Lakin Phillips (1977) says that behavioural psychotherapy aims at 'skill development, positive problem solving and greater behavioural adequacy'. And of course these disciplines are even more limited than psychoanalysis, since they usually set up precise targets and have no place for the psychodynamic aspects of the person.

In recent years the cognitive behavioural tradition has become much more popular, as witness such books as Dobson and Dobson (2009). This again has quite limited aims. The typical statement is that the client is encouraged to state specific outcome goals, which the therapist endeavours to help the client to achieve. The drawback with this is that the client's goals may be just as much a product of mental distress as anything else about the client. It also assumes that the client is consciously aware of the ultimate goals, which may not be true.

The approach of this book

What we say is that the psychotherapist has unlimited aims. What we do is to set the client's feet on a path which has no finite end. This path does, however, have certain recognizable way-stations, and one of these is by far the most significant from the point of view of what can be achieved in therapy. This is what we call the real self.

The notion of the real self is one of the key concepts. But it is not unique to us. Table 5.1 demonstrates that numerous writers have expressed some version of this idea.

What all these investigators are saying is that the ordinary ego which is presented to the world, and which other people know us by, is false. It is a made-up thing, a mask, a fiction. We may have spent many years building it up, and have invested a lot of energy in it, but it is unreal. Benson (1974) calls it the Public Relations Personality, and emphasizes how desperately it depends upon other people's opinions. It essentially arises out of an attempt to protect the real self from pain. It puts up boundaries and walls between the various parts of ourselves, so that pain will not be felt, or so that familiar pains are held on to lest they turn into something worse. A common way of

Table 5.1 Inner and outer

	Central	*Peripheral*
C. G. Jung	Self	Persona
A. Adler	Creative self	Guiding fiction
P. Federn	Id	Ego-states
F. S. Perls	Self	Self-image
R. Assagioli	I	Subpersonalities
D. Winnicott	True self	False self
H. Guntrip	Primary libidinal ego	Internal objects
R. D. Laing	Real self	False self
A. Janov	Real self	Unreal self
J. Love	Primal intent	Conscious will
R. E. Johnson	Real self	Symbolic self
P. Koestenbaum	Transcendental ego	Empirical ego
K. Wilber	Centaur	Mental ego

representing this is by way of the concentric ring diagram (see Figure 5.1). This diagram can be made much more complex. Lowen has one with four rings, Perls one with five, and Elliott has one with ten, but the basic principle can be well illustrated with these three.

Most of us are quite conscious, as soon as it is pointed out, that our positive self-image is an illusion, but our next thought is that underneath this we are bad. Each person has a different notion of what this badness is, but the three most common feelings about this are:

a) If they knew how nasty (evil, bad, horrible, hating) I really am, they would all hate me;
b) If they knew how inadequate (weak, worthless, inept) I really am, they would all reject me;
c) If they knew how needy (insatiable, sucking in and then destroying, attracting and then devouring) I really am, they would all avoid me.

In extreme cases, we may even believe all three of these things at the same time! All three of them pertain to the false self and its definitions of the world.

It is because we are aware (perhaps vividly, perhaps only vaguely) that we are bad behind our facade of goodness, that we resist therapy. The discoveries we might make, once we start questioning our false front, might be too terrible to bear. The false self defends itself against such discoveries.

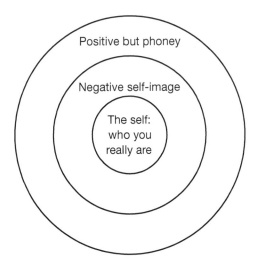

Figure 5.1 Circles of the self

And so people put off therapy in the same way that they put off going to the dentist – until the pain gets to be too much to bear.

But our approach says that underneath all this positive and negative stuff there is the real self, which is perfectly OK. We will have to work through the good and bad stuff to get there, but this will be all right, because the bad stuff is just as illusory as the good stuff. It, too, was just a story we made up and lived out for neurotic reasons. It is no more fundamental, no more basic, than the positive self-image which it balances.

Our prime aim, then, in psychotherapy, is to enable the person to get in touch with their real self – to gain an actual experience of the real self. And so we encourage clients all the time to question all – all without exception – of their taken-for-granted images of themselves, having only quite a limited degree of respect for their defences.

Defences

This question of defences is one of the key areas where we differ from the psychoanalysts, and it is easy to see why. Psychoanalysis, as put forward by Freud, has no notion of the real self. (Though this is not true of some of the later people such as Horney, Winnicott, and Guntrip.) Consequently it takes the negative self-image as being the basic truth about the person, and sees the person as a permanent battleground for good and evil. The good Ego must be strengthened and buttressed against the evil Id. Certainly the way of doing this is not the blind suppression that we find so often prescribed by more ordinary teachers, but a much more sophisticated 'know your enemy' investigative weakening process which involves getting to know the Id much better; but still defences are going to be necessary, only perhaps healthy ones such as sublimation or suppression rather than unhealthy ones, such as projection and repression.

But we don't have any need for defences in our system, because the person would only be defending themselves against their own real self – and there is obviously no point in that. So our policy with regard to defences is continually to chip away at them, in a manner and at a speed which is only limited by the need to maintain rapport between therapist and client. We obviously don't want to be hurtful to the point where the client breaks off therapy. And in this respect we are exactly like the psychoanalysts: we pay a lot of attention to the quality of the relationship. I suspect that the same is true of a good behaviourally oriented or cognitive psychotherapist, even though it forms no part of their theory.

Our psychotherapy, then, is a process of questioning all that is false in the person, and its object in doing that is to lay bare what is true in the person, in the confidence that what is true in the person is always OK.

The real self

So what is this real self, and what does it feel like to open it up? This whole area has become a lot clearer since Ken Wilber (1980; 1981; 2000) defined the Centaur level, as distinct from the Mental-ego level on one side and the Transpersonal levels on the other. What we are dealing with mainly and essentially in our psychotherapy is this centaur level. This level is variously referred to as the 'integration of all lower levels' (Sullivan *et al.* 1957), 'integrated' (Loevinger 1976), 'self-actualizing' (Maslow 1968), 'autonomous' (Fromm 1941; Riesman 1954), 'with individual principles' (Kohlberg 1969), 'integrating persons' (Mahrer 1989) and so on. Broughton (1975) in his research found that this stage was one where 'mind and body are both experiences of an integrated self'. And Wilber (1980) says: 'This integrated self, wherein mind and body are harmoniously one, we call the "centaur". The centaur: the great mythological being with animal body and human mind existing in a perfect state of at-one-ment.' What this achievement of integration brings with it is a great sense of what the existentialists have called 'authenticity'. And indeed the existentialist thinkers have done a great deal to outline this stage in some detail. According to general existential thought, when an individual's self is taken fully as autonomous, he or she can assume responsibility for being-in-the-world. And if we do this we can, as Sartre put it, choose ourselves. Here are some other existentialist texts to give the flavour:

> The 'I' casts off its shells, which it finds untrue, in order to gain the deeper and authentic, infinite, true self
>
> (Jaspers 1931)

> Before his death, Rabbi Zusya said: 'In the coming world, they will not ask me: "Why were you not Moses?" They will ask me: "Why were you not Zusya?"'
>
> (Buber 1961)

Rogers is one of the great names in therapy, and he certainly saw the matter in this way, as can be seen in all his writings. Here is a passage in which he is most explicit about this:

> I have been astonished to find how accurately the Danish philosopher Søren Kierkegaard pictured the dilemma of the individual more than a century ago, with keen psychological insight. He points out that the most common despair is to be in despair at not choosing, or willing, to be one's self; but that the deepest form of despair is to choose 'to be another

than himself'. On the other hand 'to will to be that self which one truly is, is indeed the opposite of despair', and this choice is the deepest responsibility of man.

(Rogers 1961)

What we are saying, then, is that the real self which we are aiming at in psychotherapy is not something very abstract and hard to pin down – it is situated very concretely both in the empirical realm of psychological research and in the conceptual realm of philosophy. It is contrasted very sharply and clearly with the aims of other forms of therapy, though it is closest to existential psychotherapy, as described by Friedenberg (1973):

> the purpose of therapeutic intervention is to support and re-establish a sense of self and personal authenticity. Not mastery of the objective environment; not effective functioning within social institutions; not freedom from the suffering caused by anxiety – though any or all of these may be concomitant outcomes of successful therapy – but personal awareness, depth of real feeling, and, above all, the conviction that one can use one's full powers, that one has the courage to be and use all one's essence in the praxis of being.

And this means that there are certain things that the real self certainly is not. It is not the transpersonal self, the higher self described by Assagioli (1975) and others. It is not the ultimate all-embracing God of Christianity, Judaism or Islam. It is not the ultimate formless void of Eastern mysticism and the perennial philosophy. It is simply the real self – that which was buried and put away as being too weak and too vulnerable for everyday life. We put it away – very often in a moment of panic or terror because that seemed the only way to survive. We developed enormously effective systems of blocking it off and pretending it was not there. But at certain moments – often called peak experiences – we get back that freshness of experience, that marvellous sensitivity to the world.

When we get close to the real self in therapy it feels awfully dangerous to go any further. This is for two different reasons: first, the way in lies through all our most negative self-images, which have been experienced as painful and shocking, and so we are scared of meeting even more, even dirtier secrets as we dig down further; and second, there seems to be something 'ultimate' about the real self, so that when we get to it, it seems like a breakthrough into a whole different world. We are promised that this different world will be better, but it is the difference which appals us. It seems that we almost have to die to get there. In fact, Alvin Mahrer (1996) has been quite explicit about this.

Getting close to the real self, then, almost inevitably brings with it feelings that have to do with extreme good and extreme evil, with Heaven and Hell, with death and destruction as well as with life and growth. And in fact, contact with the real self is often experienced as a breakthrough. Finding suddenly that we are able to let go of all those false pictures of ourselves which the mental ego took for granted, can bring feelings of bliss or ecstasy. An example:

> Then one cold Saturday in February we had an all-day [primal] marathon and I had the most profound experience of my life. On that day I fell in love for the first time. It was the first time because my head, heart and body were involved. I was no longer stone cold rigid and unavailable. I experienced my own beauty that day, as a woman, as a person. I really felt it on the inside. I loved everyone as they were. With each person and with each moment I was different. I saw their perfection and I also saw their limits. I was not judging. I was just appreciating. I went through a door to a place I could only call whole, clear vision. A sight that sees all undisturbedly. The endless self judgements had quieted. I was. I felt very young, open, vulnerable, not afraid and at peace.

> (Anonymous participant)

It doesn't have to happen that way, but I have seen that sort of thing happen many times in therapy, and it is genuinely impressive when it does take place. A common image for this process is the dark tunnel which we go through, sometimes in a boat. The darkness which we have to go into may seem very frightening and very hard to enter. But once the journey actually begins, it then seems easier than we thought. We see a light at the end of the tunnel, and when we come out, it is into a bright world where a sun or star or moon illuminates everything. We then rise to that light and become one with that light. It is then that we experience the ecstasy.

Now these images – both the descent into darkness and the ascent into white light – are essentially spiritual images. They are found in many accounts of religious experience of a mystical kind worldwide (e.g., Cohen and Phipps 1979). And this has deceived many people into thinking that this ecstasy is an experience of God. Obviously this attracts some people and repels others; it is hard to be unbiased about something such as God, which has aroused so much passion and so many wars down the centuries. But when we look more carefully at the matter, we find that any breakthrough into a new awareness or a new consciousness brings with it these same feelings of exposure to danger, of possible death, of falling through the bottom into infinite emptiness. And so at this relatively early stage on the spiritual path, where all we are discovering is the real self, it is important not to kid ourselves into a belief that we are entering some high mystical state. It is really what the Buddhists call the 'pseudo-Nirvana' (Goleman 1978). This is rather a put-down phrase, and there is really nothing pseudo about the experience, so long as we do not mistake it for what it is not. Actually it is very important, because it allows us, for the first time, to have a genuine experience of who we are, underneath all the trappings and all the roles. Dick Anthony and his colleagues state that these are 'glimpse experiences' on the psychospiritual path, and very much worth having (Anthony *et al.* 1987). Who we are is perfectly ordinary and perfectly ecstatic at one and the same time. The earlier experiences of the real self – which tend to last for short periods only, which is why they are called peak experiences – are often more ecstatic; the later experiences of the real self become more ordinary, partly because ecstasy becomes more ordinary, and partly because we are getting ready for the next breakthrough.

This is important too: the discovery of the real self is not the only and final breakthrough, as Figure 5.1 earlier in this chapter suggested. We can go on working on ourselves, if we want to or need to, either in the same way (psychotherapy) or by using methods such as guided fantasy, ritual, meditation or prayer. And in these ways we can experience even bigger and more difficult breakthroughs (see Figure 5.2). Of course we are interested in this, and we shall see later how important it is for a whole-person therapy. The interested reader is directed to Ken Wilber (2000), where these matters are dealt with in admirable clarity.

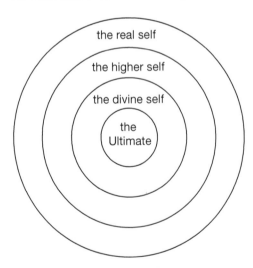

Figure 5.2 Deeper circles of the Self

James Bugental (1978) has an interesting discussion of these matters, and talks about levels of therapeutic goals. Level one is adjustment – the minimal removal of symptoms without any real change of outlook. Level two is coping effectiveness – the idea here is that the person can cope better than before. Level three is ego renewal – the person feels refreshed and more able to face the world. All these three are labelled as deficiency motivated – that is, they go from a need to a goal in a very direct way. All forms of therapy have to cover these levels, but the more advanced practitioner prefers the ones following. Level four is growth in personal and interpersonal actualization – the person has moved on from one outlook to a new one, where the old ego dominance is not so strong. Level five is existential emancipation – this is what we have referred to as the centaur level, the discovery of the real self. Level six is transcendence – we are ready to move on in our psychospiritual development. This second set of three levels is labelled as growth motivated. This seems to me a practical and helpful set of distinctions, and obviously the form of therapy will differ depending on which level one is tackling.

The real self, then, is not an ultimate stage of development. It is not strange, alien or mystical. It is just the innermost and truest part of the separate individual, seen still as a separate individual. It can be described as the existential self, the authentic self, the real self, or the integrated body/mind centaur. And as such it offers a centre for the full integration of the person, as has been very thoroughly discussed in Mahrer (1989), particularly in his chapter on the 'optimal state'. What this means is that the usual splits that are found in so many people, between body and mind, intellect and emotions, duty and inclination, topdog and underdog and all the rest, can now be healed very simply. It may take a little time to work through all the implications of this healing of the splits, and there may be some painful choices to be made along the way, but the essential blocks to full integration have now been removed, and the process is not so hard as all that.

And this means that the person now experiences a sense of personal power (Rogers 1978) which is quite different from the old kind of power associated with the mental ego. Power at the mental-ego stage is always power over other people; power at the real-self stage is power with others. And this means that the whole person is acting at once, with no splits, no reservations and no holding back; this is the 'spontaneous will' described by Rollo May (1969).

Yet sometimes it can be quite ordinary, as we saw in Chapter 3. The way Bugental puts it is modest indeed:

> Intensive psychotherapy of the sort discussed in this book is not a problem-solving technique. Not infrequently, the client at the end of

several years of hard, costly, demanding work will recognize, 'I still have the same hang-up I had when I came, but somehow it seems different now, smaller, less threatening. It's like it's remained the same, but I've grown so much larger, so it doesn't seem so important or bothersome any more'.

(Bugental 1981, p.60)

This is also amazing, but in a much quieter way, that does not arouse the same high expectations as some of our earlier formulations. Perhaps all we can say is that the person who realizes their own reality is in a better position to choose, and to learn, and to be, and to be with another person. In a later book, Bugental urges – 'Psychotherapy isn't what you think'. And he goes on to say: 'The difference between a psychotherapy that is chiefly concerned with *information* and a psychotherapy that centers on the *actual experiencing* of the client in the living moment has great significance for life-changing psychotherapy' (Bugental 1999, p.xv).

Some questions answered

Of course we need nourishment as well as autonomy. Just because we have found our real self doesn't mean we don't need nourishment. And self-actualizing people, as Maslow suggested, can be good choosers, choosing good food, good companions, good work, good art and so forth, that will be beneficial, both to them and to those around them. So we can be good at providing ourselves with the nourishment we need, not ignoring or setting aside any of our needs, and not denying our dependency needs. It seems much more important to satisfy our dependency needs in an elegant way than to pretend we don't have them at all.

If we can see the world in this way, the question of personal power becomes much more easy to handle. We are just not so panicked by the issue. It becomes something we can discuss without being scared all the time about the implications. Just because this new personal power has been gained by a total integration of the person, it takes more into account than the old mental ego was ever able to do. And because more is being taken into account, action is more rational (in the best sense of that word) and more adequate in social terms. We can act spontaneously and well at the same time.

Work by Hall (1977), Miyuki (1979) and Marlan (1981) suggests that it makes sense to say that the ego is never given up – all that happens is that false images of the ego are abandoned, and we end up with a new and improved ego. In one sense the real self is non-ego; in another sense it is the very core of the ego. Edinger (1960) calls this the basic paradox of therapy. If this were true, it would mean that the mental ego is transcended and transformed and included, rather than left behind. It is not dumped or got rid of – it just feels as if it had been. Wilber is very clear (1980) about this process, and talks about the death-seizure of the mental ego. But this is an illusion; the ego does not really die – it just has to change, by removing some of its boundaries, some of its assumptions, some of its identifications.

The key issue is that we have to move from the assumption that we are machines to the assumption that we are people. A machine has buttons to press. A person does not. A machine has triggers to pull. A person does not. A machine relates in an I/It fashion. A person relates in an I/Thou fashion. As Fritz Perls used to put it, we have to peel away the cliché layer and dump it. The aim of therapy is to become a person and give up all vestiges of being a machine.

If we want to know more about what exactly this is like, a good reference is the book by Will Schutz (1988), which explains in fine detail what it is to live at the centaur level, the level of the real self.

The transpersonal

It is here that the transpersonal comes in.

Transpersonal psychology forms a kind of bridge between what is properly psychological and what is properly spiritual. Psychosynthesis (Assagioli 1975) is very much in that position, making heavy use of symbols, which are ideal for this Janus task of facing towards the psychological for one set of people, and towards the spiritual for another set. But it seems clear that moving on from the real self to the higher self is just as problematic, just as difficult, just as much of a breakthrough, as moving on from the mental ego to the real self was. In fact, more so.

The general experience seems to be that if we want to move on from the real self, having reached that and digested that, we have to find some support group, using ritual and ceremony to enter the divine realm. Wilber calls this the Subtle stage of development, and says that this is the realm of concrete expressions of the divine, such as archetypes, angels, nature spirits, standing stones, sacred wells, and so forth. The great names in this field include Jung (2009), Grof (1975), Joseph Campbell, Jean Houston and Marie-Louise von Franz, whose many books are filled with the spirit of the Subtle. We are all familiar with the Subtle in a way, because it is the land of dreams. Psychosynthesis is one of the main accessible roads in to the Subtle for therapists, and has indeed much to offer, because it is prepared to admit that there is a divine realm to explore, accessible and meaningful to all.

And this realm opens us up.

When we realize that we are connected to everyone and everything else, we start to have a different perspective on time and space. In reality we are no less connected to an ant on a distant island in the South Pacific than we are to our noses! While it may be very rare for us humans to realize this connection, we can start moving our awareness in that direction. We can start to cultivate within ourselves a sense of this 'global consciousness'.

(Parfitt 2003, p.108)

In recent years psychosynthesis has started to move on from the original work of Roberto Assagioli and add some very important ideas (Firman and Gila 2002). Also we start finding much to reward us in the field of myth and legend. Joseph Campbell has written many books on the application of mythology to everyday life, which are very rewarding to anyone at this stage.

One of the very interesting books in this area is the one by Jean Houston (1996), where she sees her own life through a Subtle lens, and shows us how this works in practice. Another one is by Starhawk (1989), who makes important links with the Neo-Pagan movement and with the world of politics. For the therapist these are crucial links: the Subtle area, the land of dreams, is very accessible to all clients, because virtually all clients have dreams from time to time. The statistics say that everyone dreams about five times a night. To encourage clients to remember their dreams, they can be given instructions: 'When going to sleep, tell yourself that you are going to dream, and remember at least one dream in the morning; when you wake up, have a pen and a pad ready to hand; when writing, get into the same position you were in when you had the dream'.

The Subtle realm is also the home of the basic attitude of surrender, of going into a place of not-knowing and waiting. This is the most powerful kind of intuition, and intuition is what we use a great deal at this level of consciousness. It is a kind of not-doing, which Keats called 'negative capability' (Snell 2013). (See Figure 5.2.)

There is another level in transpersonal consciousness, which is not so often used in psychotherapy, called the Causal (no connection with determinism, just a conventional label). At this level there are no deities, no symbols, no images, no experiences, just a complete absence of distinctions, except the conviction that everything is one. If everything is one, there can be no problems, and so at this level there is no empathy. The therapist at this level is highly perceptive, but not about to underwrite the assumption that the client's phenomena are real. Phenomena are all separate things, and at this level there is no separation, just a oneness.

Beyond this there is an even rarer level, called the Nondual, where even the assumption that everything is one drops out, and we are left with nothing at all. In spite of the fact that this level is impossible to talk about, there are many many books about it, many of which do not separate it from the Causal, and hence are quite confusing. You never know whether they are talking about the Causal or the Nondual, as if they were really the same thing, which they are not. This one is of even less use to the therapist, so we will say no more about it here.

What we are saying, then, is that the best therapist is always aware of the transpersonal, though not necessarily practising in that mode much of the time, and very often has a regular spiritual practice of some kind. He or she is usually particularly tuned in to the Subtle level, because most clients have some sense of that in their lives, through dreams or visions. We shall have more to say about this in Chapter 14.

Useful websites

International website of the psychosynthesis approach: www.psynthesis.net/ps/index.htm

6 Ways and means

Over the past 30 years or so, an enormous number of new techniques have been introduced. In this chapter we want to look at just the main categories of work, giving references to more detailed sources as appropriate.

One way of breaking up this field is that used by William Swartley (see Table 6.1) which takes the four functions mentioned by Jung – sensing, feeling, thinking and intuiting – as the basis for division.

Sensing

Many of our techniques start from the body. As we saw in the last chapter, the integration of mind and body is crucial to the aims of the practitioner, so it is not surprising that the body can feature so directly in therapy. Wilber (1980) points out that our whole culture encourages us to see ourselves as sitting on our bodies as if we were a horseman riding on a horse:

> I beat it or praise it, I feed and clean and nurse it when necessary. I urge it on without consulting it and I hold it back against its will. When my body-horse is well-behaved I generally ignore it, but when it gets unruly – which is all too often – I pull out the whip to beat it back into reasonable condition.

Indeed, Wilber goes on, our bodies seem to just hang on underneath. We don't approach the world in our bodies but on our bodies. We are up here, in our heads, and it is down there. Our consciousness is almost exclusively head consciousness – we are our heads, but we own our bodies. There is a boundary between us and our bodies – a boundary which is like a fissure, a split, or as Lowen (1967) calls it, a block.

So all the 'sensing' approaches start off by encouraging awareness of the body. One of the simplest ways of starting this is the Gestalt approach, where you ask the client simply to pay attention to what is going on right now:

Table 6.1 Historical components of primal integration (W. Swartley and J. Rowan)

Techniques which depend primarily on Jung's four functions

Sensing function	Feeling function	Thinking function	Intuiting function
Conception trauma M. L. Peerbolte 1975 Includes twin psychology	*Cathartic method* Breuer and Freud 1880–1889 An active provocation of emotional abreaction via hypnotic suggestion	*Psychoanalysis* Freud 1900–1939 Passive, non-judgemental acceptance of verbal behaviour in order to get material for rational analysis of dreams, transference, and similar unconscious behaviour	*Analytical psychology* C. G. Jung 1985–1965 Intuitive and semi-rational analysis of dreams, active imagination
Birth trauma Otto Rank (student of Freud) 1884–1939 *Trauma of Birth* 1924	*Psychodrama* J. L. Moreno 1892–1968 Structured provocation of acting out emotional behaviour on a stage	*Child analysis* Melanie Klein 1920–1960 London (student of Ferenczi) Rene Spitz 1945–1974	*Followers of Jung* Hillman, von Franz, and others all offering ideas and methods for exploring the Subtle realm

Character analysis
Also *Gestalt therapy*
Fritz Perls
(student of Reich)
1936–1970
Combined stage techniques:
Reich's focus on body
language with an active
dream technique

Directed fantasy
Robert Desoille
1938–1966
Paris
(influenced by Jung) Technique
permits active participation of
the therapist via manipulation
of symbols

Person-centred therapy
Carl Rogers
1951–1987
Introduced a more active
acceptance of emotion
during psychotherapy

Group analysis
W. Bion
1948–1979
Tavistock Clinic (student
of M. Klein) Analyse the
psychodynamics of the
interaction between the
members of a group

Psychosynthesis
Roberto Assagioli
(friend of Jung)
1920–1974
Popularized transpersonal
values and related techniques

Group dynamics and T-groups
Kurt Lewin
1920–1947
Introduced feedback of group
dynamics of the group

Character analysis
Wilhelm Reich
1920–1957
Systematic provocation
of emotional discharge
via massage of chronic
muscular tensions

Implantation trauma
R. D. Laing
1976–1989
Introduced importance of the
implantation of the fertilized
egg on the uterus 8 days after
conception

Primal therapy
Arthur Janov
1976–present
Popularized the re-emergence
of cathartic techniques:
First-line primals

Second-line primals
Encounter groups
1963–present
Combined many influences
into a very effective form
of therapy.

Third-line primals
Transactional analysis
Eric Berne
1910–1968
Simplified Freudian theory
for use in groups.

**No interest in the
transpersonal**

continued ...

Table 6.1 Continued

Primal Integration was created to cover all four functions, by the staff of the Center for the Whole Person (Broder, Freundlich, Smukler, Swartley, etc. beginning in 1962). Later adopted by and added to by Frank Lake and William Emerson, also using ideas from Stanislav Grof. Combines all the above techniques, plus additional techniques:

Sensing function	Feeling function	Thinking function	Intuiting function
Primal massage of muscular 'triggers': • Intensification of symptoms • Massive skin contact	Intensification of acting out, transference and incest	Deconditioning cf interpersonal phobias	Completion of dreams with guided fantasy Acting out a fantasy Psycho-ritual Group guided fantasy Pre-conception primals
Guided fantasy First trimester	Guided fantasy Second chance family	Guided fantasy Oedipal pattern	Guided fantasy Death experience
Psychodrama Birth experience and other early experiences	Psychodrama Sexual relations, emotional relations, etc.	Psychodrama Facing parents, siblings, other internal objects	Psychodrama Previous lives, meeting spiritual scenes
First to develop	Second to develop	Third to develop	Fourth to develop
Lower brain stem	Limbic system	Left hemisphere	Right hemisphere

Sense organs, esp. in the skin and internal senses	'Guts' (stomach) Heart Centre	Head (brain) Neurophysiology	'Third eye' or above the head
Birth trauma Maternal deprivation Surgical trauma Umbilical affect Caesarian section Circumcision	Hysteria Incest trauma Schizoid syndrome Phobias, anxiety Depression	Pseudo-rational symptoms: obsessions, compulsions, delusions, paranoia	Blocked creativity and/or spiritual development Denial of psychic potentials Denial of higher self
Abreaction of painful sensations followed by substitution of positive sensations	Abreaction of painful feelings followed by substitution of positive feelings	Analysis of transference, dreams and free association, ego-states	Guided fantasy Art therapy Meditation Dance therapy Sand play
Complete a sensation and replace with new sensations	Complete an emotional reaction and replace with new feelings	Change a destructive logical conclusion	Change a symbol
Catharsis alone does not change behaviour	Catharsis alone does not change behaviour	Insight does not necessarily change behaviour	Creative and spiritual development does not necessarily change other behaviour

Get in touch with [whatever is coming from your senses] from inside, gently – like getting acquainted with it. Stay in touch like a spotlight that doesn't push anything around and doesn't keep anything the way it is. 'Stay in touch' means so lightly that if somewhere else in your body calls – any kind of pain or tension or discomfort – you can move to it, as easily as moving your eyes from a window to the door. Let the pain be. If it becomes more intense or less intense, let that happen – or any other changes. Let be what is . . . No straining, no pushing, no trying in that sense . . . No jumps, jerks, pushing, persevering or holding on.

(Stevens 1975)

This is a good method of approaching the body, because it is non-threatening in its invitation. It can lead to deep feelings coming up sometimes, but that is not the aim. The aim is simply that the body be allowed to exist and have its say. Awareness (what is now more often called mindfulness) is enough.

Another very simple way of getting in touch with the body is to get the client to try the three-step exercise of Masters and Houston (1978):

1   Take an imaginary walk, trying to notice what you do while you are walking. Come back to where you started, and reconstruct what you did.
2   Now actually get up and walk around, paying close attention to your movements and sensations. Come back to where you started, and recollect what you did in detail.
3   And now be aware of your present position and sensations in detail.

Again this is very simple and non-threatening, but a few questions will be enough to show how out of touch we are with our bodies. Questions suggested include the following:

When you got up in imagination, what did you do? When you started walking, which foot took the first step? When you turned, did you turn to the left or to the right, or perhaps left on one occasion, to the right on another? Whatever you did, it will have been the same as what you normally do when you walk. While the left foot and leg were going forward, what were you doing with the left arm? As you were walking, what part of your foot made contact with the floor first, and what part left the floor last? . . . When you got up to start walking, did you use one or both arms to help you, how did you use them, and did you use first one and then the other, or one more than the other? Did you push down harder with one foot, and if so, which one? As you walked, what were the feelings in the ankles, the knees, the hip joints, the shoulder joints? How extensive were the movements in the joints?

How freely did your arms swing? Did you notice what direction you turned in, and what you did with your hands and arms, your shoulders, your neck and head, and your eyes, when you turned? Were you aware of your breathing, whether it was free or whether you held your breath as you tried to concentrate on your movements? Were you, until now, aware of your breathing as you tried to answer these questions?

This is a very simple exercise, yet most people are shocked to discover how few of the questions they can answer. This demonstrates how little attention we normally pay to our bodies. Becoming aware of this is one of the first steps towards changing it.

Of course this simple awareness of the body, which seems so easy, but which actually has been made very difficult for us by our cultural assumptions, has been noticed by Eastern thinkers. The Buddhist concept of mindfulness is particularly relevant here, and of course has been discovered and used wisely in therapy recently, and also Gurdjieff's concept of self-remembering, derived from Sufi thinking.

The therapist, however, sometimes goes further than this, and actually touches the body of the client. The skin covers us all over; it is the oldest and most sensitive of our organs, our first medium of communication, our boundary and protection:

> In the evolution of the senses the sense of touch was undoubtedly the first to come into being. Touch is the parent of our eyes, ears, nose and mouth. It is the sense which became differentiated into the others, a fact that seems to be recognised in the age-old evaluation of touch as 'the mother of the senses'.
>
> (Montagu 1978)

As babies, we all had strong needs to be held and touched and cuddled. If these needs were not met, we may go through life looking for the touch we missed. Marc Hollender's research, as reported in Montagu's excellent book referred to above, demonstrates this very explicitly. More informally, Harvey Jackins (1965) said that everybody needed four good hugs a day to keep mentally healthy. Eric Berne (1972) speaking in metaphors, says – 'If you are not stroked, your spinal cord will shrivel up'.

So when the therapist touches the client, something very powerful can be set in motion, and it always needs to be carefully considered. The psychoanalytic point of view is that touching is always sexual, and that it puts too great a strain on the transference. There were great battles between

Freud and Ferenczi over this issue. But because we have a different attitude to transference (see Chapter 7) we do not have to rule out touching.

However, it is essential to recognize that there is a sexual aspect to touching, and that you as a therapist need to have worked through your own feelings about being touched in therapy before starting to touch anyone else. And it is important that just because touching is sexual, that does not mean that it is necessarily genital. As Alan Watts once pointed out, sex is like a long French loaf: one end is the lightest possible contact, like a warm handshake or a peck on the cheek, and the other end is full sexual intercourse with orgasm. We often make the mistake of thinking that if we go further than the one end, we have to go all the way to the other end, in an automatic kind of way. But in reality there is all the rest of the loaf to be explored and used – all sorts of degrees of non-genital sex. We are entitled to all of that – not just the two ends.

Touch can be used in therapy in a number of different ways. Lowen (1976) makes the interesting point that a client often has a great need to touch the therapist, but feels that this is not allowed:

> To overcome this taboo, I often ask a patient to touch my face while he is lying on the bed. I use this procedure after I have opened up some of the patient's fears. Bending over him, I am in the position of a mother or father looking at the patient as a child. The hesitation, the tentative gesture, the anxiety this manoeuvre evoked was surprising to me at first. Many touched my face only with their fingertips, as if afraid to make full contact with their hands. Some said they were afraid of being rejected; others said they felt they had no right to touch me. Without encouragement few felt they could bring my face close to theirs, although this was what they wanted to do. In all cases this procedure went to the depths of a problem that could not be reached by words alone . . .

Getting in touch with me as the therapist may enable clients to get more in touch with themselves, which is one goal of the therapeutic endeavour.

This leads on to another use of touch which is very often useful. If the client is crying, and seems to need encouragement to go deeper, it is often good to reach out and give a light hold to the shoulder or upper back. This gives reassurance of the therapist's presence and support without interrupting the flow of feelings. It is important not to hold or cuddle the client at such times, unless the client actively seeks it out. Holding the client with a lot of body contact can stop the flow prematurely. Let the emotional discharge build to a climax and resolve itself through catharsis (Nichols and Zax 1977). Then warmth and cuddling may well be in order, though not necessarily so.

Another use of touch is to go directly into muscles which are tense. Usually the client can point to the tense spot and guide you to it. With experience, you can feel it for yourself. One approach developed by Gerda Boyesen (1970) is to apply gentle circular strokes to the tense areas. These are brief and there is a pause between strokes so that the body has time to react fully. The client is encouraged to breathe from deep down in the abdomen. More about this technique is to be found in the excellent chapter by Monika Schaible in the book edited by Linda Hartley (2009). It must be emphasized that none of the techniques mentioned in this chapter should be carried out by anyone untrained in their use. Boyesen gives the case of a young woman who experienced ten days of almost constant nausea, vomiting and diarrhoea after her shoulder had been treated in this way.

With tense muscles, another approach (developed by Reich and taken further by Lowen, Kelley, Keleman and others) is to press firmly on the tense part.

> For example, screaming is blocked by muscular tensions in the throat. If a firm pressure is applied with the fingers to the anterior scalene muscles along the side of the neck while the person is making a loud sound, that sound will often turn into a scream. The scream will generally continue after the pressure has been removed, especially when there is a need to scream. Following the screaming, one moves into [the conscious ego layer] to determine what the screaming was about and why it was necessary to suppress it.
>
> (Lowen 1976)

The view here, of course, is that the muscles have been used in the client's defensive manoeuvres, and that by working directly on the defences in this way, we can get very quickly to what is really going on. And in fact this approach does very often get into deep material very fast – sometimes too fast for the material to be accepted and integrated, so that the client gets very scared. The therapist must again be thoroughly familiar with these sudden and profound effects, if this technique is to be used effectively. Variations on this are helpfully described by David Cranmer (1994) and by William West (1994). Breathing is of course an important issue in body work, and William West says – 'Over my years of work as a Post-Reichian therapist I have rarely found anyone who could breathe well, easily able to inflate both chest and abdomen'. I would confirm this from my own experience.

An even deeper form of touch is used in Rolfing. Ida Rolf (1978) invented a method which she called 'structural integration', which involves correcting all the ways in which the body has become distorted through experience, actually rearranging the muscles at a deep level. This is very specialized and needs very specific training. As done by Ida Rolf herself, it caused a good deal of pain, but some Rolfers recently have developed a more gentle form of it, which does not cause pain at all. A related form of therapy is Postural Integration, and Jack Painter (1986) has written an excellent account of this.

A different approach to the body is found in focusing, a method of working developed by Eugene Gendlin. An excellent account of this is to be found in the chapter by Marion Hendricks (2002).

There are other body approaches – an excellent summary of these may be found in Dreyfuss and Feinstein (1977). In contrast to this approach is the body work developed by a few German women, including Elsa Gindler, Magda Proskauer, Marion Rosen, Ilse Middendorf and Doris Breyer (Moss 1981). Their work promotes mind/body awareness and integration using such techniques as movement, touch, natural breathing, sensory awareness and voice work. These are much more non-stressful and non-painful practices. Some of the earlier work was very 'masculine' and almost violent, but in recent years we have all relaxed and become more 'feminine', relatively speaking. Some valuable positives and negatives about working with the body are discussed in Dreyfuss and Feinstein (1977).

Since about 1985, there has been much more suspicion of touch in therapy, because of the increased awareness of sexual and other childhood abuse first drawn to our attention by Alice Miller. Book after book came out detailing the things that can go wrong in therapy because of sexual exploitation of the client by the therapist (Russell 1993). In addition to that, clients have become more litigious and aware of their rights, and therapists no longer feel as invulnerable as they did. Petruska Clarkson (2003) has a whole section on the 'vengeance of the victim', where she says that 'a clinical practice is now developing which I would call "defensive psychotherapy"', where therapists deliberately censor themselves in the light of possible later criticism. She says that in the USA some insurance companies will not insure a therapist against malpractice if they touch their clients at all. There is a good discussion of all these issues in the excellent book edited by Smith, Clance and Imes (1998), with its fifteen chapters by different writers.

But it is possible to work with the body without touching it. An interesting version of this is to be found in the work of David Grove (Grove and Panzer 1989). He will take a bodily sensation such as tightness in the chest and work with it on a metaphorical level.

Client:	I have a tightness in my chest.
Therapist:	And you have a tightness in your chest. And when you have tightness in your chest, that's tightness like what?
Client:	Like a rock.

Therapist:	And a rock. And when it's like a rock, what kind of rock is that rock?
Client:	A hard rock.
Therapist:	And a hard rock. And when it is a hard rock is there anything else about that hard rock?
Client:	Nothing can break it.

(Tompkins and Lawley 1997)

The therapist then continues to explore the symbol of the hard rock by asking further questions, until some kind of transformation takes place. This is a surprisingly effective way of working, and works simply by taking the bodily sensation seriously and working very directly with it, taking it where it needs to go.

The work of Arnold Mindell (1985) also works without necessarily touching the body, but just following the promptings of the physical sensations experienced by the client. His excellent and very helpful book, *Working with the dreaming body*, is packed with examples of how he works on this level.

The Hakomi approach (Martin 2014) also makes much use of the body, and Donna Martin shows quite beautifully how the work of Ron Kurtz can be used to stunning effect.

Feeling

This is the approach where we start from feelings. Carl Rogers (1961) emphasized the healing quality of simply paying real attention to the client's feelings. We have already seen in Chapters 3 and 4 how important this approach can be in the early hours of the therapeutic relationship. It can of course be made the basis for the whole therapy, but many practitioners feel that it is too slow for them. Akin to the Rogerian approach is the Gendlin (1969) approach, which he calls 'focusing'. This is based on the idea of the felt experience as a kind of summing-up of the whole weight, size and pattern of a particular person or situation. The theory here is that the felt experience is prior to any analysis or intellectual elaboration, and that if we can get a shift at that level, we can do what is essential in therapy. This shift in experiencing is ultimately what therapy is all about; it is not a matter of having better conceptualizations at an intellectual (what we earlier called the mental-ego) level. So the client is encouraged to feel meanings rather than just intellectualize about them. Gendlin has taken this further in his 1996 book.

Another approach which is superficially similar to Rogerian counselling and therapy and to Gendlin's focusing is Harvey Jackins's 're-evaluation counselling'. This way of working, which is more informally known as co-counselling, lays great stress on emotional discharge as the key to therapeutic change. And because it is a method developed by Jackins (1965) for use by lay-people with just 40 hours of training, it lays a great deal of emphasis on positive feelings and a light touch. One of the key differences between the co-counselling approach and the Rogers or Gendlin approach comes in the treatment of self put-downs. The earlier approach is to go down with the client into his or her bad feelings, on the grounds that it is only when these have been fully explored that the positive impulses can be voiced. The Jackins view, however, is that the counsellor should lighten the darkness by contradiction (getting the client to say the opposite, or to repeat the accusation in a funny way, or to boast about the fault); or validation, where the client has to say how good or right or marvellous he or she is. This brings about a balance of attention between the distress material and the current situation here in the room, and this is the optimal condition for therapeutic change to take place. Jackins is admirably clear and succinct as to what he is about, and has done a lot to demystify therapy. More recently, his work has been taken up by others (Kauffman and New 2004), and I have hope that this will result in a further growth of this approach.

One of the most-used of the feeling therapies is Gestalt therapy, as developed by Fritz Perls (1969). It is important to realize, however, that what most practitioners use is not Gestalt therapy in its pure state, but rather certain specific techniques lifted out of Gestalt therapy and used in a much more eclectic way.

Gestalt therapy in its pure state focuses almost exclusively on the here and now. How is the client sitting? Breathing? What are the client's hands doing? Eyes? Feet? All these things are part of who the client is and how the client functions. The tone of voice is very important: the hesitations, the changes in pitch and volume – listening to the music as much as to the words: 'We have to become aware of the obvious. If we understand the obvious, everything is there' (Perls 1976). Perls in his demonstrations didn't ask the client what the problem was; he got the client to talk about the here and now, and then worked directly on what came up. Neither did he tell the client what the problem was – he just encouraged to emerge whatever was ready to emerge.

This is not the place to describe Gestalt therapy in detail. All I want to say is that what most practitioners do is simply to use one of the techniques from Gestalt therapy: that of the empty chair or cushion. Perls used to use chairs, because of his generation and history, but it is really better to use cushions because they are more flexible and make more distinctive and colourful anchors. All you do as a therapist is wait until some conflict emerges, such as 'on the one hand this, on the other hand that' or 'part of me wants to do this, and another part of me wants to do that', and then put one side of the conflict on one cushion, the other side on the other, and let a dialogue take place between them. Anything can be put on a cushion – people, things, events, times, qualities, expressions:

> Okay, I would like you to put phoniness in that chair; talk to phoniness. . . . Now let's finish up by putting that smirk in the chair. Talk to your smirk. . . . Put the old man [in the dream] in that chair and compare him to me. What are the similarities, what are the differences? . . . Can you talk to that memory once more? Change seats. Be the memory. . . . Say, bye-bye memory.
>
> (Perls 1976)

This is an enormously flexible technique, which can be used at the drop of a hat. It is used in self-help groups (Ernst and Goodison 1981) a great deal, and comes very easily once it has been experienced. Some people initially find it very artificial, and say they can't or won't do it. The answer to this is always to use it for the first time with a naive client when the client has already said something such as – 'It is as if there were two voices inside me'; this makes it really easy to get into this way of working. For a full rundown on all aspects of chairwork and its extensions see Rowan (2010).

Another way of getting round objections to this empty chair technique is for the therapist to role-play. This is one of the techniques also used in co-counselling, and it is quite easy to do. Let us say the client is talking about his or her mother. You can say – 'Imagine that I am your mother, and talk directly to me'. This gets the benefit of eye-contact as the action proceeds, which for some clients is more powerful anyway.

Feelings usually appear in the first instance in mild ways. It may be just one word or phrase that seems to have a little extra charge behind it. Both in co-counselling and in Gestalt therapy one of the most basic moves is to ask the client to repeat such a word or phrase, continuing with it as long as there is energy behind it. This often results in a deeper feeling being expressed, which was not apparent at first. A great deal of therapy consists in turning molehills into mountains: the reason why this works so well is because they really were mountains in the first place – they were just pretending to be molehills. The best account of the actual psychodynamics involved here is to be found in Mahrer (1989).

One of the best ways of picking up something small and amplifying it is through the use of images. I do this a lot. For example, Jean had the experience of feeling a weight in her stomach, with waves going through it – something similar to an orange, with green waves flowing past it. I got her to draw this with felt pens on paper. I then put the paper on a cushion and got her to talk to it, and then talk back, in the usual chairwork dialogue. This resulted in a very strong interaction, which led into a piece of deep work.

You can even use images when the person is stuck completely. Bill was bothered about women, but could not get any clear line on what was going wrong. I asked him to imagine two large boxes. One contains a man, the other a woman. What happens next? He told how they climbed out of the boxes, the man fucked the woman, then departed. What did the man feel? Disappointed and unsatisfied. This opened up the area for a much deeper exploration than we had been able to do up to that time. Shorr (1972) has a whole host of suggestions along these lines, which are very usable in brief and informal ways.

A similar and even more effective approach is that of Allen (1982) which I used for a while. Joe complained of a pain in the neck. I asked him to focus on the exact pain, and ask it a question. He asked 'What are you?' I then said – 'After repeating the question three times with intensity, relax and let go into a place of not-knowing, where you don't know the answer and you are not trying to figure it out or logically deduce it. (Pause) Now be aware of the next experience that comes up for you, and get in touch with it as openly as possible. (Pause) Now draw or write on this sheet of paper what you have experienced'. Then I put the drawing (of a gateway, in this instance) on to a cushion and invited Joe to talk to it, and this became a very valuable dialogue.

More recently, David Grove has been describing a way of using imagery which has the power to work completely through a trauma without the therapist needing at any time to know what the trauma actually is. He turns the physical experience in the present into a metaphor, and then works with the metaphor, using what he calls 'clean language' – that is, language which does not assume anything, which does not put any idea into the client's mind, and which sticks to the age to which the client may have regressed. Grove and Panzer (1989) have a clear account of how this is done, and make it clear that this approach is particularly suitable for cases of sexual abuse in childhood. More recently, the work of James Lawley and Penny Tompkins (2000) has shown in detail how this approach can be used very flexibly and effectively.

It is important in all this work to make it easy for the client, so that there are no awkward transitions. It is very disruptive if the client suddenly decides that the whole exercise is nonsense or artificial. So you build in to your instructions just sufficient scaffolding to hold the thing up. For example, Ellen talked about having a fog between her and other people, and I wanted to put the fog on the cushion. So I said – 'Let's imagine that we can put the fog on to this cushion' (bringing the cushion into position) 'and that by some miracle you can talk to it, and it can talk back if it wants to'. If she had said – 'I don't know if I can do that', I would have added – 'Just imagine it's a character in a play, called "Fog", and it's coming on to play its part'.

What we are trying to do all the time is to bring something which is hidden out into the open a bit more, so that we have a chance to see just how big or small it is, how important or unimportant, how shallow or deep, how much feeling is attached to it or bound up with it. There is a very full account of all the ways of using chairwork in my own book *Personification* (Rowan 2010).

Similarly if a word or phrase is uttered with a certain gesture, you can ask the person to exaggerate the gesture more and more, until the feeling behind it comes out. What we are trying to do all the time is to get down to the roots of the affect tree. The lower we go down on the tree (see Figure 6.1) the more basic and single-minded are the feelings, and the closer we are to the real self.

The crucial step is the realization of total aloneness – 'I'm all I've got!' This brings a feeling of excitement, which is perhaps the most basic feeling of all. But it can either be negative excitement – how terrible, how awful, how dreadful – or positive excitement – what joy, what bliss, what ecstasy!

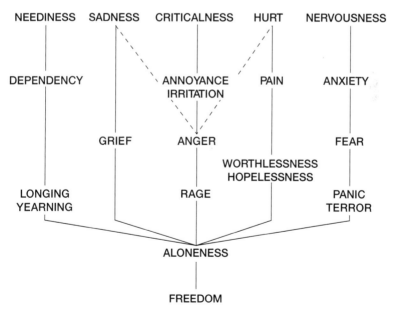

Figure 6.1 The affect tree

EXAMPLE 6.1 THE 'I AM' EXPERIENCE

Rollo May has a wonderful example of this in his 1983 book, where he quotes a patient of his who had a revealing experience of the outcome of therapy. She was walking one day under the elevated tracks in a slum area, when she felt the thought, 'I am an illegitimate child'. She recalled the anguish in trying to accept that fact. Then she understood what it must feel like to accept, 'I am a Negro in the midst of privileged whites'. Or 'I am blind in the midst of people who see'. Later on that night she woke up and it came to her this way, 'I accept the fact that I am an illegitimate child'. *But* 'I am not a child anymore'. So it is, 'I am illegitimate'. That is not so either: 'I was born illegitimate'. Then what is left? What is left is this, *'I Am'*. This act of contact and acceptance with 'I am', once gotten hold of, gave her for the first time, the experience 'Since I Am, I have the right to be'.

She then had insight after insight: it was like receiving the deed to her house, it was like a boat being given an anchor, it was like her saying to Descartes, *'I Am, therefore* I think, I feel, I do'. She felt it was like an axiom in geometry – basic and fundamental. It was like going into her very own garden of Eden. It was like owning Cinderella's shoe and looking all over the world for the foot it will fit and realizing all of a sudden that one's own foot is the only one it will fit . . . This was a huge experience for her, and she would never forget it.

It is this switch from negative to positive which is the most fundamental move in therapy. As Mahrer (1989) puts it, we have to embrace and love our deeper potentials; at the moment we can genuinely do this, they change from negative into positive. For an example of this sort of thing, see the following example.

One of the best and most direct ways of getting back to this point is through the process of regression. In regression we take the client back to the earlier days of life. The person who has done most to establish the importance of regression is Arthur Janov, and his book *The primal scream* (1973) is one of the most moving documents in the whole literature of therapy.

But the best explanation of what regression is all about is to be found in Stan Grof (1975). He says that you don't just find an emotion hanging around loose, as it were. It is attached to a situation, and forms a definite pattern, which he calls a COEX (short for constellation of condensed experience).

Now the important thing about a COEX is that it is one of a long line, a chain of similar experiences. Events from different life periods are linked together by the common feeling which runs through them – an identifiable felt sense. And the links lead back to the oldest experience, usually traumatic, of the sequence. The oldest event that forges the prototypical pattern forms the nucleus of the COEX – the core of the whole neurotic system.

When encouraging a client to regress, it is not necessary to give them LSD, or to hypnotize them, or to make them breathe in a particular way, or anything else of that nature. All that is necessary is to give the client permission to regress as far back as necessary.

For example, a client might talk about a small incident at work, being criticized by a superior. The feeling associated with this could be expressed in the words – 'It's not fair'. The client is then invited to get in touch with this feeling, to experience the weight of it, the size of it, the colour of it, the texture of it, the sound of it, the taste of it. Then comes the request – 'See if you can allow yourself to go back to another time when you had that same feeling'. The client might then go back to a time in adolescence, and be asked to get in touch with the feeling again, expressing it as appropriate in order to get a better felt sense of it. Then the suggestion again, to go back further, and so on. In this way we are, as it were, climbing back down the ladder, using the COEX units as rungs. And we may get back to the primal trauma, with the results that Janov has so graphically described. In an interesting book relating psychotherapy to physiology, Janov and Holden (1977) distinguish between third-line primals (verbally oriented, dating from the period of about 4 years old and upwards); second-line primals (largely referring to events taking place in the pre-verbal and highly emotional early years before that); and first-line primals, concerned with physical survival at the earliest times. This is a very important idea, which ties in with research on the brain (MacLean 1973). It is also important in making it crystal clear that much of our experience is pre-verbal, and that language is not primary or fundamental to experience.

We do not always get back to a single 'grand-slam' event, however, and it would be wrong to expect this, in line with our earlier warnings against being oriented towards results and success. All we are trying to do is to encourage the client more and more to open up the inner world. That is therapeutic in itself, because it enables the client to re-own more and more of that rich emotional world which had been cut off and denied. Or as Mahrer (1989) says, to get in touch with his or her deeper potentials.

Grinder and Bandler (1981) have an ingenious trick which can be used with clients who baulk at a particular scene, and will not describe it, because they know it is going to be too painful. You get them to begin the experience and then step outside of it so that they see themselves going through it. They hear what was going on at the time, but they watch themselves go through the event as if they were watching a movie. Or you can even go further:

> If you want to be really safe, have them watch themselves watching themselves go through the experience, as if they were in the projection box at a movie theatre, watching themselves watch the movie. If you have them go through an event this way, when they remember it later on, they won't remember the terror.

This is particularly suitable when events such as rape or war wounding are involved, or any incident which resulted in the client losing consciousness. You don't want the client to lose consciousness while regressing, because that interferes both with the therapeutic process and with the therapist–client relationship. This is why the approach of Grove and Panzer (1989) already mentioned is so valuable and important.

People in the Gestalt tradition are often very suspicious of the idea of regression, because they want to pay much more attention to the here and now. Similarly with people in the existential tradition: although one of the best discussions of the value of regression is to be found in Laing (1982, Chapter 12). But all therapists of all persuasions find that their clients spontaneously regress from time to time, and it is well to know how to handle regression even if it is not regarded as something to aim at. The Gestaltist Frank-M. Staemmler (1997) has an excellent discussion of this whole question, making a number of very careful distinctions. Similarly Petruska Clarkson (2003) has a good account of the relationship that is set up in the consulting room when the client regresses: she calls this the reparative or developmentally needed relationship.

Thinking

The thinking therapies are again various, but what they have in common is an emphasis on insight and clear thinking as the starting point in therapy.

My kind of psychotherapy does often start from the thinking function. The main one of these, perhaps, is simply the patient digging out of the client's system of beliefs. Often we cannot even begin to work with a client until an interlocking and self-supporting structure of beliefs has been exposed.

Bill had a belief system in which there were only two types of women he could be attracted to: beautiful women and women with problems. He couldn't get to go out with the beautiful women, so he had to go out with women with problems. But women with problems were too much for him, and made him impotent. The thing is that as soon as this type of absurd system is brought out into the open, it is so obviously self-defeating that the very awareness sets in motion a process of change, which can then be used as appropriate.

Claire had a system where washing-up was a chore so boring that she couldn't do it, couldn't find the energy to do it. But she couldn't go out of the house until the washing-up had been done. So she would wander round the house with her shopping list, not being able to do the washing-up (Can't Cope) and not being able to go out either (Bill the Jailer). This was quite literally an imprisoning system. Chairwork could again be used in dealing with this sort of problem.

Beck (1979) points out that people often have a story that they keep telling themselves, a kind of running commentary going on in their heads. He calls these 'automatic thoughts'. Surprisingly often, these are self-put-down thoughts, such as 'they won't like that'.

Ellis (1970) has collected a whole anthology of such thoughts, stories that people tell themselves in order to avoid ever winning or being happy. I should be thoroughly competent, intelligent and achieving in all possible respects. I must be loved by everyone for everything I do. What I have done is awful or wicked, and I should be punished for it. So if something once strongly affected my life, it should go on, doing so indefinitely. I must have certain and perfect control over things. There are many more of these statements, guaranteed to keep you miserable.

One of the best books showing how people's belief systems are constructed to be self-defeating is Dorothy Rowe (1978). The heart of this book on depression is a set of nine case histories, told almost entirely through extracts from therapy sessions. I think I would disagree with Rowe when she just regards the statements such as: 'I despise myself', 'My husband spoiled my life', 'Animals are better than people', and so on as propositions. I would regard them as decisions, made at some specific time under some specific pressure, and linking back to more fundamental decisions, such as: 'My mother is part of me', 'I don't trust women', 'I don't know what love is', 'If I am on my own I cease to exist', and so on, also made at some specific time under some specific pressure.

Greenwald (1974) has taken the view that all therapy is about decisions such as this. Find out what decisions the person had made about their life, and you will be able to go back and change those decisions. This is similar to Berne's (1972) idea that what you need to know is the person's script: 'A script is an ongoing program, developed in early childhood under parental influence, which directs the individual's behavior in the most important aspects of his life'. The client is almost always unwilling to give up the script, because it makes sense of life. Without the script, the world would no longer make sense, and would become a frightening and unpredictable place.

But it ultimately has to be given up if therapy is to proceed. In Mahrer's terms, we have to be prepared to surrender our operating potentials in order to realize our deeper potentials.

This is now very close to the neuro-linguistic programming (NLP) ideas of Bandler and Grinder (1979). They say that each thing that a person does is done for a reason, because it seems the best choice possible in the circumstances. If we want to change a neurotic pattern of behaviour, we have to find out what it is doing positively for the person, and then we find out how the person could get the same result by more healthy means. In other words, we go back and question the original decision to operate in that way. This is a very sophisticated form of decision therapy which they call 'reframing', and it is particularly useful where a very visible and overt pattern of behaviour can be found, such as a phobia or obsession.

As well as these approaches via the thinking function, there is also the question of 'direct teaching' in the therapy session. Many therapists are very opposed to teaching, saying that it is untherapeutic to give explanations or to attempt to persuade the client of anything. But when we examine the matter more closely in practice, we find that therapists of every persuasion do a good deal of actual direct teaching in the session. They tell clients what to expect, or what their experience might mean.

One of the best examples of this is in rational-emotive therapy (RET) where Ellis (1970) talks to clients about the ABC theorem:

ACTION > BELIEFS > CONSEQUENCES

When you do something to another person, he tells the client, its effect on that person depends entirely on the beliefs that person has about what your action means. You may try to punish a 3-year-old for some transgression of your household rules, for example, but unless the 3-year-old has a notion of what a rule means (which most of them do not as yet) he or she will merely experience you as being in a bad mood, or being inexplicably disagreeable, or proving once again that he or she is bad or worthless. (RET has now been renamed as REBT – rational-emotive behaviour therapy (Ellis 1995)).

Similarly, if you try to reward someone, it will only work as a reward if it is something that the other person believes to be valuable and interesting. Otherwise it will be experienced as just another odd or even oppressive act – as for example the famous white elephant.

By teaching the client this theorem, we can give a very useful hint as to how to take up the most productive stance in therapy: the stance which says – 'I create my world'.

Now we have to be very careful about this notion, which is used so consistently and thoroughly by people such as Schutz (1988) and Mahrer

(1989). Let us stay with it for a moment, because it is so important. The standard misunderstanding that arises is for people to think that we must then approach clients, and other people generally, by saying in effect, as Jill Tweedie once put it – 'You're wretched, mate, because you chose to be wretched. So rot'. To understand why this is wrong, and not our position at all, we have to distinguish between saying that I create my world, and saying that they create their world. This is the difference between first-person use and third-person use.

In first-person use, I say – 'I create my world', and this can be an incredibly liberating thing for me to say and fully believe. It can give me the energy to lift myself up by my own bootstraps – or more accurately, it can give me access to my own energy, which was there all the time. Charles Hampden-Turner (1977) movingly describes the Delancey Street project, a house for ex-convicts in San Francisco. It is full of people who are victims of society, if that phrase ever had any meaning, and yet he says that for each person there, it was only at the moment that they said – 'I create my world' – that they could change their destiny. Once they had said that, they could create a healthy community with a genuine capacity for healing and for survival. Few of us are buffeted by fate as much as the men and women in Delancey Street; for most of us it is easier to take control of our own lives. And this is one of the main effects of personal growth – this ability to say: this is my life, and I run it. In doing this, we are not denying that the world is complicated, or that we are subject to many pressures. We are just saying that we decide which pressures to respond to, and how to respond to them. Different people respond differently, choose differently, as Mahrer (1989) has so brilliantly laid out, and as the existential position insists. But if I pretend that I have no choice, I am just copping out, avoiding the issue, letting myself off the hook, and therefore not learning anything, not changing. As someone once said, the distinguishing feature of all victims is that they tell themselves that they have no choice.

Taking this attitude, of taking responsibility for creating my own world, is not like hiding behind a role. It is more exposed, more honest, more risky. It is responsive as well as responsible. It makes me feel like a complete human being. When I do this, it makes me into a person, and takes me away from behaving like a thing. I become an origin rather than a pawn; an end rather than a means. So I value this as a key part of the whole message of psychotherapy.

But look what happens when I move into third-person use. I change it just slightly, it seems, and say 'He creates his world', 'She creates her world', 'They create their world'. Immediately this turns me into an observer, a commentator, even a judge. I am standing outside the person and the situation, and making myself superior to them both. And I am implicitly withholding any help, assistance or sympathy I might be capable of offering: it is a cold thing to say. It is a statement that removes me far away from the person and the situation: it is nothing to do with me.

And so the third-person use of this kind of phrase is a denial of solidarity, a negation of community. It is also a contradiction of my own responsibility for the situation that people find themselves in; I am not owning up to my part in the social situation in which a person may be suffering. I am a bystander, in the terms that Petruska Clarkson (1996) has so clearly laid out.

So there is nothing healthy or productive at all in the third-person use of this statement. It is not conducive to growth at all: neither mine nor that of the other person. So using such a statement in a third-person way is not part of our philosophy at all.

Now, in the light of all that, what are we to say about the statement in its second-person form – 'You create your world'? It must depend on context. In a context where I am identified with you, or empathetic with you, or very close to you; a situation where you trust me and feel my support; it may be just what you need. It may be the spark that ignites you. Even in this situation, however, it will be most effective when you see it for yourself; and the least effective thing I can do is to lay it on you as a truth. The nearer to first-person it gets, the better it will be.

But in a context where I am not at all close to you, and where you do not trust me at all, such a statement will be seen as an even further reason for distance and mistrust. In that situation, it will seem more and more like the third-person use, and will be useless and even harmful.

There is one more thing to say about this issue before we leave it. The statement of self-responsibility, even in its good first-person form, is often taken quite wrongly as a statement of one-sided autonomy, some kind of a claim that I don't need other people any more. Nothing could be further from the truth; the people at Delancey Street, for example, support each other in a very striking and effective way. The point is that *you alone can do it, but you don't have to do it alone*. Both sides of this new statement are true, and they must not be separated from one another. Autonomy is important, but love and mutual support and nourishment are important too.

It can be seen how closely we are approaching the ideas of existentialism. And there is indeed a form of therapy called existential analysis (or sometimes *Daseinsanalyse*) which should be part of our approach. The reason why it is not squarely within is that it does not believe in the use of any techniques. This makes it the purest form of therapy there is, in a way, and yet there is a curious contradiction about the whole thing. By just sitting there and 'being authentic', the existential therapist is not far away from the original psychoanalytic model pioneered by Freud. There is the same silence, the same sense of frustration and deprivation for the client, and the indications are that it is just as slow (Shaffer and Galinsky 1989). Yet existential therapy is developing too, and a recent text (van Deurzen-Smith 1997) makes it clear that even though existential analysts are still suspicious of questions and interpretations, they do still use such things on occasion.

A fascinating dialogue between Martin Buber and Carl Rogers shows how similar and yet how different are the old existential approach and the HEART approach. Buber (1965) makes it clear that for him Rogers is too technique-minded. Rogers is still trying to do something, whereas Buber says that being is more important than doing. There is a good discussion of all this in the *Handbook of humanistic psychology* (Schneider *et al.* 2015), in chapters by Ernesto Spinelli and me.

As I say, this is very pure and very simple. But in practice it is very boring and slow, and also, like most of the 'thinking' approaches, it completely ignores the body. The result is that violence tends to erupt outside the therapy room, because it can find no expression inside. My psychotherapy wants to make the best use of all the skills available, on whatever level they may be.

Intuiting

Here we are concerned with work that starts from the transpersonal level. In other words, we are concerned with the spiritual aspects of the client. These include intuition, the higher self, higher archetypes from the collective unconscious, and so on. In practice, this means using symbols a great deal, sometimes to supplement language and sometimes to replace it.

Work with dreams often touches on this area. For example, Ernst and Goodison (1981) describe work on a dream involving an 'androgynous figure from Mars, supple and radiant in white and silver'. On being asked to 'get into and be' this person (in the usual manner of Gestalt therapy) she realizes that this is her spirituality, which she has repressed and been scared of. Similarly Perls (1976) gives a fully worked example of a dream (Madeline's Dream) where it is quite clear (and even more so from the film which was made of this piece of work) that the client has got in touch with her spirituality.

How do we detect when we are beginning to work in this area? Grof (1975) gives a good hint when he says that we are looking for: 'experiences involving an expansion or extension of consciousness beyond the usual ego boundaries and beyond the limitations of time and/or space'. He has a whole list (Grof 1988) of such experiences and shows how they can be ordered and classified.

But as well as just waiting for this kind of material to come up spontaneously, we can work directly to evoke it. This is often done in psychosynthesis (Assagioli 1975) where guided fantasy is used a great deal.

Through guided fantasy we can introduce symbols to the client which can be useful in opening up spiritual areas, to the extent that the client is ready for that and needs that. Assagioli has a discussion of four critical stages in spiritual awakening, which can happen at any age. A good rundown, with some excellent examples of guided fantasies to use, may be found in Ferrucci (1982). Stevens (1971) gives us an excellent manual of guided fantasy, and a number of fully worked-out examples. Usually in this work, an upward journey takes us towards the spiritual (what Assagioli calls the 'superconscious') while a downward journey takes us into the personal unconscious. But these are just conventions which suit a patriarchal culture, and there is no reason why an upward journey should not represent the more materialistic and superficial types of consciousness, and a downward journey represent descent into the depths of spirituality. Stanton Marlan (1981) has suggested that attention to the depths of the psyche is actually a more valid way of exploring spirituality than any of the more usual aspirations to the heights.

Hillman (1979) made a striking and very disturbing extension to this way of seeing the matter. He suggested that it is wrong to treat dreams merely as clues to day-world problems. Before going into Hillman further, let us look at this question of dreaming.

In the area of dreamwork, there are traditionally three broad ways of working. The first is to see dreams as having to do with the past. This is the psychoanalytic approach. The work on dreams is then retrospective, using the dream material to guess at what is coming up from the unconscious, distorted and censored as it usually is.

The second way of working with dreams is to see them as about the present. This is the approach of Gestalt therapy and existential analysis, as well as of Corriere and Hart (1978) with their idea that, as therapy continues, the client comes more into the active central position in the dreams they have.

The third way is to see them as about the future. This is the Jungian approach, where the work we do is prospective, and refers to our aspirations and our directions in life. The dream is seen as referring to our journey towards individuation.

It is important to realize that these different approaches to dreams can all work because the dream is symbolic. A symbol can and does stand for layer after layer of different things. For example, a Tarot card such as the Wheel of Fortune symbolizes, on the most gross and material level, the ups and downs of life. On another level it is about being able to 'stop the world' and sit on top of all the cycles. On another level it is about going to the still centre and resting there, part of the movement and yet not moving round. On another level it is about standing back and being able to look at the whole Tarot card. And this is just a beginning – there could be a million other interpretations, any one of which might be the best on a particular occasion. This is why there is no way of working on a dream without the client being present.

Coming now to the Hillman revolution, what Hillman (1979) does is to say that all of these methods without exception are wrong. What we need to do instead, he says, is to treat the dream-world as a world in its own right. The world of the dream is a night-world, different from the day-world. It is a soul-world, a spiritual world which needs to be done justice to in its own terms. Instead of interpreting the dream symbols, we must live with them and get to know them and learn how to relate to them:

> It is not what is said about the dream after the dream, but the experience of the dream after the dream. A dream compared with a mystery suggests that the dream is effective as long as it remains alive. . . . It is better to keep the dream's black dog before your inner sense all day than to 'know' its meaning (sexual impulses, mother complex, devilish aggression, guardian, or what have you). A living dog is better than one stuffed with concepts or substituted by an interpretation.
>
> (Hillman 1979)

By really getting into the underworld in this way, Hillman says, we deal with what the dream really has to offer, which is our own soul. He calls therapy soul-making rather than analysis:

> Growth lets the soul do its own thing, like a plant. This organic mystique implies minimal work. Soul-making, too, has a mystique, the mystery of death, which encompasses organic growth and employs its images in the work of soul. Making is a term which reflects what the psyche itself does: it makes images.
>
> (Hillman 1979)

Because the client is a human being, he or she may be at any point of development, or may be partly here and partly there. It is all too common for people to try to work at more advanced levels when they haven't dealt with the basic ego stuff yet. Being able to talk about the mental ego in lofty terms doesn't always mean that it has been adequately dealt with. So the therapist needs to know and be able to work with these other levels even though they have different and incompatible aims.

The beautiful thing about dreams, however, is that they can be worked with at all levels. We can do mental-ego work on dreams, as the Freudians and the person-centred people do; we can do real-self work on dreams as the Gestaltists and the Mahler people do; we can do transpersonal-self work on dreams, as the psychosynthesis people and the Jungians do. But in all cases we shall need to get the client to remember and record dreams, and keep a dream diary. The best set of instructions for this is to be found in Garfield (1976), who says:

> Remind yourself before going to sleep that you will remember your dreams. . . . Knowing that you have just completed a dream, the next step is crucial: Don't open your eyes! Lie still with closed eyes and let images flow into your mind. . . . When you feel as though your dream recall is complete in the position in which you awoke, move gently into other sleeping positions which you use, with eyes still closed, and you will often find additional dream recall . . . record your dreams, preferably with eyes closed [Garfield explains how to write in the dark], in the order that you recall them . . . record a unique verbal expression immediately. . . . Note your unique productions first. . . . Try to at least identify the elusive elements of your dreams. . . . Share your dream experiences with a friend, if possible, as well as record them. . . . Select titles for your dreams from their unique characteristics. . . . As you practise valuing, recalling and recording your dreams, you will increase your recall. Your dreams will become more vivid, complete and relevant to waking life.

To close this chapter on techniques, let us just note that the practitioner has a wealth of methods available. There is no shortage of techniques and methods. But it is important to have the aims and implications of the techniques clear in your mind.

Groupwork

One of the most characteristic features of our approach is that everything we are saying about one-to-one therapy also applies to groupwork. This certainly applies to the encounter group (Rowan 1992a) and the work on couples and families of Virginia Satir (1988), as well as to the leaderless group described by Ernst and Goodison (1981). Satir's work is well described in the chapter by David Cain (2002), where he says: 'Satir focused on the growth process – how it takes place, how it becomes distorted, and how it can be restored' (p.42).

My own work in encounter started in 1970, when I went to groups at the biggest growth centre at the time, *Quaesitor*, which at that time was located at Avenue Road in St Johns Wood. It was there that I actually went to a weekend workshop led by Will Schutz, who impressed me very much. Later I also attended groups led by Jim Elliott and Elizabeth Mintz, and met Will Schutz many times in different contexts.

What I like about encounter is the way in which it allows the practitioner to use the whole range of his or her talents, and to explore the gamut of the group's capacity for healing and discovery. I find that I can stretch my capacities to the full in following the energy of the client who is focal at a given moment.

Learning in the group

It may be useful to point out that the kind of learning that tends to happen in an encounter group is of a very special kind. It is what Gregory Bateson called 'Learning III'. Let us examine this for a moment, because it is a point which is not often made. The kinds of learning are as follows:

Learning I: trial and error processes through which the individual adapts to his environments, finding new responses or patterns of response to given situations. Learning practical or communicational skills takes place at this level. Learning at this level has its joys and its miseries, as anyone who has sought to master, say, a musical instrument or a sport will know.

Learning II: processes through which the individual comes to modify the way he views (or construes) the context in which he applies the knowledge and skills he has gained through Learning I. This is sometimes called 'learning to learn'. There are many kinds of experiential groups where this kind of learning can take place. It is generally regarded as valuable when it does so. For example, if a doctor comes to see his role as that of helping a person in physical or mental distress, instead of repairing a faulty biological mechanism, he may begin to make use of his medical knowledge and skills in different ways. Such a reorientation may be very painful, and/or may be a great release. Once it has taken place, it seems to be self-validating, and is therefore more or less irreversible.

Learning III involves processes though which the individual learns to attend to, and question, and hence bring within conscious control, the habitual ways of construing situations which are the outcomes of Learning II. Learning III entails a much fuller and deeper reflexive awareness. This means a radical questioning of the self. Our imaginary doctor might for example learn to monitor the idea of his role which was implicit in the way he was dealing with this patients, with the possibility of continuing Learning II. In so doing, he would find himself reflecting upon his deepest beliefs, about himself and his patients and about human life, suffering and death. Thus Learning III involves the whole man, and is likely to initiate change in other areas of his life. Such disturbance is frequently frightening and painful; and once again, it may also be a matter of joy and gratitude. These ideas come from Gregory Bateson (1972).

In saying, therefore, that an encounter group enables Learning III to take place, we are maintaining that it is or can be a truly radical experience, which can lead to real restructuring of a man's belief system. In particular, it can lead to a deep questioning of the self and whatever the self takes for granted. And ultimately it involves taking nothing for granted. Barry Palmer, in a very thorough discussion of Bion's groupwork, says the same thing about the deepest kind of group in psychoanalysis:

> [This kind of group] even 'proposes' Learning III. It invites participants to become reflexively aware of the person who is committed to certain ways of construing his role relationships rather than others and who invests them with personal meaning . . . it is assumed that people can look after themselves.
>
> (Palmer 1992, pp.293, 300)

And it is interesting that Palmer, as a psychoanalytically trained group leader, sees clearly that it is in this area that encounter is strongest:

> Recognition of this factor may be seen as a major influence in the development of all those techniques which attempt to outmanoeuvre or dismantle the defences of the ego, such as the techniques of the encounter or personal growth movement. Some of these are defined as therapeutic, others are derived from 'ways of liberation' originating in the East. Their goal, in the terms used here, is Learning III.
>
> (Palmer 1979, p.179)

What we are saying, therefore, is that the integrative nature of the encounter group makes it particularly suitable for breaking down existing patterns of relating and patterns of social assumptions. It is therefore very suitable for the kind of group where men can re-examine their assumptions about masculinity, and where women can re-examine their assumptions about femininity. The new thinking is well described in the chapter by Page and others (2002) in the recent handbook.

The advantage of the integrative approach is that it enables the practitioner to do what is appropriate in a given situation, rather than sticking to some previously worked out theory. It enables, in particular, the regressive, the existential and the transpersonal all to be given their due weight. In this way theory and practice are in a dialectical relationship, each informing the other. The theory gives rise to the practice, and the practice in turn enables the theory to be further developed. (See Appendix 5: Doing good therapy and Example 6.1: The 'I AM!' experience.)

7   The dialogical self and transference

In the last edition of this book, there was a long chapter on transference, with all sorts of details and references, but now it seems to me that there is no need for all that. The current theory of the dialogical self, which I have been working on for many years now, takes its place.

This theory comes from Hubert Hermans, who was influenced by Mikhail Bakhtin (1981), a literary intellectual from East Europe, and his colleague Voloshinov (1986).

Most of us have had the experience of being 'taken over' by a part of ourselves that we didn't know was there. We say – 'I don't know what got into me'. This is generally a negative experience, although it can be positive too, as for example when we find extra strength in an emergency. The way in which we usually recognize the presence of what is now called an I-position is that we find ourselves, in a particular situation, acting in ways that we do not like or which go against our interests, and unable to change this by an act of will or a conscious decision. This lasts as long as the situation lasts – perhaps a few minutes, perhaps an hour, perhaps a few hours – and then it changes by itself when we leave this situation and go into a different one. As long as 40 years ago it was possible for a good and quite uncontroversial text on social psychology (Middlebrook 1974) to say such things as – 'Thus the individual is not a single self, but many selves, which change somewhat as the individual shifts from situation to situation and person to person. We are, in short, what the situation demands'. More recently, David Lester (1995) has said:

> It seems wrong to single out one of the subselves as a core self and also to have only one façade self. It seems more reasonable to propose several subselves that are equivalent (though differing in their influence on behaviour), in much the same way as a person can have several roles without one being seen as a core role and the others as façade roles.
>
> (p.128)

And more recently again Donald Pennington (2003), in using the concept of self-schemas as an equivalent to subpersonalities, has made the point that:

> A strength of the self-schema approach to personality is that it is strongly embedded in the scientific tradition through extensive use of experiments. The self-schema also takes the concept of traits or personality differences into looking at cognitive structures or mental representations. This aids understanding the relationship between personality and behaviour through an appreciation of the mental processes causing the behaviour.
>
> (p.235)

This concept of self-schemas, because it has been used in many research projects (e.g., Markus 1977), has recently been a point of entry into the major texts on personality, and this is a beginning for the full entry of such a concept into the mainstream. This seems confirmed by the current emergence of Schema Therapy (Young *et al.* 2003) as a free-standing school of therapy and counselling.

The question of whether there are parts of a person that can be talked to and worked with as if they were separate little personalities with a will of their own is one which has fascinated nearly everyone who has had to work with people in any depth. Phrases such as – 'On the one hand I want to . . . on the other hand I don't', 'I don't know how I could have done it', 'It was as if a voice was telling me off' – are so common that they inevitably give a counsellor or therapist the cue that more than one system is at work. Internalized mothers and fathers are so common that it has almost become a joke. All these are examples of ways in which the idea of I-positions presents itself very patently and obviously. In fiction and in plays the idea often comes to the surface. I became interested in the idea and decided to do some research of my own.

Regard the problem: how to reconcile the Freud (1923) who wrote of the ego, the id and the superego; the Jung (1928) who talked about the complexes or the archetypes; the Lewin (1936) who wrote about subregions of the personality; the Klein (1948) or Fairbairn (1952) or Guntrip (1971) who talked about internal objects; the Gurdjieff (1950) who introduced the concept of little I's; the Federn (1952) or Berne (1961) or John Watkins (1978) who spoke of ego-states; the Perls (1951) who referred to the topdog and the underdog, or retroflection; the Balint (1968) who delineated the child in the patient; the Winnicott (1965) or Lake (1966) or Janov (1973) or Laing (1976) who referred to the false or unreal self; the Gergen (1972) or Martindale (1980) or O'Connor (1971) or Shapiro (1976) who refer to subselves; the Strauss or Rossan who talk about subidentities; the Goffman (1974) who referred to multiple selfing; the Assagioli (1975) or Redfearn (1985) or Rowan (1990) or Sliker (1992) who talk about the subpersonalities; the Mair (1977) who opened up the possibility of a community of self; the T. B. Rogers (1981) who writes about prototypes; the Beahrs (1982) who refers to alter-personalities; the Mary Watkins (1986) who described imaginal objects, such as the imaginary friend; the McAdams (1985) who deployed the concept of imagoes as a key to life histories; the Hilgard (1986) who discovered the 'hidden observer' in hypnotic states; the Tart (1986) who spoke of identity states; the Denzin (1987) who talked about the emotionally divided self; the Stone and Winkelman (1985) who used the concept of energy patterns; the Mahrer (1989) who theorized deeper potentials coming to the surface; the Ornstein (1986) who spoke of small minds; the Gazzaniga (1985) or Minsky (1988) who discovered agents and agencies within the brain; the Markus (1987) who speaks of possible selves; the Crabtree (1988) who refers to multiple personalities; the Kihlstrom and Cantor (1984) or Young *et al.* (2003) or Pennington (2003) who introduced the concept of self-schemas; the Hermans (1999) who introduced the notion of I-positions; the Mearns and Thorne (2000) who speak of the configurations of self: the Bogart (2007) who refers to personas – all the time we are talking about the same thing – this thing which is not mentioned in the major textbooks of personality.

This is all in the past, but what about the present? The new thinking comes from a number of different angles. The first and most prominent is the work of Hubert Hermans at Nijmegen University in the Netherlands. It was he who coined the term 'the dialogical self', partly inspired by Bakhtin (1981). The eighth international conference on the dialogical self took place in 2014 in The Hague. What he did was to shift the nomenclature from the older ideas of subselves, subpersonalities, ego-states and so forth, all of which lent themselves to misunderstanding as solid entities all too easily, and introduce instead a new vocabulary based on I-positions.

> The notion of the 'dialogical self' deviates from those associations and considers the self as a multiplicity of parts (voices, characters, positions) that have the potential of entertaining dialogical relationships with each other . . . The self functions as a society, being at the same time part of the broader society in which the self participates.
>
> (Hermans 2004, p.13)

Hermans and his colleagues, for example Giancarlo Dimaggio, have conducted many research studies to explore their theory, and it is now well established.

What is remarkable, however, is that this is not the only approach that is now opening up the realm of multiplicity within the person. William Stiles, who goes back and forth between Ohio and Sheffield, has developed what he calls assimilation theory, which again has produced a large research programme to explore the idea of listening to the different voices that emerge during the course of therapy (Stiles *et al*. 2004).

The person-centred school has in recent years begun to use the concept, under the heading of *configurations of self*, particularly in the hands of Dave Mearns and Mick Cooper. And this has enabled them to speak freely of the parts of the person that are negative.

> It is important that the person-centred therapist offer an equally full therapeutic relationship to *not for growth* configurations, like: 'the "me" that just wants to curl up and do absolutely nothing'; 'the part that wants to go back'; and 'the bit of me that wants to destroy this therapist'.
>
> (Mearns and Thorne 2000, p.115)

This is quite a new departure for the person-centred school, and begins to sound much more like the psychoanalytic position about resistance.

Philip Bromberg, in the psychodynamic school, has made some very interesting points, showing that multiplicity is not at all foreign to that outlook.

> A noticeable shift has been taking place with regard to psychoanalytic understanding of the human mind and the nature of unconscious mental processes – away from the idea of a conscious/preconscious/unconscious distinction per se, towards a view of the self as decentered, and the mind as a configuration of shifting, nonlinear, discontinuous states of consciousness in an ongoing dialectic with the healthy illusion of unitary selfhood.
>
> (Bromberg 2004)

Of course it is well known that transactional analysis and Gestalt therapy speak often of different parts of the person, but recently the torch has been taken up by experiential process therapy – much more interested in research than these earlier advocates.

> Process-experiential therapy has attempted to provide a comprehensive theory of treatment by integrating Gestalt and client-centered approaches. It combines the relationship conditions of empathy, prizing and congruence with more active interventions like empty-chair and two-chair work from Gestalt therapy, and focusing and evocative unfolding from Gendlin's and Rice's developments within client-centered therapy.
>
> (Watson *et al*. 1998, p.14)

The handbook edited by Leslie Greenberg and his collaborators (Greenberg *et al.* 1998) makes creative use of these ideas to intervene very effectively in research terms with people who have problems such as depression, posttraumatic stress, anxiety, psychosomatic disorders, sexual trauma, borderline personality disorder, dissociated and fragile process and so forth. This is exciting new work which needs to be better known.

And of course we must not forget the recent work in narrative therapy, based on the pioneers David Epston and Michael White at the Dulwich Centre in Adelaide. They and their collaborators (such as Michael Durrant and Cheryl White) have developed some fascinating ideas using person-ification to bring to life some important creatures, such as the Fear Monster, Sneaky Wee, Sneaky Poo, Concentration, Tantrums, Misery, Guilt, Bad Habits, Zak (cannabis) and Sugar (diabetes). By working directly with such characters, they found that they could confirm the adage – 'The person is not the problem. The problem is the problem'. Jill Freedman and Gene Combs have added such things as Bravery and Self-Blame (Freedman and Combs 1996).

Nor must we forget the recent work of Jeffrey Young and his collaborators in schema therapy. Their reseach has suggested that there are only eighteen basic early maladaptive schemas, and only three modes of dealing with each one. This theory comes out of cognitive-behavioural therapy, and represents a much more sophisticated version of that basic outlook. 'Schema therapists view experiential techniques as one of four equal components of treatment and devote considerable time in therapy to these strategies' (Young *et al.* 2003, pp.51–2). In a later discussion, the authors have this to say:

> Patients learn to conduct dialogues between their 'schema side' and their 'healthy side'. Adapting the Gestalt 'empty chair' technique, the therapist instructs patients to switch chairs as they play the two sides: In one chair they play the schema side, in the other they play the healthy side.
>
> (p.100)

This again is personification, and it seems clear that it fits well with the basic orientation.

Of course the astute reader will have noticed that all this material is highly compatible with the basic case of constructionism, while avoiding the excesses of a one-sided postmodernism. The important book of G. S. Gregg put it very succinctly:

> The central point here is that the self consists not of a collection of Me attributions, as cognitive personality theorists would have it, nor

of ego-syntonic identifications, as most psychoanalytic personality theories would have it, but of a system of Me/not-Me oppositions.

(Gregg 1991, p.120)

Gregg pertinently asked the question as to how a unitary self, a single overarching system of symbols, could split felt experience, encode moral imperatives, and reconfigure itself according to the context. His answer was – very simply, in the same manner that a sentence can articulate double entendre, or a figure/ground illusion can switch between two pictures, or two notes an octave apart can be heard to be both the same and different. John Shotter (1999) adds some interesting ideas from the work of Bakhtin.

There are basically three forms of personification in the world of therapy, counselling and coaching.

1   Empty chair work. This is the basic idea, pioneered by Jacob Moreno, of asking the client to imagine that the object of his or her affections or enmity is sitting on an empty chair. The client then first of all describes and talks to the character involved, and then moves over into the other chair and enters into and speaks for that character. In recent years this has been formalized by the Integral Institute as the 3–2–1 method: first we describe the character in the third person (he or she is like this or that), then in the second person (addressing the person as 'you'), and finally in the first person (turning the person into an 'I'). Fritz Perls was the great master of this method, and showed that we could put into the empty chair such things as 'the number plate in your dream', 'your smirk', 'the dream you did not have' and 'your aborted fetus'.

2   Two chair work. In this version we identify two (often incompatible) parts of the client, and put each one on to a separate chair. The client is then encouraged to speak for each of the parts in turn, and may then be encouraged to engage in a dialogue between the two parts: perhaps they may want to convince the other part that they are more necessary or more valid. Robert Elliott has done much research on this technique in recent years.

3   Multiple chair work. This is particuarly often used by the Voice Dialogue school, who may use up to ten or more chairs to personify different parts of the person. Again they may speak individually or engage in dialogues with other 'persons' on the other chairs. The Voice Dialogue people always insist on having an Aware Ego which is above and beyond the other characters, but this does not seem to be essential. Again the idea goes back to Moreno. It has been used very creatively in the last few years by Genpo Roshi in his Big Mind workshops.

This is therefore a very flexible idea, which can take a number of forms. In recent years I have been urging that it is now possible, using the idea of I-positions, to have dialogues with one's Soul or even one's Spirit. This idea was pioneered by Moreno again, who sometimes asked a protagonist to stand on a chair and be God. But it was refined and developed further by the psychosynthesis people, particularly Molly Young Brown. More recently, Kellogg has introduced the idea of 'transformational chairwork' which seems like a good addition to the repertoire.

It is obvious that the notion of an I-position makes all these moves more transparent and less worrying conceptually. John Beahrs put it very well when he said:

> When is it useful or not useful to look upon an individual as a single unit, as a 'Cohesive Self'? When is it useful or not useful to look upon anyone as being constituted of many parts, each with an identity of its own? When is it useful to see ourselves as part of a greater whole? I use the term 'useful' rather than 'true' since all are true – simultaneously and at all times.

Transference

How does all this help with the notion of transference? Let us look at an example. Supposing that a therapist says to a client – 'I shall be taking six weeks off for my holiday'. The client may look brave, and say – 'of course, that is OK'. The psychoanalyst might say to herself – 'He says that it is OK, but at an unconscious level he might think otherwise, and we shall have to probe that on my return'. But the dialogical self thought might be much more precise: 'He says that it is OK, but perhaps there is an adolescent I-position who is very angry; or perhaps there is a child I-position who is very scared; or perhaps there is an infantile I-position who is just screaming, and we shall have to probe all that on my return'. It can be seen how much more specific the dialogical self thought is, and how much more helpful it could be.

In other words, the dialogical self position can be much more specific and fine-tuned than the general idea of the unconscious. Looked at in this light, the idea of the unconscious seems very general and much too blunt and insensitive. If we talk instead about a number of different I-positions, this not only clarifies our thought, but it also opens the way to approach alternate realities through questioning or chairwork designed to explore the matter in detail. I have explained all this in detail in my book *Personification* (2010).

Therefore the broad idea of transference drops out, to be replaced with the more subtle and specific idea of I-positions. For example take the case of erotic transference. We would now say – 'One of the I-positions of the client is sexually attracted to one of the I-positions of the therapist'. This immediately sounds less threatening and more open to modification than any recourse to notions of transference. And it suggests that the therapist had better take something to supervision, in a way that transference does not.

The same reasoning applies to countertransference. Instead of a supervisor saying to the counsellor – 'The way you are talking reveals that your unconscious is taking the side of the child against the mother' – the new statement would be more – 'The way you are talking reveals that you have an I-position which is on the side of the child against the mother'. This leaves the way open to talking to this I-position directly, and finding out more about how and why this should be taking place.

Instead of having to work out which form of transference is involved (and there are many) all we have to do is to pick out the I-position and chat with it. This is both more simple and more direct, and so, I believe, more effective. (See Appendix 2: Ground rules for groups, and Appendix 6: Dangers and traps.)

Useful websites

International Institute for the Dialogical Self: www.dialogicalinstitute.com – This is the main reference for the history and other features of the dialogical approach.

8   Resistance

We saw in Chapter 5 that the aims and underlying assumptions of our psychotherapy are very different from the aims and underlying assumptions of psychoanalysis. For Freud, the Id is the fundamental bedrock. For us, the real self is the equivalent foundation.

Yet it is curious how virtually all the people who broke away from Freud, whether the break came early or late in Freud's life, did come to believe in the real self, as something healthy and trustworthy. Some of them did so while making huge revisions in the theory, while others did so with very little change at all. And this suggests that the idea of the real self may not be so remote from Freud after all – maybe it is really very close to Freud, rather than being at the other end of a long line.

Suppose, for example, we look at Paul Federn (1952), a psychoanalyst of the 1930s and 1940s. He has an outer layer of the person which he calls the ego-states, rather similar to Eric Berne's ego-states or Assagioli's subpersonalities, and an inner centre which he calls the Id.

Real self and Id

Where would it take us if we simply said that Freud's Id was the real self? At first it seems quite ridiculous. The Id is seen in psychoanalysis as the basic foundation of all motivation in the individual. It is an extraordinarily dramatic concept. It seems to be impossible to describe it without excitement. It is a 'seething mass', 'primitive', 'repository of primitive and unacceptable impulses', 'completely selfish and unconcerned with reality or moral considerations', or 'unorganized chaotic mentality'. Freud's own words are 'a cauldron of seething excitement'. The Id works on the pleasure principle – that is, it uses primary process thinking, attempting to discharge tension by forming an image of the object which will remove the tension. There is no time in the Id – past, present and future mix without distinction. The laws of logic and reason do not exist for the Id, so that contrary wishes can exist side by side quite happily. One thing can stand for or symbolize other, incompatible things, and so on. If the Id were a person, it almost sounds as if he or she would be mad!

I don't want to exaggerate this, because Freud talks in one place quite positively about 'the Id's will', but certainly Freud and his commentators see the Id at least as unreliable, not to be trusted.

Contrast this with what people say about the real self. Jung says – 'The self is our life's goal, for it is the completest expression of that fateful combination we call individuality'. Reich says that the deepest layer of the human personality is a place where the impulses are no longer distorted and pathological, but spontaneously decent. Maslow says that:

> self-actualisation means experiencing fully, vividly, selflessly, with full concentration and full absorption. . . . At this moment the person is wholly and fully human. . . . Peak experiences are transient moments of self-actualisation. They are moments of ecstasy which cannot be bought, cannot be guaranteed, cannot even be sought.

Janov says that 'to be totally oneself is a spectacular feeling'.

These seem to be two very different things, then, don't they? The Id and the real self are both supposed to be somehow at the base or centre of the person, and to represent the person's most fundamental bedrock, but it is as if one were black and the other white. Or as if one were a mess, and the other a jewel. And yet. . . . And yet there is something that doesn't fit about that way of putting it. And what doesn't fit is that getting in touch with the real self is very scary. Everyone seems to agree that it's a good thing, and well worth getting in touch with, and yet everyone avoids getting in touch with it like mad. People appear to be just as scared of it as they would be of the Id.

The way this comes out is in the phenomenon that Freud called 'therapeutic resistance'. What Freud discovered was that people came to him saying they wanted to get rid of their neuroses, and then proceeded to hang on to them and grab on to them and dig their heels in to keep them in every way possible, and even found whole new ways of expressing them better. And this was easy for him to understand, because he could see how people would naturally want to avoid admitting all the nasty impulses coming up from the Id – all about desperately unsavoury things such as incest and destruction and horror and fear. So he felt very comfortable about resistance and devoted a lot of time to thinking about it.

But we as psychotherapists find plenty of resistance too. I've been around most kinds of therapy in my time, and I've certainly felt it in myself and seen it very clearly in others. And it arises in just the same way as it does for the Freudians: people come to a group or an individual session to work on their problems, and then proceed to avoid them, sidetrack them, not know how to work on them, get interested in other people's problems, smoke a lot, drink cups of tea, go to the toilet a lot and all the rest of it. And then maybe start working, but find that the therapist isn't doing it right. . . . But we as psychotherapists don't talk much about resistance at all. Rogers only mentions it as a temporary stage in the life of a group. Perls plays it down and treats it as just another split in the personality. Corsini says that it only really arises in long-term therapy, so he advocates short-term therapy. The NLP people say – 'There is no resistance, there are only incompetent therapists'.

But there is one person who does justice to the whole thing, and shows us where the answer might be, and that is Reich. I didn't realize until recently that Reich's whole early approach was being worked out in a seminar that he ran at Freud's request, which was mainly devoted to the study of resistance. And the way he came to look at it was that the human personality is something like an onion, with layers. The deepest and innermost layer – the centre – was what we have been calling the real self – healthy and fundamentally OK. But surrounding it on all sides was another layer just like what we have been calling the Id – a layer of distorted impulses and dangerous fantasies.

What we are saying, then, is that by his deep and extensive studies of resistance, Reich (1950) came to the conclusion that the real self was 'inside' the Id. This would mean, if it were true, that in order to get through to the real self, the route would go through the Id. This radically changes the definition of the Id, though not its nature. Instead of the Id being seen as the biological bedrock of the personality, it is seen as just another false self – a set of mistakes we have made about ourselves. But each of those mistakes may need to be picked up, and seen, and dealt with, before we can leave them behind or transform them. So there is no way, either for Freud or for Reich (or for us), of avoiding the need to deal with that layer. (Compare our account in Chapter 5).

If this way of putting it is anything like the truth, as I believe it is, then resistance is understandable once again. The reason why we avoid the real self is because we have to walk through hell to get there. This means that we can accept the Id as a perfectly valid description of the way things appear, and of what we have done to ourselves and had done to us. It does have to be dealt with, just as Freud said it did. Only when we have done that, instead of just going back to our boring old over-socialized ego, we can go on to the ecstasy of the real self. It was James Bugental who made the link with existentialism. He says: 'Resistance is the name that we give to the general defensive wall the patient puts between himself and the threats that he finds linked to being authentic. Resistance is anti-authenticity' (Bugental 1981, p.103).

So the real self is the authentic self. And the way to it comes through a thicket of threats. One of the most important aspects of resistance is the way we can let our catastrophic expectations get in the way of the work. One of the best accounts of this is by Beth Erickson (1993).

Brammer, Shostrom and Abrego have a very good discussion of resistance, and one of the things they say which has really stuck in my mind and resonated there, is: 'The job of the therapist is not to overcome this resistance, but to explore it, because it can reveal the answer to the question – "How does the client hide his or her secret?"' (Brammer *et al*. 1989, p.225).

This idea of hiding secrets, and of this being a useful skill as well as whatever else it may be, is very close to the ideas of Reich mentioned earlier. These authors go on to say that resistance may vary from rejection of therapy and overt antagonism, on the one hand, to subtle forms, such as hesitation and inattention on the other.

> For example, the client criticizes the counselor, expresses dissatisfaction with the results of counseling, fails to hear or to understand the counselor, comes late or fails to keep appointments, remains silent, forgets the fee, engages in intellectual discussion using complex psychological terms, expresses negative attitudes toward psychology, desires to end counseling prematurely, is unproductive in associations or with unfamilar material, introduces irrelevant topics, makes unreasonable demands on the counselor, is pessimistic about counseling, or expresses skepticism about interpretations.
>
> The client's resistance may take less aggressive forms as, for example, agreeing unequivocally with everything the counselor says, refusing to get emotionally involved, being overly cooperative, prolonging a dependency transference, maintaining persistent facetiousness, forcing the process into a semantic wilderness of abstractions and philosophical notions, pressing the limits of the relationship by asking for overtime, perhaps, and expressing strong interest in the counselor's personal life.
>
> (Brammer *et al*. 1989, p.224)

What does this mean in practice? Well, for me it means that I can now go to all the wealth of knowledge and experience that therapists of all persuasions have built up over the years about resistance, and learn a hell of a lot from it. For example, we can now distinguish five different kinds of resistance.

Repression resistance is just due to the person not being aware of all the games they are playing. The unconscious defences remain unconscious because of the weight of repression still operating on them. This is the most common and basic kind of resistance. The client is fighting against becoming aware of painful feelings that are coming up, and may suddenly switch to a different subject, or switch off altogether.

Secondary gain resistance is all about the set of satisfactions the person gets from being neurotic – all the advantages you get, such as gaining attention, avoiding things you don't want to do anyway, getting looked after and treated specially, and so on. This is all about the dangers of improvement:

> If one loses weight, one will have to alter or buy a whole new wardrobe; if one feels more confident, others may then not hold back on unleashing criticism they have withheld 'while you were down'; in performing better sexually one may feel impelled to make up for lost time and neglect other necessary activities, or one's partner might not be able to keep up; and so forth.
>
> (Fisch *et al.* 1982)

These drawbacks are very real, but they are often pooh-poohed by the client at the conscious level, even though they do affect behaviour.

Superego resistance comes out in the client's unconscious need for punishment or rejection. We would of course not use a word such as 'superego', which belongs to a different theoretical position. It would be for us just another instance of Mahrer's (1996) disintegrative relationships between operating potentials and deeper potentials.

> This feeling is painful, but muted. It is an uncomfortable feeling, but soft and subtle. It consists of a little internal whimper, a delicate inner voice which says, 'You should not do this; that was a real mistake'. It is the voice which psychoanalysis attributes to the superego, and which humanistic theory attributes to the deeper potential which is blockaded in the service of preserving the self.

'The self' in Mahrer's quote here means the unregenerate neurotic self, the self that does not want to change, the unexamined operating potentials.

Repetition-compulsion resistance is that where the person maintains their fixed patterns in spite of all the insights and catharses they may attain to, and which seem to be deep and genuine. This is a particularly difficult form of resistance to handle, and it gave rise to Freud's idea of the death instinct. It can be a particularly frustrating one for the therapist.

Transference resistance is where the client tries to get from the therapist true love, or a magical cure, or tries to be like the therapist, or is competitive with the therapist, and so on. We can easily see how this can arise, from our discussion of transference in the previous chapter.

Therapist response

Jim Bugental (1978) has a very good analogy to show how we should think about resistance. He says that when we are travelling on a motorway and come to roadworks causing a diversion, and find ourselves on side roads that are much slower, we are disappointed and inconvenienced. But if we are a member of the crew working on the road and come to that same set of roadworks, we say 'Aha, this is what I am looking for'. So it is in therapy, he says. We are looking for what interferes with the free flow of awareness of the full creative potential of consciousness (p.89).

What I have learned from all this is that the best thing for the therapist to do is to interpret the resistance. We saw in the last chapter how widely that has to be understood by the practitioner.

One of the best ways I have found of doing this is to personify the resistance and talk to it, and let it answer back. This is a good recourse. Mahrer says very directly:

> While the patient is 'resistant' to the deeper process, the deeper process has no 'resistance' to the patient, so the interaction is free to occur. The problem of 'resistance' is solved by giving the integrative, 'unresistant' deeper process a form and shape and voice with which to interact with the patient.
>
> (Mahrer 1986, p.115)

Mahrer has his own way of carrying this out. I find a good way, which is compatible with most of the usual ways of working, goes like this:

Step one in this is to wait until the person comes up with an image of the resistance: 'It is like a wall'; 'It is like a porcelain bath with no way out'; 'It is like a fog'; 'It is like a huge door'; 'It is like a huge ball with hooks on it'; 'It is like a death skeleton' – and so on. Step two is put it on the cushion or chair. This may be done quite directly, and it has worked well just like that; but more recently I have started to get the client to draw a picture of it, and then put the picture on to the cushion. This acts as a very powerful 'magnetic' focus of attention, which seems to bring the thing alive more vividly. Of course the theory of the dialogical self, that we met in the last chapter, helps us a lot in this endeavour.

Step three is to talk to it. What I usually say is – 'Wait until you can really see it there on the cushion, and have a real sense of its presence. When it is really here, start saying any words that come up, without thinking about them or censoring them, addressed directly to it. Let's suppose that by some miracle it can hear you, and talk back if necessary'. If the client doesn't accept this, and argues that a fog can't talk back, as with the example discussed in Chapter 6, I simply say – 'If it makes it easier, just imagine that it is a character in a play, labelled "Fog". This character comes on and represents Fog, and talks as if it were your Fog'. This then gets over the logical objection, which is of course just another aspect of the resistance itself. Once the talking starts, let it continue for some time. Now we are in touch with the relevant I-position, and can let it speak for itself.

Step four is to get the client to change over and sit on the other cushion (putting the drawing under the cushion so that it doesn't get torn or crumpled too much, if one is being used). I say – 'Take a moment just to get into the feeling of being that character. Sit the way it would sit, breathe the way it would breathe, think the way it would think, feel the way it would feel, and just be it more and more. And when you are ready, see if there is anything you want to reply. (Name of client) is sitting there on that other cushion. S/he has just been talking to you, and saying various things to you. (Perhaps repeat some of them.) See them sitting on the cushion. Notice how they are dressed, what their expression is, how they are sitting and all that. And then see if there is any response you want to make'. It is important to put it in this permissive way, because sometimes the resistance takes the form of an I-position that won't talk, and it is important not to rule this out.

When the resistance has talked back, the dialogue carries on. People sometimes ask – 'How do you know when to get the person to switch from one cushion to the other?' The basic answer to this is that you must allow the client to finish with one cushion before moving to the other, otherwise you can miss important spontaneous material that may emerge. It is like a conversation, and as with all conversations, eye contact is used as punctuation; so when the client pauses and looks at me, I know it is time to switch over.

Sometimes when the interaction has moved into its middle phase, I hurry things up a bit, by just waiting until one important phrase is uttered by one side or the other – something that if replied to will move the interaction along – without waiting for the client to give the signal. But this needs to be very carefully considered, because it puts the therapist into a more pushy and controlling position, and it should be abandoned as soon as possible. The client should always feel as if it is them doing it, and not that the therapist is doing it. This is of course highly compatible with the theory of the dialogical self that we met in the previous chapter.

There are obviously many other ways of dealing with resistance. Sometimes it is enough just to talk about it directly – things such as arriving late, forgetting appointments, leaving one's cheque-book behind, can all be directly faced and commented on. For example, when a client is late by a quarter of an hour or more, a good question to ask is – 'When was the first moment when you knew you were going to be late?' After all, if it were an examination that only took place once a year, and on which one's whole future depended, one would not be late no matter what. So it is largely a matter of choices and priorities, and that is where resistance comes in.

James Bugental has a very full and clear discussion of resistance. He remarks on how it can reveal not only what the person is doing in the session, but how they relate to the outside world. And in order to track a particular type of resistance, he advocates tagging it. This idea of tagging seems to be very important.

> Tagging the resistance is a matter of again and again pointing to the resistive pattern as it is occurring. This means that the pattern chosen for therapist attention must be one that is manifested frequently and is interfering currently with the client's inquiry into her own subjectivity. This means also that it is usually best to select only one such pattern for attention at any given point ... With accelerating frequency the therapist needs to point to the client's dependence on this way of managing his in-the-moment experience ... As the client becomes aware, through the tagging, of how frequently she relies on the pattern, the tagging needs to be extended to show how it affects the work.
>
> (Bugental 1987, p.184)

How one deals with resistance says a lot about one's own personality as a therapist, and also about one's aims. The more limited one's aims, the less resistance is going to matter. The more far-reaching one's aims, the more resistance is likely to play a major role. But the therapist can certainly exaggerate and overemphasize resistance – Reich himself was a classic example of this. He would have angry shouting matches with his clients, because that is the kind of person he was. He was a good therapist, but he probably aroused more resistance than was really necessary.

Our approach is not to oppose the resistance, but to let it speak, let it have its day. Usually it thinks it is doing a great job in protecting the person from non-survivable threat. But of course in reality the threat was survived – otherwise the client would not be here today – so there must be some flaw in the logic of that.

It often pays off to ask the question of this I-position – 'When did you last succeed in protecting the person from anything at all?' Usually the answer is a lemon, and then the whole set-up can be abandoned.

Usually there are two levels involved: at one level there was an external threat that needed to be defended against; at another level there was a destructive response, where the client went beyond defence into attack. Most therapists, myself included, would say that the first came first, and the second, second. Melanie Klein says that the second comes first. But either way, feelings of guilt will be associated with the second part, because the person being attacked by the infant client is usually the mother, and you just naturally feel guilty about trying to destroy your mother.

So the pain arises from intolerable threat and intolerable guilt, in some painful combination. No wonder that, as we get closer to this syndrome, resistance increases. All that I, as a therapist, can do is to work through this material myself, in my own therapy, and then encourage the client to follow my example.

9   The process of development

At the end of the last chapter we started touching on the question of theory. If we want to do good therapy, we must have some notion of what is going on inside the person. Obviously our ideas about what works in therapy must be based on our ideas about where problems come from. The psychoanalyst has a clear set of ideas about the Oedipus complex, about the Id, ego and superego, and about the psychosexual stages of development. The behaviourist has a clear set of ideas about stimuli, responses, reinforcement and extinction. The cognitive therapist has a definite set of ideas about automatic thoughts and so forth. I am in a more difficult position, because there are a number of separate disciplines within me, each with its own notion of development, often not very well worked out or spelled out.

In my own work, I find I have three different theories which I use at different times. In the first edition of this book I had to say that I could not see how they could be reconciled, but now I can. Each of the three seems to have something which is missing in the others, and which is true and has to be taken into account in any adequate way of looking at these matters. And I now think they fit together in a convincing manner. The three are: primal integration theory; Mahrer's humanistic theory; and Wilber's transpersonal theory. Let us look at each of these in turn, and see what they have to offer.

Primal integration

In this theory we say that neuroses and psychoses often come ultimately from early trauma. At some point in our history we meet a situation that is intolerable – it is too painful to be borne. And at that point we resort to a defence that is generally known as splitting.

Frank Lake (1980) is clearest of all about the different levels of stress and the different levels of trauma which result from them. The highest level he calls 'transmarginal stress' (after Pavlov's research terminology) and it is this which leads most catastrophically to the splitting defence. Lake shows how by applying his four levels of stress to Grof's (1975) four stages of the birth process we get sixteen cells which between them account for most of the neuroses and psychoses seen in clinical practice. But the person who has spoken most eloquently about these matters is Arthur Janov, who says:

> This separation of oneself from one's needs and feelings is an instinctive manoeuvre in order to shut off excessive pain. We call it the split. The organism splits in order to preserve its continuity. This does not mean that unfulfilled needs disappear, however.

(Janov 1973, p.22)

This process has been well diagrammed by Winnicott (1975) (see Figure 9.1). He says that after a trauma where splitting takes place:

> The infant gets seduced into compliance, and a compliant False Self reacts to environmental demands and the infant seems to accept them . . . The False Self has one positive and very important function: to hide the True Self, which it does by compliance with environmental demands.

So the split is a defence against the annihilation of the experiencing subject. This is the same process that Michael Balint talks about as the 'basic fault'. He points out that we are probably not talking – though we may sometimes be – about a single event:

> The trauma itself, of course, is not necessarily a single event; on the contrary, usually it amounts to a situation of some duration caused by

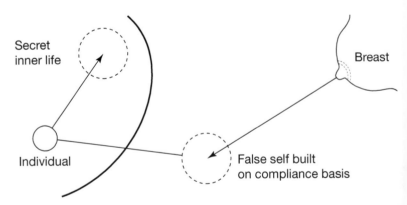

Figure 9.1 The Winnicott view

a painful misunderstanding – lack of 'fit' – between the individual and his environment.

(Balint 1968, p.82)

This very early splitting is a source of psychosis as much as of neurosis, particularly where the split is deepened and confirmed at a pre-verbal stage. So we should never be surprised when psychotic material comes up in any form of therapy. And this means that we as therapists need to work through our own psychotic material first, if we are not to be overpowered and overwhelmed by the depth of feeling involved in these very early traumas.

How early are they, in fact? Different researchers give different answers to this. Duval and Wicklund (1972) see the major trauma happening at about 3 years old; Mahler *et al.* (1975) see it happening at about 1 year old; Klein (Segal 1979) and the rest of the object relations school put it within the first 6 months of life; Grof (1992) and Lake (1980) say that it most often happens at birth, and have a lot of evidence to support their contention; Noble (1993) and Feher (1980) say that it can happen in the womb; Mott (1969) and Laing (1976) say that it can happen at implantation; Sadger (1941) and Peerbolte (1975) say that it can happen as far back as conception; and Roger Woolger (1990) is willing to go back into past lives in order to find the major trauma which has to be dealt with. One of the best and most fully thought-out accounts of all this material is to be found in Firman and Gila (1997): John Firman comes from the psychosynthesis school, but has a wide-ranging set of sympathies and is very well read in these matters.

It doesn't seem to matter very much what we believe about this – it is what the client believes that matters. As long as we as therapists keep an open mind, we can go with the client to wherever the client needs to go. The important thing is that crises in the person's life tend to reactivate the defences which were used before. This means that we have to go back down the chain of crises to find the original trauma or traumatic situation.

The basic thought, held by many different theorists, is that crises form a series, such that the way the early crises are dealt with form the pattern for dealing with new crises as they arise. This position has been put forward most classically by Erikson (1965), but Grof (1975) has his version, the NLP people have their version, and so on. Janov (1977) says it this way:

In the maturation of the brain each new trauma is represented and then re-represented holographically on higher and higher levels of the brain neuraxis. In this way a Primal chain is developed, with later traumas reactivating related first-line Pains. What this means is that at each stage of brain development an imprint of the trauma occurs, and as the brain develops each imprint joins other related imprints of traumas, the early imprints becoming connected to the later ones. This fusion and representation continues to occur and becomes more elaborate and complex as maturation goes on.

Janov is here trying to work out what must be happening at a neurophysiological level. I don't think we need to get too hung up about the details of that, but it is important to show that in principle the brain is capable of working in this way, starting back before birth, to produce a chain or relay system of experiences which we can use in therapy as a kind of rope-ladder, going down step by step. Verny (1982) has collected a good deal of research which again shows that very early memories are indeed possible, and Chamberlain (1998) has demonstrated convincingly that many people can remember their own birth. The research is now there, reported regularly in the *Journal of the Association for Pre and Perinatal Psychology and Health*, and summarized helpfully in the Chamberlain book just mentioned.

Once we have this basic split into the real or true self and the unreal or false self, it becomes easy to grasp how false selves can proliferate, thus producing the phenomenon which is variously known as subpersonalities, ego-states, complexes, internal objects, little 'I's and so forth (Firman and Gila 1997; Rowan 2010). I call them I-positions, because that seems to be most useful for therapy purposes, and this idea comes from well-researched sources (Hermans and Gieser 2012). I have written about this at some length (Rowan 2010). One of the best descriptions of how this happens comes from Freud:

> A portion of the external world has, at least partially, been abandoned as an object and has instead, by identification, been taken into the ego and thus become an integral part of the internal world. This new psychical agency continues to carry on the functions which have hitherto been performed by people in the external world.

Here Freud is, of course, talking about the superego. What we are now saying is that there are many separated superego-like regions in the child's psychic space, each of which has its own energy and its own rules. In recent years a much more adequate theory of this has appeared, using the basic concept of the dialogical self. We now talk about I-positions (Hermans and Gieser 2012) and see them as normal aspects of development rather than something pathological.

There is much more that could be said about this process of development, but the main lines are now clear. As can be seen, this approach is not very far removed from psychoanalysis, particularly the position of the object relations school, or the middle school, as it is sometimes known. But the theory as laid down by Grof, for example, is much more flexible than the work of the object relations school, and not so hampered by the need to avoid any mention of perinatal experience or spiritual development. I find it very useful and helpful in my work, and very much in tune with the work I have done on myself. I have written it up more fully elsewhere (Rowan 2010) and a good chapter on primal integration has been written by Juliana Brown and Richard Mowbray (1994).

Mahrer's humanistic psychodynamics

The late Alvin Mahrer again is more recent and original: in fact, it has been said that he is one of the great founding fathers of humanistic psychology, and his work should be much more widely known. According to Mahrer (1989), instead of talking about the self as if it were present from the start, we should talk about a primitive personality field out of which a self only gradually emerges, a year or more after birth. So there is no way that early traumas can happen, because there is no one there for them to happen to. This is the logic; but the practice is subtly different. In Mahrer's therapy (Mahrer 1996) he continually takes the client back into earlier experiences, and some of them are extremely early, going back into perinatal scenes. There is clearly someone there, someone experiencing life in the womb, life during the process of birth. So there is a self after all at these early times. My own view is that a threat to life brings a self or ego of some kind into being. Before that I may have been part of a field, or part of a symbiotic unity or a pleroma or whatever, but as soon as my life is threatened there must be me who is being threatened and someone or something else that is doing the threatening. Mahrer calls these 'catastrophic incidents' and agrees that some people call them traumas. And none of Mahrer's clinical evidence contradicts that.

Mahrer talks throughout about 'infantness'. Usually an infant means a baby who can't yet talk, but by using the word 'infantness' instead, Mahrer makes it possible to say that the idea of the infant can extend back to a year or two before conception in many cases (or even further back in more unusual cases). So the infant is being constructed by the parents as part of their external world before he or she comes on to the scene in any tangible form. And similarly at the other end, the parents can continue this idea of infantness long after the child can talk.

So the primitive personality field consists (in the usual case where father and mother are both present) of the operating and deeper potentials of the father and the mother, plus infantness.

What does Mahrer mean by potentials? This is one of his major theoretical innovations, and we must look carefully at his account:

> Each potential constitutes its own zone of experiencing, more or less distinct and independent of the other potentials. It is as if each potential is its own mini-world of experiencing. In this sense, we are indeed multiple selves, multiple consciousnesses, even multiple personalities. Each potential has its own centre, its own self system, its own personality.
>
> (Mahrer 1989, p.29)

This makes it clearer. We are talking about something resembling sub-personalities, ego-states, complexes, internal objects, little 'I's, I-positions once again. This enables us to feel that we are on familiar ground to that extent. So when he talks about relations between potentials, it is similar to talking about relations between persons – only this time they are internal persons:

> The nature of the relationships among potentials is the major determinant of problems. A disintegrative relationship among potentials is probably the major factor in the occurrence of bad feelings, in the occurrence of bodily pain and suffering, in the construction of a person's unhappy world and . . . as the key determinant of human problems and pain. . . . Our theory turns to the distintegrative relationship among potentials not only for 'neuroses', but for the whole spectrum of human suffering.
>
> (Mahrer 1989, p.28)

The primitive personality field, then, going back to our discussion of early development, consists of the parents' potentials and the positive or negative relationships among them, plus infantness. And this space, as it were, of infantness, gets filled by the physical baby and infant as and when it appears, and by the embryo and foetus before that. This means that the infant has no potentials of his or her own:

> Bluntly, the potentials of the infant are the relevant potentials of the significant figures. That is, the potentials of the infant are those potentials of the figures within the primitive personality field which pertain to the infant. The same reasoning places some of the relationships of the significant figures within the larger conception of the infant. That is, the relationships among potentials of the infant are those relationships among the potentials of the figures within the primitive personality field which pertain to the infant . . . The disintegrative or integrative nature of these relationships becomes the nature of relationships within our larger definition of the infant's primitive personality.
>
> (Mahrer 1989, pp.622–3)

This is reminiscent of the Freudian saying that the superego of the child comes from the superego of the parent, in quite an unconscious way, and at first it sounds as if this is a one-way thing. It sounds as if Mahrer is sinking the poor infant quite vanishingly into the personality field set up by the parents. But he is far more subtle than that. He is saying rather that this primitive personality field, while set up in the first instance by the parents, can be seen from various perspectives once it is set up:

> In contrast to our common system of thought, humanistic theory suggests that the definition of an object varies with the context. What mother is depends on our context of understanding. Within the context of mother, mother is one thing, the centre of a given context. Within that context, baby is an extension of mother, a constructed component of her world. But when we switch to the context of the infant, and hold the infant as the centre of that context, then mother becomes a constituent of baby. . . . There are . . . as many perspectives as there are participants.

Having set up this notion of the primitive personality field, and the perspectives within it, Mahrer goes on to say, first, that the process of development of the infant into a child and into an independent adolescent and adult depend on the dissolution of the primitive personality field, and second, that the parents have a lot of power and resources, if they care to use them, to prevent this dissolution taking place.

So Mahrer is saying that the symbiotic relationship between mother and child, which has been referred to by Stanislav Grof (1992) and others, goes back a lot further than psychoanalysts say, and involves the father as well as the mother. Anxiety, for example, does not start with feeding or with birth – it may be present before the moment of conception, and may become intense for the infant at any point where it affects one or both parents. This is such an unfamiliar idea that we need to look at one piece of evidence at least:

> As reviewed by Joffe (1969) the research first indicated a high correlation between maternal smoking and infant prematurity, especially when prematurity was defined in terms of birth weight. This research was interpreted as suggesting a causal relationship between maternal smoking and premature birth. Subsequent research, however, reported similar high correlation between premature low birth weight and paternal smoking!
>
> (Mahrer 1989, p.677)

The research by Rottman, reported in the classic book by Tom Verny (1982) – and indeed much of the other research in the same book – points in the same direction. Rottman tested pregnant women for the conscious and unconscious attitudes they had towards the child they were carrying. This gave four possibilities: consciously and unconsciously positive (Ideal); consciously positive but unconsciously negative (Ambivalent); consciously negative but unconsciously positive (Cool); and consciously and unconsciously negative (Catastrophic). At birth, the babies of the Ideal mothers were physically and emotionally healthy, and thrived. The babies of the Ambivalent mothers tended to have behavioural and gastrointestinal troubles. The babies of the Cool mothers tended to be apathetic and lethargic. And the babies of the Catastrophic mothers tended to be premature, low-weight and emotionally disturbed. The rather similar research of Lukesch, also reported by Verny, showed that the fathers were implicated too.

So this primitive personality field, which includes both parents and the infant, is powerful indeed. And it carries on its work of constructing the infant without needing the awareness of the participants. The entire scene may be carried on without anyone being conscious or even half-sensing what is going on. In constructing this field, parents can use any one or more of four basic methods or mechanisms:

Inducing behaviour from scratch – 'By organizing the primitive field in a very particular manner, only certain infant behaviour can occur as the other side of the behavioural coin'. For example, if the parent engages in a high rate of interaction with a baby, at least three types of response are automatically induced (Beckwith 1972). The infant has no way of avoiding this.

Developing behavioural nubbins – The baby does something small, a hint of some later action, if taken in a certain way. The parent then takes it as a fully developed indication of that later action, and treats it in such a way as to turn it into that action. 'Mother will see before her a baby who is demanding immediate gratification, who is demanding that things be done right now; she will not see a mere behavioural nubbin, a whimper or a little cry'.

Attributing intentions to behaviour – 'All the baby has to do is to behave in the most ordinary ways. Indeed, baby's role is so easy that often all baby is required to do is not behave in some way . . . Any infant can be interpreted as behaving in a cold and unresponsive manner'. The number and variety of actions that can be attributed to very young babies is extraordinary, only limited by the imagination of the parents. But once an interpretation has been made, the actions of the parents are such as to confirm and reinforce their interpretation, and this is very effective because of the extensive contact of the parents with the baby.

By being part of the field that is the infant – 'Here the connection is intimate and inescapable. It is not a causal connection, but a relation of identity. It is an almost magical relationship between the behaviour of infants and the personality processes of parents'. For example, Glauber's (1953) research found that very young stutterers were acting out their mother's tendency to stutter. All the material on the family as a system can now be seen in this light.

These, then, are the four methods, and by using them the parents have the power to imprison the young child within the primitive personality field long after it could have been dissolved. (All this material comes from Mahrer 1989, Chapter 14.)

Some of Mahrer's most moving and distressing material concerns the way in which parents maintain the field and stop the child's own self from emerging, even right up into school age and beyond. If they want to do this they must:

> (a) maintain ownership of the child's behaviour, (b) maintain ownership of the child's external world, (c) maintain ownership of the child's relationship with himself, and (d) prevent escape from the encompassing primitive field.
>
> (Mahrer 1989, p.723)

To stop a child developing a sense of self, parents can initiate the child's behaviour, take over the child's behaviour, take ownership of the child's thoughts, prevent the child from defining its centre of attention, serve as model and leader, take over the child's perception of reality, neutralize the child's attempts to own its own behaviour, disqualify attempts to define equal stature relationships, and so on. They can determine the nature of the child's external world, they can uncouple the child's behaviour from consequent changes in the external world, they can stop the child owning any part of the external world. And this is just a list of the headings for (a) and (b) above – we do not have space here to do more. Mahrer goes on to give many moving examples of all this – a part of his work that I found very painful to read. It all sounds horribly familiar. He tells of how children's thoughts are monitored, contradicted, twisted and fed back in distorted ways so that the child doesn't know if he/she is coming or going.

> Little wonder that some adults have practically no memory of huge slabs of their childhood; they were engaged in responding to parents, in carrying out what parents got them to do, in never owning their own behaviour.
>
> (Mahrer 1989, p.730)

The parents will tend to hold on to the primitive personality field in this way to the extent that it is expressing in a successful way their own potentials and the disintegrative relationships among them. If there is a disintegrative relationship between the parents' potentials, then to that extent they will want to project their conflicts into and on to the child. So the dissolution of the primitive personality field depends upon the parents achieving some measure of integration:

> If parents do not let go, then the self cannot occur. The act of dissolving away the primitive field is more than the passive freeing of shackles. It is an active step in the development of the sense of self. . . . If the parent hasn't achieved intactness, the parent cannot enable the child to achieve intactness.
>
> (Mahrer 1989, pp.760–1)

Mahrer is very acutely aware of the difficulties involved in the process of emergence into selfhood, to the point where it sometimes seems a miracle that anyone ever achieves it. But of course this fits with his insistence that virtually all of us have some disintegrative relationships with our deeper potentials – this results very clearly from our experience within the primitive personality field. But there are ways out, both for parents and for children. Here is an example, one of many given in Mahrer's book:

> From the beginning, Helen was mother's closest companion and confidante. Helen did not exist as a person, though she was six years old. She was run by mother, encompassed and owned by mother. When mother was ready to undergo her own personal change, she entered into the kind of psychotherapy which brought to an end her owning of her child. . . . As the bonds dropped away, as Helen came forth out of the primitive field, little by little, in subtle ways. Helen's mother felt sad. Mother knew that Helen was not, and had not been, the perfect companion. In many ways, Helen had no understanding at all of her mother. Helen preferred to have other friends, and was not really interested in hearing mother's thoughts and feelings. Each tiny increment in the dissolving of the old field had its own entitled bit of sadness as mother became a new person with a new daughter. It was a good sadness, accompanying the dawning personhoods of both Helen and her mother.
>
> (Mahrer 1989, p.762)

Now this is a striking, simple and self-consistent theory, and it has many merits. It is profoundly social, and it leads to a view of psychodynamics which is very usable in therapy. Mahrer died in 2014, and this has led to a renewed interest in his work. It is certainly well worth our attention as a true humanistic version of psychodynamics. But there are three things I disagree with in it.

The first is the overemphasis, as it seems to me, on the idea of parental pressures in forming the infant's personality. Although the resources of the infant are relatively restricted by comparison with the resources of the parents, it does have some, as all parents well know. And in my view the infant is always interpreting the world from its own perspective, right from the start. This is of course allowed for in the quotes above, but Mahrer never really does justice to the infant's point of view, and seems to lose touch with his own insights.

This ties in with my second disagreement. Mahrer always presents the dissolving of the primitive personality field as a positive process – perhaps some sadness goes with it, as in the example just given, but on the whole it feels good. In my view, the emergence of the self can come about (and often does) as a result of trauma, as suggested in the work of Winnicott (1975), Janov (1973), Duval and Wicklund (1972) and the other investigators referred to earlier in this chapter. The split into the real self and the false self would be equivalent to the split between operating potentials and deeper potentials in Mahrer's terminology. The operating potentials would be false selves or I-positions, and one of the deeper potentials would be the real self. The other deeper potentials would be other false selves, repressed and denied for various other reasons.

My final disagreement is about the lack of any spiritual element in the theory (except for a few references to Zen). It seems to me that since Mahrer does provide for different levels of the deeper potentials – he speaks for example, about 'mediating potentials' and 'basic potentials' – it would be an interesting extension of the same idea to say that there are some very deep spiritual potentials that may arise and need to be dealt with. That is precisely the view of Ken Wilber, whose position has also influenced me very much.

Wilber's transpersonal theory

Wilber says that we start life with a spiritual nature that has been developed in many previous lives, and which lies within us as a potential that requires to be unfolded during the process of our current life. Enfolded and enwrapped in the ground-unconscious of the newborn lie all the higher states of being. They were put there by involution, and they exist there as undifferentiated potential. 'Development or evolution is simply the unfolding of these enfolded structures, beginning with the lowest and proceeding to the highest: body to mind to subtle to causal' (Wilber 1980).

The last few words may be unfamiliar or confusing. Wilber has a well-worked-out map which clarifies his meaning. From this map we can see that the early stages are much as they have been laid down by the Jungians, by the object relations people and the primal integration people. Then comes adolescence, which has been well described by the social psychology people. Then comes adult life, which is the most researched part of the arc, though much of the research is not at all good, as we have pointed out elsewhere (Reason and Rowan 1981). Then comes the centaur stage, which most of this book is about, and which also forms the centre of my earlier books, particularly of course *Ordinary ecstasy* (Rowan 2001). Then comes the subtle stage, which Wilber divides into two – the lower subtle and the higher subtle (see Figure 9.2).

The lower subtle, which he also calls the psychic, is where we are concerned with things such as out-of-body experiences, auras, ESP, clairvoyance, dowsing, healing, etc. By some form of spiritual discipline we acquire skills that are not reducible to the ordinary material categories we have been using up to now. (I would argue, however, that some of these skills can come through quite other means, and that they should therefore be treated with great caution as evidence of spiritual progress.) At this stage we are transpersonally sensitive, and this intuitive power can be developed by practice. We are going beyond the centaur categories of 'meaning in my life'; we are giving up intentionality and self-actualization; we are letting go of self-autonomy. We are thinking more in terms of obedience and surrender.

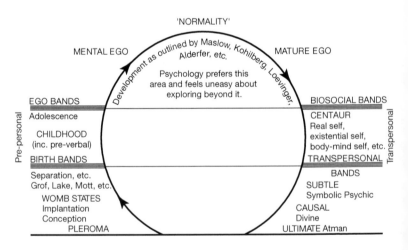

Figure 9.2 The Wilber diagram

In the high subtle all these things go further, and we really get in touch with higher powers outside of ourselves, which we may see (depending on our cultural surroundings) as gods or goddesses, higher presences, guides, guardian angels, ishtadevas, higher archetypes, the higher self or the overself. We can have symbolic visions, religious inspiration, literal dictation, experiences of blue, gold and white light, audible illumination, brightness upon brightness, experiences of rapture, bliss and compassion. Bijas and affirmations become particularly powerful tools at this stage, being given to us rather than chosen by us.

The causal realm is the realm of the divine proper, where the archetypes and other entities dissolve into final-God, the source of all archetypes and angels. And in the higher causal, the final-God itself dissolves into the Ground of formlessness which lies behind. To put it simply, everything is One. At the Nondual stage, this Ground itself disappears. My own opinion is that Wilber is less good a guide at the causal stage and beyond, because he performs the amazing feat of talking about the Divine without ever mentioning Adonai, Allah or the Holy Trinity! Any account of the Divine which is going to be worth listening to must include these somehow, even if only to explain them away.

So that is the map, but the most interesting thing about it is the precise way in which Wilber says we move from one stage to another through the process of development which is what the map describes.

At each stage, he says, we have to give up one notion of the self and adopt another. We actually have to revise our whole self-image or change our ego. This is very clear and familiar at the earlier stages. We know how difficult it is to leave the womb and become a separate body – Grof and others have described this very well. We know how difficult it is to leave the primitive personality field and be born psychologically – this is Mahrer's great area of expertise. We know how difficult it is to leave the family and become a separate individual – Madison (1969) has given a very fine account of this. At each of these stages we had to give up our safe identity and pick up a new and less certain identity.

Thus, at each point in psychological growth, we find: 1) a higher-order structure emerges in consciousness (with the help of symbolic forms); 2) the self identifies its being with that higher structure; 3) the next-higher-order structure eventually emerges; 4) the self disidentifies with the lower structure and shifts its essential identity to the higher structure; 5) consciousness thereby transcends the lower structure; 6) and becomes capable of operating on that lower structure from the higher-order level; 7) such that all preceding levels can then be integrated in consciousness, and ultimately as Consciousness (Wilber 1980).

This is a dialectical model of self-actualization through self-transcendence. There is no smooth evolution – we have to say a loud No! to our previous sense of self. This is exactly what Alvin Mahrer says happens in therapy, when we move from the mental ego to the real self. We have to abandon our existing self-image (what he calls in his terminology our operating potential) and plunge into and identify with that which we fear (what he calls our deeper potential):

> The centre of the person or self or person-as-operating-potential kills itself by hurling itself into the very core of the deeper potential. No longer is the centre of the person lodged within the domain of the operating potentials; no longer is the centre of the person separate from the bowels of the deeper potentials. . . . In this adventure, the very core of the person plunges into the metamorphosis of self-transformation. Nothing is held back or withdrawn.
>
> (Mahrer 1989, pp.480–1)

What Wilber is saying is that this process continues. Having got to the integrated and actualized stages that Mahrer talks about, there are further stages to go through, and they require more of that same process of losing the self to find it again. At each stage, Wilber says, there is incest and castration. The incest is the hanging on to a self which we should have outgrown; the castration is the fear of losing it – of having it taken away before we are ready. But we are never ready – it is always scary.

What we are really about, says Wilber, is Ultimate Unity with whatever is behind everything. This is what we most desire; that is what we have inside us as our deepest and most important potential. And we resist this and fight against it with every means in our power. At each stage in development we say, in effect, 'Let me have some peace now – I've been through such a lot.' But there is no peace to be had. There is only stagnation, unless we go on, and on. Ken Wilber puts this with eloquent concision:

> We have seen that psychological development in humans has the same goal as natural evolution: the production of ever-higher unities. And since the ultimate Unity is Buddha, God or Atman (to use those terms in their broadest sense as 'ultimate reality'), it follows that psychological growth aims at Atman. . . . From the outset, the soul intuits this Atman-nature, and seeks, from the outset, to actualize it as a reality and not just as an enfolded potential. That drive to actualize Atman is part of the Atman-project. But it is only part, because – even though each stage of psychological growth is a step closer to God – each stage is still only a stage. That is, each stage towards God is still not itself God. Each

stage is a search for God under conditions which fall short of God. The soul must seek Unity through the constraints of the present stage, which is not yet Unity. And that is the other side of the Atman-project: each individual wants only Atman, but wants it under conditions which prevent it. . . . And that is why human desire is insatiable, why all joys yearn for infinity – all a person wants is Atman; all he finds are symbolic substitutes for it. This attempt to regain Atman consciousness in ways or under conditions that prevent it and force symbolic substitutes – this is the Atman project.

(Wilber 1980, pp.100–103)

This seems to me a very powerful statement, and it makes sense of so much of my own experience that I feel I cannot ignore it. And I find it helps very much to clarify what is happening to those of my clients who are getting into transpersonal material. It is a much more persuasive and well-worked-out map than the Assagioli egg or the Jung diagrams of Esther Harding (1965) or Erich Neumann (1963).

Attachment theory

So what are we to say about attachment theory? It is extremely popular at the moment, and it seems wise to say something about it. For example, Hardy *et al.* (2004) write about formulating attachment issues and styles in psychotherapy as useful in assessing an individual's suitability for psychotherapy. And the reviewer of Jeremy Holmes' third book on the subject (2001), says: 'There cannot now be many psychotherapists not influenced in their clinical practice by attachment theory' (Linington 2003). But does it deserve the status that it has apparently reached?

In my opinion, attachment theory is basically trivial and simplistic and says nothing much at all in any human way. The paper which really brought this home to me was by Kim Bartholomew (1997). This author finds (both here and in some earlier papers) that we can derive a four-category model of adult attachment: the two dimensions are 'Positive model of other' and 'Negative model of other' across 'Positive model of self' and 'Negative model of self'. That gives us four quadrants: Secure; Preoccupied and Ambivalent; Fearful and Avoidant; and Dismissing.

This seems to me to have an extraordinary and suspicious similarity to the idea of Eric Berne (or his follower Ernst (1971) or *his* follower Harris (1973)) that there are four basic 'existential positions'. In other words, we have the TA model (sometimes known as the 'OK Corral') of 'You're OK' and 'You're not OK' across 'I'm OK' and 'I'm not OK', giving us the four quadrants – Basic Trust and Intimacy, Dependency and Pleasing, Victim or

Table 9.1 Attachment and the OK Corral

	Positive Model of Self (I'm OK)	Negative Model of Self (I'm not OK)
Positive Model of Other (You're OK)	Secure (Basic Trust and Intimacy)	Preoccupied and Ambivalent (Dependency and Pleasing) Dedicated and Committed
Negative Model of Other (You're not OK)	Dismissing (Bossy or Arrogant) Authoritarian and/or Patronizing	Fearful and Avoidant (Victim or Patsy) Overcommitted and Work Enmeshed

Patsy, Bossy or Arrogant. If that is a trivial and simplistic theory, and I believe it is, then attachment theory is also quite trivial and simplistic. Table 9.1 puts the two together.

Petruska Clarkson (1992) has pointed out that the OK Corral fits very well with the ideas of Freudenberger (1975) on burnout, and his categories of different types of worker have been added in to Table 9.1 above. She also links it with the three 'racket systems' described by Freudenberger.

The more recent paper by Stein *et al*. (2002), whose ideas have also been added in to the table, makes it even clearer that these categories hold, and indeed quote an earlier Bartholomew paper. Obviously this is about adults and not children, still less infants, but if we look at the work on children, the same simplifications can be found.

It seems to me, therefore, that attachment theory falls into the same trap as does the OK Corral, in that it makes perfect sense, but does not tell you much. What it does tell you is diagnostic or descriptive, rather than helping in any way to tell the therapist what to do or avoid doing. For any help for the therapist, we have to go elsewhere.

So why has attachment theory become so popular? It may perhaps be because it is one of the few theories coming from the psychoanalytic camp that is related to evidence. We all know how crazy everyone is these days for evidence-based practice, and here is a theory that not only has evidence but also a test. But in my opinion this is no justification for devoting so much attention to something that is basically so trivial and non-actionable.

Conclusion

These, then, are the three theories of development that have helped me at various times. The primal integration story is very flexible, and can deal with the mental ego, the centaur and the subtle stages very well, as I have explained in detail in an earlier chapter (Rowan 1997b). The Wilber story is very wide-ranging, and really covers the whole gamut in an extraordinary way. But the Mahrer story deals almost exclusively with the centaur stage, so of the three I think it is the most pertinent to the aims of this book. And the more recent work on the dialogical self is even more relevant. What I find remarkable is the way in which these developmental ideas are ignored in academia and in the practice of psychotherapy generally. They must not be lost or forgotten.

But all these theories fall short of doing justice to the political and social considerations that bear on therapy and the counselling situation. It is this which we must now look at.

Useful websites

Information about the Whole-Self Institute: www.whole-self.info

The Association for Pre and Perinatal Psychology and Health: www.birthpsychol ogy.com

More about the APPPAH: www.theconsciousbaby.com

Article about Primal Integration by John Rowan, in three parts: www.primals.org/ articles/rowan01.html (also parts 2 and 3)

Website of the Primal Integration Association in Britain: www.primalintegration. com

10   Listening with the fourth ear

In 1967 an extraordinary book appeared – *The politics of experience*, by R. D. Laing. During the next 10 years, all the issues raised in that book were acted on in various ways by different groups. In the Introduction, Laing says:

> We are bemused and crazed creatures, strangers to our true selves, to one another, and to the spiritual and material world – mad, even, from an ideal standpoint we can glimpse but not adopt.
>
> We are born into a world where alienation awaits us. We are potentially persons, but are in an alienated state, and this state is not simply a natural system. Alienation as our present destiny is achieved only by outrageous violence perpetrated by human beings on human beings.

If anything such as this is true, the whole task of psychotherapy has to be seen in a new light – not as helping people to adjust to a world that is basically all right, but as freeing people from their internal shackles so that they may effectively go about ridding themselves of their external shackles.

Social awareness

This means, however, that anyone working in the field of personal growth has to be aware of the way in which mental disturbance is systematically created by the conditions in which we live. Robert Seidenberg (1974) put this in a memorable way when he said: 'Often the therapist is still listening with the "third" ear when the times call for a fourth'. This was in the context of a case history of a woman who came to him with symptoms of 'fear of losing her mind, episodes of severe apprehension in the street and in stores, and fear that she might harm her 3-year-old daughter'. This woman seemed to have no external problems, and so she was referred for psychotherapy on the assumption that the problems must be internal and neurotic. So Seidenberg set out to discover what her blocked impulses were, what traumas she might have had, and so forth.

What he found himself impelled more and more towards, however, was the discovery that her problems were current and external, and even about the future, rather than internal and in the past. Her life had been chosen for her by her husband and her father – it was a secure trap. Her life would be the same for the next 30 or 40 years as it had been for the last 20. There would be no challenge, no decision-making, no problem-solving, no choices. And she could see her daughter going the same way. The realization came to her that her brother had been treated quite differently because he was male. Her destiny was to be a female and therefore to be basically unimportant, pushed around and controlled by men, in a safe, cared-for but featureless world. Seidenberg called this 'the trauma of eventlessness', and said:

> A lack of external events and appropriate internal responses can constitute a trauma no less than the 'dramatic' assaults against the ego. More than that, the anticipation of more and more eventlessness may similarly constitute a danger of severe proportions to one's well-being.
> (Seidenberg 1974)

Recognition of this made it possible for this woman to take herself seriously and to start to think in terms of what she needed for her own survival. She got a part-time job which involved going into unfamiliar parts of the city, and here she experienced no fear, only exhilaration. She refused to have any more children.

Once this area has been opened up, it is easy to see how it applies in many other areas as well. We start looking for external factors and for anticipatory factors. We look not only at what is inside or what is in the past. We look not only at the emotional, the intellectual or the spiritual, but also at the political. As Jean Baker Miller (1974) put it:

> One permits all so-called symptoms to be seen in a new light – no longer merely as defences, manoeuvres or other such tactics, but as struggles to preserve or express some deeply-needed aspects of personal integrity in a milieu that will not allow for their direct expression.

The point is that if the therapist is unaware of these issues, the client may ignore them too. In all counselling and psychotherapy, the unspoken assumptions of the therapist can have a profound effect on the client, in what she says or does not say. It is not necessary for the therapist to do anything wicked to miss all this important material – all that is necessary is that the therapist pays no attention to the fourth ear. As one of the authors says in Ernst and Goodison (1981):

Yet [my analyst] was obviously a kind man, he never told me what to do, or what I should think, or laid interpretations on me. He was not oppressive in the blatant ways that feminist writers on therapy have documented. He didn't try to seduce me, tell me I should use make-up or dress differently, accuse me of being incapable of real love because I didn't have orgasms. I have no doubt that overt oppression of women does go on in therapy . . . but I think what happened to me is equally common and perhaps more difficult to particularise. The oppression lay in who he was, the questions he didn't ask and the material I didn't present. It lay in the way I felt when I arrived at his house on my bicycle and he drew up in his large car; the sense I had that he must see his wife and family and home as normal and my household as a sign of my abnormality. To be cured would be to be capable of living like him.

But if we can open up the fourth ear, we can become much more open to noticing this sort of thing.

There are some good examples of this in the book by Jill Freedman and Gene Combs. They speak very thoroughly about the social context in which all therapy takes place. They have a perspective which locates the individual client in a matrix of supporters, antagonists, reference points and social realities. And they are prepared to enter into this social process and get involved with it. They talk about not just having these ideas, but living them.

> When people, through the 'unmasking' process of relating problems to societal discourses, see their local problems as particular instances of political problems in the larger society, they can become motivated to deal with them differently. When people stop living by the dictates of a political problem at a local level, they help deconstruct the problem at a societal level.
>
> (Freedman and Combs 1996, p.68)

They talk about 'an insurrection of lost knowledges', and there is a radical flavour about their whole approach. They look on the list of people who have abused the client in the past as the 'abuse team', and encourage the client to look around for a 'nurturing team' to compensate and help in the fight back against such treatment. Instead of relying solely on autonomy and self-reliance, they see the social context as having a part to play in the ultimate mental health of the person. Instead of criticizing the person for being too dependent, the aim is to set up good forms of dependence and interdependence which will be genuinely nourishing for the person. For example, the client may be encouraged to join or help to set up an 'Anti-Anorexia and Anti-Bulimia League'. Or a book may be put together by several therapists and several clients (who may be adults or children) such as 'The Temper Tamer's Handbook' and 'The Fear Facer's Handbook'. There is a good discussion of ethical principles in relation to community and social context. There are some good examples of this in the Ernst and Goodison (1981) book already mentioned:

> In a separate therapy group women were able to explore feelings of loneliness, lack of confidence, anger, exhaustion in the struggle to establish any independence; this activity ran parallel to the more outward looking activities of the food co-op and the community issues raised there.

But in a way this enables us to avoid the awkward questions about the one-to-one relationship between therapist and client. If one of the main external reasons why women feel bad is the oppression of a male-dominated society, then there is something very curious about women coming to a male therapist. A therapist is an authority figure (and as we have seen, this is so irrespective of orientation or of subjective wishes) and perhaps the woman's whole problem is with very real and very present male authority figures. In such a case, maybe a male therapist is the last thing she needs. Certainly some women feel this. Nadine Miller (1973) writes a moving piece about a woman saying goodbye to her therapist, in which she says: 'I was lucky enough to realise that my hostility toward men was real, and was not an individual problem. You bet I had reasons to hate men – you not being the least'. But is this fair? Certainly Robert Seidenberg (1974) thinks it is. In his discussion of power he draws attention to the very unequal gender distribution of power, such that women defer to men, and men expect women to defer in that way, to their expertise and their egos. And Jean Baker Miller (1978) has explained in great detail, from a psychological standpoint, exactly how this works. This is a book that anyone interested in this whole area must read.

The patriarchal culture surrounds us all. There is a very good discussion of these matters by Betty McLellan (1995), who takes a very tough line on it all.

Integral psychotherapy

More recently, Ken Wilber (2000) has been arguing that in all serious attempts to deal with individual or social problems, we have to pay attention to the four quadrants: the individual consciousness (the 'I'); the personal background including basic cultural impressions (the 'We'); the broad social setting (the 'They'); and the objective individual being, including the body and brain (the 'It'). This seems to capture the whole problem admirably, and offers us a viable model for taking care of all these important matters. His ideas have now been taken further by others, and in the book by Ingersoll and Zeitler (2010) we have a full treatment of this idea, which I find quite inspiring.

Not only do we have to pay attention to the four quadrants, we also have to pay attention, they say, to the levels within them. Of course, these are the same levels we have already met in our earlier discussions – the Magic-Mythic (not much found in the everyday life of the West), the Mental Ego (highly prevalent in the West, but restricted to First Tier thinking, and distressingly reliant on self-image rather than self – often called the conventional approach to life), the Centaur level (also labelled as the authentic self, the existential self, the real self, and so forth – often called the post-conventional approach, and characterized by Second Tier thinking), and the Subtle level, characterized by Third Tier thinking or true spirituality. I have gone into this in detail elsewhere (Rowan 2012).

There is also the excellent book by Mark Forman (2010) which explains how we can use the four quadrants in all our work in therapy. He makes the valuable point that there is not just one line of personal development, but many different lines. We may be well developed along one line but quite undeveloped in others. For example, it is quite common to find people who are highly developed in intelligence and social ability, but quite undeveloped in the moral or ethical line. Similarly, it is possible to be highly developed in social interaction and relatively undeveloped in the mathematical line. The idea that we develop all our abilities and capacities at the same time is not realistic, we can now say.

Co-counselling

Although there are several schools of co-counselling, they all have in common the idea of two people meeting and each spending half their time together as counsellor and half as client. There is no mystification, because they have both learned the same techniques, often from the same person at the same time. There is no authority problem, because the relationship is precisely equal in its basic assumptions. And no money changes hands, which eliminates another source of imbalance. The only exception to the money question is for the initial training: this takes two weekends, or some equivalent period of time – about 40 hours. It is not expensive, but for those who reject paying even this amount, or who don't even have that much money, one co-counsellor can teach another in a quite informal way.

It then becomes clear that all therapy requires a differentiation of roles. I am either the counsellor or the client and the role of the counsellor is quite different from the role of the client. This is an enormous clarification at once, because once we see through the authority and power question, we often tend to go to the opposite extreme, and assume that the good, radical, non-authoritarian therapist must be just the same as the client – not using techniques, not playing any role, denying all special expertise, and so on. This is rubbish, because it just doesn't work, and there is no way of making it work. Therapy and counselling are essentially role-oriented relationships, where the initiating activities are different from the responding activities – both being equally necessary and equally capable of being done well or badly.

And just here there arises a most important paradox. Usually there is a contradiction between playing a role and being authentic. But a therapist or counsellor is playing a role which essentially involves and entails being authentic. It is 'the game of no game' as someone once put it. This belief makes it impossible for therapists such as me to go along with the idea that everything in the therapeutic relationship must be either transference or countertransference. The authentic relationship is one of the five (Clarkson 2003) which are continuously operating in all therapy.

There is a corresponding paradox on the other side. The client has to try hard to let go. Of course, trying hard is the opposite of letting go. This is the central paradox in all personal growth, and also in activities such as meditation and the Zen koan solution. The harder you try, the more the letting go means when it finally does happen. Through the medium of co-counselling, all these things can be seen much more clearly, because it removes all those awkward and confusing questions about authority figures, whether they be therapists or gurus. We can then see the process as it is, and this takes away all our fears about being manipulated by techniques we do not understand (Kauffman and New 2004).

Another insight which becomes crystal clear through co-counselling is that therapy takes a long time. As long as we were worried about getting into the hands of the therapist, and worried about the money being made by keeping the client dependent, we could not look straight at the question of how long therapy might take. And of course we were further confused by new innovators in therapy, because each one always claims that their new method is really fast and effective, and that the old methods were designed to prolong therapy for the benefit of all the unscrupulous therapists. Co-counselling helps us to see that this is not so, and that any real attempt to change the personality is going to take years of effort. Someone told me once that the CG Jung Institute in Los Angeles had a motif on their letterheads which looked at first like a mandala; but when one looked more closely, it became clear that it was actually a picture of four snails following each other round in a circle. This is a good symbol of therapy, in my own opinion, because it emphasizes the slowness of it all. Someone else told me of the slogan – 'Fast as a speeding oak' – which again seems a helpful sketch of the issue at hand.

Once we fully realize and accept this, we can then look much more rationally at the question of which practitioner we are going to see, and how much we are willing to pay. And as therapists, it makes us less worried about our own motives. We can be more relaxed about the whole thing, once we see that our role is a legitimate one. And we can recommend co-counselling to our clients when extra sessions are required, or when the client runs out of money, without feeling that there is anything second-best about this.

The patripsych

There is, however, an even deeper way in which we can listen with the fourth ear, and that is to listen for the patripsych. This is a word invented by John Southgate to represent the internalized patterns of patriarchal thinking, and is pronounced pay-tri-syke.

> The patripsych is a shorthand term for what we have called the 'internal constellation of patriarchal patterns'. By this we mean all the attitudes, ideas and feelings, usually compulsive and unconscious, that develop in relation to authority and control. This development is closely related to learning about sex roles – learning about whether you are a little boy or a little girl.
>
> (Southgate and Randall 1989)

It is the patripsych we have to contend with when we are touching on compulsive feelings of dependence on authority figures, so that I assume they know best, I want to get near them, I want to be like them, and so forth. It is also the patripsych I have to contend with when I have a compulsive need to fight authority figures, opposing them regardless of what they do, dedicating my life to their destruction and seeing them as symbols of evil. And it is also the patripsych I have to contend with when I am touching on compulsive needs for flight from authority figures, withdrawing into myself, refusing to compete, being uncommunicative, not engaging in any way and avoiding all the issues of control. Southgate and Randall (1989) say:

> It is important to remember that we not only develop compulsive ways of relating to people who are in authority over us but also develop compulsive ways of relating when we are in positions of authority ourselves. The general point about this is that it is very difficult for anyone to relate to authority (theirs or others) in a fully creative way.

There is frequently little choice in our actions (although we may think there is) and power relations are mystified and confused.

And they make the point that the patriarchal family continues to exist still, even though the outward appearance of many families may be relaxed and equal. This usually becomes more apparent when children come along, and the 'crisis of parenthood' (Neugarten *et al.* 1964) pushes men and women into more one-sided roles.

This kind of insight is of course very similar to what Mitchell (1975) has said about the extraordinary way in which patriarchy has entered into our language and our thinking at deep unconscious levels. It seems closely parallel to the kind of thing that Wyckoff (1975) classically said about the Pig Parent:

> In women's groups, women can become familiar with what insidiously keeps them down – not only the obvious, overt male supremacy of which many of us are already aware and struggling against, but also oppression which has been internalized, which turns women against themselves, causing them to be their own worst enemies rather than their own loving best friend. This internalized oppression I have called the Pig Parent. It is the expression of all the values which keep women subordinate . . .

The idea of the Pig Parent is again an internal pattern of responses – the voices within us which tell us that we are no good, that we need good pure strong figures to lean on and depend on and admire, that we can never make it on our own, that it is wrong to aim at equality. Another version of this has been described as the self-hater by Starhawk in her excellent book *Dreaming the dark: magic, sex and politics* (1982). The self-hater can be a powerful subpersonality.

And this applies to men just as much as to women. Both men and women have internalized the oppression of a patriarchal society, and both have these internal voices. It is just that society tells men that they have to be leaders, and so they lead, but still with the voices telling them that they are no good, that they are unworthy, that they have no right to be equal or to be loved for themselves. And so they perpetuate the structures that will make it all seem impersonal and objective, and nothing to do with them personally.

Masculine bias, thus, appears in our behaviour whenever we act out the following categories, regardless of which element in each pair we are most drawn to at any given moment: subject/object; dominant/submissive; master/slave; butch/femme. All of these false dichotomies are inherently sexist, since they express the desire to be masculine or to possess the masculine in someone else (Dansky *et al.* 1977). Under patriarchy, it is the stereotyped masculine qualities that get all the acclaim and all the interest, and this is true both for men and for women. I have discussed these issues in much more detail elsewhere (Rowan 1997a).

This is all very reminiscent of the discussion about penis envy, except that as Firestone (1972) puts it, we should talk rather about power envy. And except that we now see it as applying to men as well as women, and as being much more complex – not only wanting to be close to penis-power, but also wanting to oppose it or withdraw from it – and all these in a compulsive way, driven by unconscious demands. One of the best writers on the whole male–female relationship question is David Deida (2004), and his book should be read by anyone seriously interested in this fraught area. He holds the balance very well between saying too little and saying too much, and he includes the spiritual dimension which is so important.

It is extraordinarily difficult to deal with the patripsych in therapy – all the most successful attempts seem to have been in groups, rather than in one-to-one work. This is simply because as fast as we break down the patterns in our therapy sessions, society puts them back again. If we really want to deal with the patripsych, it seems that we have to set up some kind of living community which will have different values; but then it seems that we lose all power to change the broader society.

Ultimately, then, we are faced with the answer that in order to deal with this aspect of therapy thoroughly, we have to change the whole society. I have dealt with this problem elsewhere (Rowan 1997a) and this is not the place to go into it fully. Enough to say that this is one of the most important areas, and that it is therefore imperative to sort out one's own personal attitude to it. Someone who has been writing about this in recent years is Andrew Samuels.

He draws attention particularly to the question of subjectivity. While it has been downgraded in most of our discourse, in psychotherapy it is respected and taken seriously and disciplined. And now he says that in politics, too, our subjectivity must be reframed and re-evaluated. Our feelings, our sensations, our wild fantasy even, must be taken seriously, disciplined, and used constructively to inform and inspire our politics. Far too much of politics is deadly serious and deadly dull and mind-numbing to most of us. We seem to have forgotten, he says, the late sixties in France and the USA and elsewhere, when politics came alive. But Samuels is not a romantic, and has a very full discussion of the possible dangers of taking our subjectivity seriously.

One of the dangers of therapy, some interested in politics have supposed, is that it may divert the feelings which could be used to change the world into a private examination of private troubles and private solutions. Samuels has a spirited answer to this concern:

I do not agree that therapy inevitably syphons off rage that might more constructively be deployed in relation to social injustices. In fact, I think that it is the reverse that often happens: Experiences in therapy act to fine down generalized rage into a more specific format, hence rendering emotion more accessible for social action.

(Samuels 1993, p.51)

Samuels has also pointed out with good evidence that psychotherapists are often deeply involved with politics. He actually carried out a postal survey of 600 psychotherapists in seven countries, including Freudians, Jungians and humanistic psychologists. He asked them many questions about politics, including what political issues arise in the course of therapy. Number one on the list was a range of gender issues.

The questionnaire asked how therapists responded to political material. Did they deal with it on a symbolic and intrapsychic level, treating it as fantasy referring to the inner world? Did they deal with it by exploring its meaning for the client, without any concern for its external reality? Or did they explore it with the client as reality, as real concern about the external world? There was much overlap, with a number of therapists adopting more than one of these approaches, but the overall figure for those who did deal with the issues raised as reality was 71 per cent. The overall figure for those who did not deal with reality at all was only 22 per cent. These are quite exciting and unpredictable figures. Therapists of even the most rigid theoretical positions proved to be far more political, far more open to discuss reality, than anyone would have supposed.

In a more recent book, Samuels (2001) argues that 'Political dispute and struggle give life to a society. They also serve to define the society generally and act as an access route for those who want to participate in politics' (p.183). So instead of searching for the one right view we begin to value the differences, the divergencies, the incompatibilities in politics. Again this is very reminiscent of Wilber's recent work on the different groupings in politics. 'Passion can abide in dialogue and tolerance as much as it does in monologue and fanaticism' (p.184).

Implications

It seems very important for any therapist or counsellor to know how to listen with the fourth ear, particularly when working with women, children, immigrants, working-class people, handicapped people or anyone else defined by society as second-class or third-class. And this will be in two main areas: first, the environment – what needs changing there; and second, (but not less important) the therapist himself or herself – what am

I as a therapist standing for in the client's eyes, and how can I bring that out and use it?

As I have said already, the majority of the most penetrating thinking on this topic has been done by feminists, and there is a huge literature now available to women on the subject, some of which has been referred to in this chapter. Much of this literature is less helpful to men, though men should certainly read it to pick up on the strength of feeling that comes through, and to empathize with that strength of feeling. More directly useful to men are the books written specifically for men, such as those by Osherson (1986), Kupers (1993), Meade (1993), Levant and Pollack (1995) and the masterly book by Bob Connell (1987).

One of the best exercises I ever went through myself was at a conference of the Association for Humanistic Psychology at Princeton University, where we were asked to 'be gay for part of a day'. We started off lying on the floor, while a tape was played giving typical phrases and news items and snatches of conversation that might be particularly relevant to gay people, and might make them feel bad about being gay. This built up until it became clear that to be gay was to live under a considerable burden of prejudice and ill-will. Then we were told to get up and walk around feeling the fear: it is not OK in our culture to be gay: you might get found out. You mustn't look anyone in the eye: they might find out, it might slip out suddenly, it might reveal itself in a glance – so keep your eyes down. Then some more tapes were played, bringing us to the point where we had decided to take a risk and look for a member of the same sex to be with. I chose somebody (can't remember how) and sat opposite him; we had to interact non-verbally. I was hot and embarrassed and sweating, and found it really hard to do. We held hands. I put my hand on his knee (he was wearing shorts). I found that the flesh contact was easier than the eye contact. If I could keep it all below the neck it somehow felt safer than if I engaged with the man above the neck. This was a powerful experience for me.

Then there were some more fantasy suggestions about having now decided to come out, and feeling more confident about our gayness, and now being able to have fun with other gay people. We had to form groups of three or more, and just interact in any way we liked. I found myself in a group of three, with two men I didn't like particularly, but by talking about my feelings I got to the point of feeling a lot of warmth and sympathy for one of the guys, who was gay and married and not sure where to go from there. Then we had to write a letter to a close relative or intimate person, saying that we were gay, and how we wanted the other person to feel about that. I wrote to my father, and halfway through changed it to father and mother. Then we discussed in small groups (single sex or mixed) about what had happened. And so it ended.

It seems to me that this basic format could be adapted in various ways, and used for initiating people into what it feels like to be in someone else's shoes, over quite a wide range. People who have unorthodox sexual preferences often experience prejudice and misunderstandings, and any therapist who wants to do a good job with clients such as this really needs to study them properly, perhaps with the help of books such as Davies and Neal (2000) and contact with organizations such as Pink Therapy.

But I think it is also important to remember that a therapist is always bound to be a limited person, with a restricted range of sympathies and abilities, and there is no point in trying to be perfect. One should not take oneself too seriously as the only recourse the client has. Society is rich in all manner of resources which may be much more use than a therapist at a given time. So it is good for a therapist to have some contact with available resources, whether it be women's groups, co-counselling networks, Alcoholics Anonymous, local residential facilities, legal aid or whatever. But unless we first cultivate the fourth ear, we shall not know when to call on these other resources; it is this awareness which is so important.

Useful websites

Co-counselling: www.co-counselling.org.uk
Andrew Samuels: http://andrewsamuels.com
Pink Therapy: www.pinktherapy.com
The United Kingdom Council for Psychotherapy: www.psychotherapy.org.uk. This is the umbrella organization for psychotherapy in Britain. It keeps a record of all the training organizations that have passed certain standards of excellence. These standards are maintained by a system of 5-yearly examinations by outside experts. It also provides a list of approved psychotherapists, all of whom have been accredited by formal means.

11 Research

The question everyone asks is – how do you know that counselling or psychotherapy works? And there are basically three possible answers to this: *I don't care if it works or not – I just get so much satisfaction from doing it.* This is the 'faith' answer. *I see such good results in my work with clients.* This is the 'anecdotal' answer. *Well-designed research studies say so.* This is the 'research' answer. Most counsellors and psychotherapists are quite happy with faith or anecdotes, but hardy souls such as me are eager to have research answers.

Unfortunately, good and relevant research is hard to find. Most researchers in this field seem to be more interested in what is measurable than what is important. For example, in the 1,024-page handbook of Garfield and Bergin (1978) there are no entries in the index for bioenergetics, birth, conception, foetus, Gestalt, implantation, memory, potentials, primal, psychodrama, regression (one reference to mathematical regression to the mean!), resistance, transpersonal, trauma, umbilical or womb.

This means that most of the specific things that we have been interested in as practitioners do not figure in the research reports. So in this chapter we need to do two things: first, to see what the existing research does say, and second, to see what new research needs to be done, and how.

Existing research

Luckily for us, the major work has been done for us by Roberta Russell (1981) in going through the literature and spelling out the main results. She gives extensive references for all these statements, and the interested reader is referred to her report for checking all the many sources. Although her report is now quite old, nothing published since seems to contradict it. A useful summary of some of the more recent work is to be found in Reeves (2014). Russell's six conclusions are as follows:

1   Comparative studies show that the outcome of psychotherapy does not depend on the school to which the therapist adheres.
2   Experienced therapists are generally more effective than inexperienced therapists. Experienced therapists resemble each other to a greater extent than they resemble less experienced therapists trained in their respective disciplines.
3   Paraprofessionals consistently achieve outcomes equal to or better than professional outcomes.
4   A professional training analysis does not appear to increase the effectiveness of the therapist.
5   Therapists who have undergone traditional training are no more effective than those who have not. Microcounselling and skills training appear to be useful procedures in the training of therapists.
6   Congruent matching of therapist and patient increases the effectiveness of therapy.

Now in view of our criticisms of the body of existing research, how should we regard these conclusions?

Item (1) probably needs to be checked out much more thoroughly before we accept it. If hardly any of the existing research deals in any way with Gestalt therapy, psychodrama, bioenergetics, transpersonal therapy and so forth, how can we say how they compare with psychoanalysis or behaviourism or cognitive therapy? And also we need to be very critical of the use of the word 'outcome'. If the outcome is that someone stops washing her hands thirty times a day, that is easy to check on and easy to keep track of; if the outcome is that someone gets in touch with her real self, that is much harder to pin down and measure. If we look at the more than sixty case histories in Corsini (1981) we see that each of the cases is rated as successful, but the criteria of success in each case are different. Some of the shifts are very small, others are very large.

So the whole question of values comes in here. When we accept a client for therapy, what are we trying to achieve? And does that client know that this is what the aim is? Unless there is some agreement worked out, therapist and client may be at cross-purposes. If there is agreement, it may still be hard to compare one client with another. The whole idea of adding up outcomes as if they were apples may be a nonsense.

Item (2) is in two parts. The first sentence is contentious for the reasons already advanced – the concept of 'more effective' entails and takes for granted the concept of 'outcomes' which we have seen some reason to doubt. But the second sentence may well make sense. It would certainly be much more amenable to test, and a variety of dimensions might be used; this would be a much more possible area for research efforts of one kind or another.

Item (3) again uses the concept of 'outcomes' and has to be questioned on that basis. So do items (4), (5) and (6). The second sentence of item (5) is more testable and more interesting for that reason.

It seems that not much is left, if we don't believe in measuring outcomes; so let us have one more look at that concept. In the masterly paper by David and Diana Shapiro (1982) we find the outcome study to end all outcome studies, putting together the results of no less than 143 carefully evaluated pieces of work. The first thing we find is that the source studies were primarily of behavioural methods, with systematic desensitization the most widely represented method, followed by relaxation and rehearsal/self-control monitoring. Cognitive and minimal therapies were less widely represented, and verbal methods figured very little in the data. So once again there is very little information about what we are interested in. It is clear that this kind of outcome research much prefers very specific outcomes, preferably small and easily measured. The predominant mode of therapy was group, and the average therapist had some 3 years of experience, the level of an advanced post-graduate student. Therapy typically lasted for around 7 hours, and most procedures were at least moderately reproducible. How much change can take place in 7 hours? It seems to be getting more and more obvious that research in this area is subject to the besetting sin of all academic research, a trap which it falls into again and again in every psychological field – do studies that will represent another notch on your academic belt, rather than studies that are useful to anybody (see Rowan 1974).

The most common target problems were performance anxieties, followed by physical and habit problems, social and sexual problems and phobias. (In fact, the biggest single group suffered from test anxiety.)

Again it becomes obvious that the clients in these studies were students – the usual subjects in university laboratory work. The university causes test anxiety by setting test after test and making academic progress dependent on the results, and then kindly provides a group to get rid of the anxiety so produced, thus providing material for another academic paper.

If this is what outcome research leads to – which of course it does – it seems not only worthless but actively harmful. The search for outcomes is the search for numbers; the search for numbers is the search for things to count; human beings are not things. It is all right to count human beings if all you want to know is where they are or what they have done; but the moment you want to count what is going on inside them you run into trouble. Human beings are freedoms and choosers.

The later research

One of the best books in this field is the one by Wampold (2001), which represents a very thorough examination of the research, and comes to the conclusion that: (a) therapy does work very well, and (b) we now have a pretty good idea of what works in therapy. And the outcome is very revealing. It turns out that there are some quite solid figures here, which have been summed up as: Outcome results in psychotherapy run as follows: 40 per cent of them are due to extratherapy factors (that is, the client's experience outside the therapy room, which is always, of course, quantitatively larger in time terms than the few hours spent with the therapist); 30 per cent of them are due to common factors (that is, factors common to all therapies, such as empathy, warmth, acceptance, encouragement of risk-taking and so forth); 15 per cent are due to expectancy factors (sometimes called the placebo effect, coming from the sheer fact of turning up and taking part); and 15 per cent from the techniques used.

What then strikes us is that virtually all the research done by the behavioural schools is on the techniques used. It seems that these researchers refuse to take seriously the research in this field and hold fast to the faith that it MUST be the techniques that do the work. This is clearly an irrational stance, and it is a source of some puzzlement to the rest of us that it is still held so rigidly. This is not research on the whole person, which is the only research that makes sense, but rather research on something relatively small but more easily accessible. We all remember the old joke about the person who looked for his missing watch far from where he lost it, because the light was better there!

A new approach

One of the most important new approaches comes from our old friend Alvin Mahrer, in a book called *Psychotherapeutic change*. This talks about a type of research called 'in-session outcome research', which Mahrer has pioneered and written about a good deal now.

Mahrer (1985) was very struck by the early work of Carl Rogers (1961) in the research field. He quotes Rogers as saying that he was particularly impressed by the presence of 'moments of movement' – moments in therapy where it appears that change actually occurs. These are often moments of strong emotion. What Mahrer has done is to specify in some detail what these moments actually consist of. He found thirteen indices of psychotherapeutic movement, and gives examples of each of them. Here they are:

1 providing meaningful material about personal self and/or relationships;
2 describing/exploring the personal nature and meaning of feelings;
3 emerging of previously warded-off material;
4 showing insight or understanding;
5 communicating expressively;

6 manifesting a meaningfully significant working relationship with the therapist;
7 expressing strong feelings towards the therapist;
8 expressing strong feelings in personally meaningful life contexts;
9 radical shifting into deeper personality states;
10 risking new ways of being and acting within the real world of the imminent future;
11 expressing or reporting positive target actions;
12 expressing or reporting reduced negative target actions and ideas;
13 expressing or reporting a state of well-being.

In the piece of research I am now going to talk about (Mahrer *et al.* 1987), categories 1, 5, 8 and 9 were the most often used. Would this be the case with other clients, other therapists, other approaches?

For each of these categories, it was true that the good moments came in bursts or series rather than as isolated events. From 5 to 10, the statements tended to follow one another. And it also seemed that one could detect stages within each session.

It was also found that certain categories clustered together. Categories 1, 5 and 8 tended to go together, and also whenever category 9 was found, category 8 was also found. Mahrer says:

> These findings suggest that for a therapy which values very good instances of the client's expression of strong feelings in extratherapy contexts (category 8), it may be useful for the client's voice quality to be alive, vibrantly energetic, with vivid and rich language (category 5), and for the client to be providing meaningful material about personal self- and/or interpersonal relations (category 1). For a therapy which values very good moments in which the client undergoes a radical shift into a qualitatively altered personality state (category 9), the findings suggest that this is facilitated when the client expresses strong feelings in extratherapy contexts (category 8).

I think it is worthwhile looking at these findings simply to see what sort of results can come out of this type of approach. The methodology does not really come alive unless we can see something of how it can be used.

Mahrer and his colleagues also looked at the question as to which actions of the therapist were associated with these good moments and clusters of good moments. In this way we can investigate the associations of therapist actions with client responses. They would of course be different for other types of therapy. This sort of research seems to me much more useful than most, because it actually refers to recognizable things that we can work on and take account of in the actual session with a client.

New paradigm research

So we need a new approach to research if we are to do any kind of justice to the way human beings work, and what goes on inside them during the process of therapy. And it so happens that over the past 40 years or so, another kind of research has been slowly growing up – and in the recent past it has accelerated its progress considerably.

It will help us to see the similarities and the differences between new paradigm research and old paradigm research (such as that quoted so far in this chapter) if we construct a diagram of the general research cycle (see Figure 11.1). This is the cycle that is common to all forms of research without exception. We start at the point of BEING. This is where I am working in my own field – in this case as a student of the process of therapy. All goes as normal, until some problem or insight comes along, something which seems to be a matter of fact, such as 'Does a depressed person respond better to being pushed deeper into the depression (in the Rogerian or existentialist manner) or to being pulled in the opposite direction (in the co-counselling or transpersonal manner)?'

We then move into the THINKING mode, where we get information which is already available, and combine it in our own minds. Maybe the answer is there already, in some book or paper, or maybe one of our friends knows the answer; we keep on searching until we have tracked down all the hints we can find.

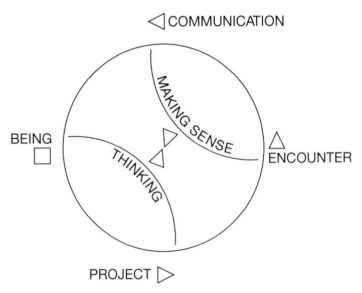

Figure 11.1 The cycle model

Assuming that we cannot find the answer, we move on to the point of PROJECT. Here we start to ask the question – 'What kind of investigation would in principle give me the answer I need?' And here immediately at this point the difference between the two paradigms starts to appear, because in the old paradigm I was alone in this search for a plan or design, apart from the help given by colleagues, perhaps. In the new paradigm I search for a plan together with a number of people who have the same problem from the inside. In other words, they are people who have suffered from depression or who do at present suffer from depression. And together with them I work out what form of questioning would be possible and acceptable; what form of observation or self-observation would be all right; what forms of recording would be suitable and so forth. And when we have agreed, these are the people who will carry out the research, on themselves, not on others.

At this point we move on to the ENCOUNTER, where we actually try something out for real. There is some action, some engagement, such that reality can come through and be registered in some way. At this stage I must lay myself open to the possibility of improvisation and spontaneity, based on the very specific plan which has been agreed. Real involvement is needed in this phase, so that we are genuinely open to what may happen. This is the crux of the whole process.

But at a certain point we have done enough of this very intense work, and the time comes to make sense of it all. So we go on to the MAKING SENSE section of the figure, where we stand back from what we have done and what we have all been through, and ask ourselves – 'What did it all mean?' And we may answer this question in very crude terms, or in terms of a rough model, or in terms of a very elaborate theory; this is the stage at which we see what kind of a story can be extracted from the activities in which we have been engaged, and what happened as a result.

And when we have done this to our satisfaction, we move on to the point of COMMUNICATION, where we communicate among ourselves, or to others, about what we have discovered. This may go on for a brief moment, or for several years, it all depends on how deep or elaborate the information is. But at the end of this process we are ready to come back into our field with this new knowledge at our fingertips. Perhaps one cycle is enough, but more likely we shall still be dissatisfied, and start out on another cycle, only this time we shall be able to be more specific and more differentiated because of what we have found out from the first cycle. The idea of multiple cycles is very important in this approach, forming a spiral in this case, or perhaps running parallel to each other in other cases, and knitting together in some pattern.

Now we said that all research styles used this cycle, but they use it in different ways. The two main dimensions on which they differ are alienation and involvement round the cycle. Here is a list of twenty-seven research traditions, each of which has produced a substantial body of highly regarded research. They are listed in order of alienation, the most alienated at the beginning of the list, and the least at the end:

Tradition	Example
1 Pure basic research	These are the four orthodox forms of research found in most textbooks.
2 Basic objective research	
3 Evaluation research	
4 Applied research	
5 Participant observation	Polsky (1969)
6 Language and class research	Labov (1972)
7 Personality and politics research	Knutson (1973)
8 Ethogenic research	Harré (1979)
9 Phenomenological research	Giorgi (1975)
10 Ethnomethodology	Turner (1974)
11 LSD research	Grof (1980)
12 Dialectical research	Esterson (1972)
13 Action research	Sanford (1981)
14 Intervention research	Argyris (1971)
15 Personal construct research	Fransella (1972)
16 Existential research	Hampden-Turner (1977)
17 Experiential research	Heron (1981)
18 Endogenous research	Maruyama (1978)
19 Participatory research	Hall (1975)
20 Co-operative inquiry	Heron (1996)
21 Interactive holistic research	Cunningham (1988)
22 Collaborative inquiry	Treleaven (1994)
23 Transformational research	Rowan (1997b)
24 Integral inquiry	Braud and Anderson (1998)
25 Intuitive inquiry	Braud and Anderson (1998)
26 Organic research	Clements *et al.* (1998)
27 Hermeneutic research	Bentz and Shapiro (1998)

Now we can introduce one or two simple conventions for diagramming different research styles. If we use a dotted line to represent alienation, we can show pure basic research as shown in Figure 11.2.

The circle represents the researcher going round the whole cycle. The line represents the participant meeting the researcher at one point only – the point of ENCOUNTER. What results is an alienated encounter, where there is a meeting of role to role, rather than that of person to person.

The next diagram represents existential research, such as that which is reported in my T-Poems (Rowan 1976) (See Figure 11.3).

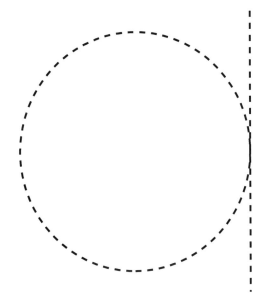

Figure 11.2 Pure basic research

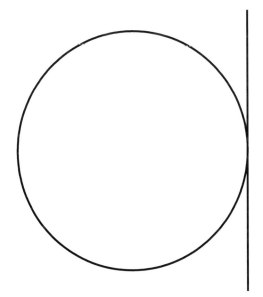

Figure 11.3 Existential research

Here again the researcher meets the participants only at the point of ENCOUNTER, but this time both researcher and participants are non-alienated, or authentic. There is a genuine meeting in which there is mutual disclosure; the researcher and others are open to each other, not hiding behind roles. So this diagram and the one previous show how the dimension of alienation makes a difference.

If we then use a dashed line to represent a situation where the researcher or the others may or may not be alienated, depending upon circumstances, we can represent action research, intervention research and personal construct research as in Figure 11.4.

This is a quite different level of involvement, which makes a huge difference to the way in which people can participate in the research. It makes it almost inevitable that the research project will affect the lives of all those involved in some way. This social effect is very important.

And finally, Figure 11.5 shows how we can represent experiential research, endogenous research, participatory research, co-operative inquiry, interactive holistic research, collaborative inquiry and transformational research. All seven of these have in common a commitment to full engagement on the part of the researcher, and a refusal to let the others hide behind a role. These are the most change-oriented of all the methods, because they set up a context of mutual trust, within which support and confrontation can take place. One of the most striking things about research done in this way is the amount of energy released. That is why it seems fitting to call it a high-energy type of research. What is more, energy seems to be released

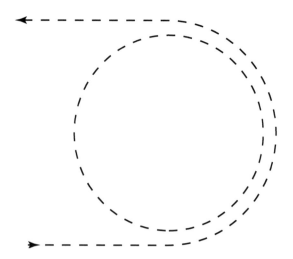

Figure 11.4 Action research

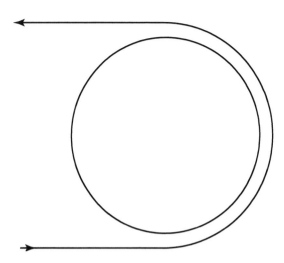

Figure 11.5 Authentic research

as each point on the cycle is left behind. It seems that the point is not just left behind, it is contradicted in a more or less negative way. This seems to be to do with the much higher degree of involvement and commitment required of the investigator. The researcher is in touch at several levels, not just the one level favoured by old paradigm research.

We can in fact say that there are three kinds of knowledge involved here. As John Heron (1981) says:

> Propositional knowledge is knowledge of facts or truths as stated in propositions: it is entirely language-dependent. Practical knowledge is knowing how to do something, as exemplified in the exercise of some special skill or proficiency. Experiential knowledge is knowing some entity by direct face-to-face encounter with her/him/it; it is direct discrimination of what is present in relation with the knower.

Traditional quantitative research is for the most part content with propositional knowledge, though some studies in the field provide some practical knowledge. But qualitative research essentially and necessarily provides propositional, practical and experiential knowledge – the knowing that comes out of it is 'thicker' and more substantial than that coming out of quantitative research.

In the book by Reason and Rowan (1981) there are given fourteen full examples of this kind of research in action, and further studies are given in

Reason (1988) and Reason (1994). Some excellent later work is contained in the book edited by William Braud and Rosemarie Anderson (1998). It is important to realize that with this kind of research the propositional knowledge of 'what the research says' is only a part of the story. One of the best brief accounts of the available research is to be found in the book by Paul and Charura (2015), particularly Chapter 2.

One interesting piece of research is that carried out by Ninoska Marina (1982) on the process of psychotherapy. She enlisted the help of five people who had been in therapy for at least a year, using humanistic approaches, and went into great depth with them on the question of what changes exactly had happened, using their own statements and their own way of seeing the question, and covering five periods of time: Pre-Therapy; Therapy; Post-Therapy; Now; and Future.

What she found is that people always have certain major dimensions along which they seem to move, or want to move. And these tend quite independently and spontaneously to be very similar as between people (see Table 11.1). It seems obvious that much of this could be summed up by saying that therapy is about self and others. But one of her findings goes rather deeper than this. She says that what comes out very strongly is 'A sense of self different to what it had been at the pre-therapy period'. This is extraordinarily important, in view of what we have been saying in this book about the aims of therapy.

She also draws attention to the way in which language is important in enabling people to understand themselves:

Table 11.1 Categories used by people in describing their changes (Repertory Grid method)

Person	Categories
Person No.1	Relating to people
	Relating to women
	Getting to know myself better
Person No.2	Self-knowledge
	Relating to people
Person No.3	Having more energy
	Liking myself more
	Enjoying sexuality
Person No.4	Self-image
	My view of and relationship with the outside world
Person No.5	Accepting and liking myself better
	Relating to people

Source: Marina (1982) Table 5.1.1

Synergy has been defined within this context as a state brought about by the simultaneous availability for access of all parts of the cognitive-affective system taken as the person. It is possible through the availability to access appropriately both the cognitive-affective level and the alignment level. This availability can be achieved if a person has been able to develop a double language; that is, to create a language of interpreting what is accessed. Given this development a person is able to reach a state where s/he acts, thinks and feels in an integrated way.

This point about a double language is very important, and ties in with the work of Luria (1969) who talks about the way in which inner plans can be formed for getting access to one's own system. It seems clear that research can be useful in finding out what goes on in therapy, but only on condition that it follows the direction pointed out by new paradigm thinking. And we now know how to do this.

12 Supervision

In previous chapters we have already touched on several issues that have to do with supervision, but it is now time to look at it in more detail. The basic humanistic position is that all therapists need supervision all the time.

What, then, is the function of the supervisor? It is to enable the therapist or counsellor to become aware of blind spots and prejudices and mistakes and inadequacies, and to work on them in such a way that professional development takes place. Because these issues are very emotive, and go to the very heart of the therapist's professional self-image, supervision is always a delicate and difficult business. This is all the more so because of the other pressures that bear on the supervisor–therapist relationship. As Ekstein and Wallerstein (1972) have pointed out, there is a rhombus of supervision in most cases (see Figure 12.1). In the diagram, S is the supervisor, A is the administrator, T is the therapist, and P is the patient. So the supervisor's role is to hold the balance between the perhaps conflicting demands of the administrator, the therapist and the client.

And in this setting the therapist experiences the three other corners in a very personal way. The patient can represent 'the archaic, unorganized

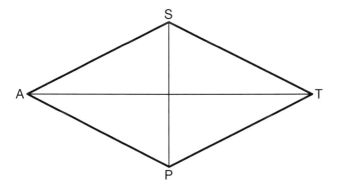

Figure 12.1 The Ekstein and Wallerstein rhombus

aspects of his professional self', but can also 'be a model of increasing mastery, external evidence of inner growth and maturation'. The administrator can represent 'the task of having to live by regulations and of having to live up to professional ideals'. And the supervisor can represent 'skills, areas of technical and human competence'.

Ekstein (1969) has a nice statement about the difficulties that the therapist may be struggling with in supervision. He speaks about the student's dumb spots, blind spots and deaf spots. Dumb spots are those areas where the student lacks the required knowledge and skill in dealing with the client. This is most likely to happen when the therapist is faced with clients who are very different, whether they be poor and disadvantaged, or whether they be the other oppressed groups we mentioned in the last chapter. The therapist just does not know enough about what it is to be like the client. Blind spots are those places where the therapist's own psychodynamics get in the way of appreciating what is going on in the client. All the phenomena of countertransference that we looked at earlier can come in here. Gardner (1971) has a very good discussion of how particular problems are likely to arise between the white therapist and the black client. The patripsych comes in here as a particularly difficult part of the psychodynamics involved. Deaf spots are those where the therapist not only cannot hear the client, but cannot hear the supervisor either. These are likely to involve particularly defensive reactions based on guilt, anxiety or otherwise unpleasant and disruptive feelings. Hostility to authority figures may come into the picture.

So we may sum up the aims of the supervision session by saying that it is about getting in touch with the covert processes that are going on between therapist and client no matter what the theoretical orientations may be. It may be done on a one-to-one basis, but nowadays in training it is more often done in a group, so it is mainly group supervision that will be dealt with in this chapter. By far the best book on the actual live process as it takes place is Margaret Rioch *et al.* (1976) and anyone concerned with supervision should read this book.

Of course we come up against the question of research here, and there is a useful summary of the recent research in the chapter by Matthew Bambling (2014). He says:

> There is sufficient evidence to conclude supervision creates a variety of positive outcomes for both therapists and clients. Supervision may enhance supervisee self-efficacy, knowledge, and skills, at least in the training setting. Most encouragingly, there is evidence that supervision might also improve the quality of client work and enhance treatment outcomes for clients.
>
> (p.453)

Supervisor styles

Increasingly in recent years we have been moving away from opinion-led practice to evidence-based practice, and many research studies have shown that this is indeed possible and desirable. And as this process has gone on, it has become evident that there is much in common between humanistic education (Rogers and Freiberg 1994) and humanistic supervision. There is also a connection between the balance of confrontation and support that is valuable in humanistic groupwork (Smith 1973) and the balance of confrontation and support that is valuable in supervision in order to avoid both the Scylla of cosy collusion and the Charybdis of over-criticalness and distance.

There are several different ways in which a supervisor might operate, and five basic styles have been found to operate in practice. First there is the laissez-faire style, where the supervisor largely leaves the therapist alone to get on with it, only making consultations where necessary. This is quite suitable for very mature therapists, but even here some lack of support may be felt at times. It is quite unsuitable for immature therapists, who need much more in the way of leadership.

Second there is the authoritative style, where the supervisor monitors and regulates the therapist's work very closely. This may be welcomed at first by the beginning student of therapy or counselling, but it becomes oppressive quite quickly, and students do not respond well to it after a time (Cherniss and Egnatios 1978).

Third there is the didactic-consultative style, where the supervisor offers advice, suggestions and interpretations. This can easily become a 'brilliant performance' that takes away the case from the student, as in the following example taken from Cherniss:

> The other day I had an emergency, a client, a couple of clients, and I was feeling upset about things. But supervision means we get into stuff about clients very objectively and analyze it. And in a way, it feels like my supervisor's show, like she's doing a performance. The main thing that happens is she analyzes the client. And that's great for her. She really gets off on it. It can be exciting momentarily for me. And you know, she can help me see a little more clearly what's happening. But for me, that takes a lot of the fun out of it. My attitude is, 'So you take that client, then!' I don't want my supervisor to take it away from me, the joy of discovering how to work with this person.
>
> (Cherniss 1980, p.118)

All supervisors do a little of this at times – the temptation is too hard to resist – but as a main style of supervision students do not like it and do not respond to it too well.

Fourth, there is insight-oriented supervision, where the supervisor asks questions designed to encourage the therapist to think through and solve problems. This works well and is liked by students (Cherniss and Egnatios 1978). The term 'empowerment' is often used in this connection, though it has unfortunately become something of a cliche in recent times.

And fifth, we have the feelings-oriented style, where the therapist is encouraged to ask questions and think about his or her own feelings and responses to the client. Supervision helps the therapist to come to terms with emotions and perceptions (Aponte and Lyons 1980). It is these last two styles that seem most suited to the needs of both students in training and experienced therapists. As Rioch (1976) puts it:

> My view is that the work of this seminar is like walking a tightrope between a therapy group and an objective, intellectual course of study. It is more personal than the latter and less personal than the former.
>
> (p.13)

In the Ekstein and Wallerstein (1972) book, there are some extended examples of exactly how individual therapists work out their problems with their clients, and this delicate balance between the personal and the professional comes out all the time. As Rioch puts it again:

> If the seminar is to study the interaction between each therapist and his client, then each therapist is part of the study. This involves attitudes, feelings and sensitivities. It requires an extraordinary degree of honesty, which can be quite painful.
>
> (p.14)

I don't think it is a good idea to call a supervision session a 'seminar', but that is a minor point. The main issue is that supervision has to maintain this position of doing justice both to the theoretical and to the personal matters that are thrown up in the process of discussion.

And one of the theoretical points that comes up here is the difference between psychoanalytic and humanistic supervision. Up to now we have been able to quote analysts just as often as anyone else, but now it is time to be a bit more specific. Let us look at an example taken from Rice (1980):

> One apprentice therapist complained that her client often got panicked in the early morning, and called her up at home. These early morning calls became mini-therapy sessions, and afterwards the therapist could not get back to sleep before it was time to get up and start the day. The crowning annoyance was that the client then sometimes cancelled a

regular appointment later in the day. The therapist wondered if she should confront the client with her 'manipulative and exploitative behaviour'. My suggestion to the therapist was to tell the client in the next session about her own limits, that she didn't like to be awakened in the early morning, and that it disrupted her night's sleep. . . . The client became angry, and accused her of putting her own comfort first. But this led to a number of explicit discussions of the relationship, and a fuller awareness of the rights and feelings of each of the two participants, which in itself seemed to be therapeutic.

(p.139)

What comes out in this example is that the supervisor refused to go along with the label of 'manipulative', and encouraged the therapist to treat the matter on a reality level which assumed the basic health of the client. Words such as 'manipulative', which can never be used other than in a negative and disparaging way, are best avoided in supervision.

There is no evidence that labelling a client is ever therapeutic, unless the label is clearly temporary and a kind of joke, such as the labels of 'zombie', 'marshmallow' or 'peanut brittle' that Eileen Walkenstein (1975) used (once only) in her work. The humanistic practitioner would do well to steer clear of labels altogether, for the reasons already outlined in our discussion of assessment.

Gossip is talking about people when they are not there. Many case conferences organized and run by people who are not humanistic practitioners consist almost entirely of gossip. They can be opportunities, as we have already seen, for experienced people to show off in front of their colleagues, displaying insights and knowledge of psychodynamics and jargon. In humanistic supervision, all the emphasis is on the person who is in the room – the therapist – not from the point of view of 'therapizing' the therapist, but from the point of view of helping the therapist face problems arising out of actual practice. As Cohen and DeBetz (1977) put it: 'The trainee's problems in doing therapy with the patient are fair game for supervisory intervention while personal problems (provided they do not interfere) are not' (p.59).

We have mentioned the three main functions of supervision as found in the literature – normative, formative and supportive – but it is worth going on from there and starting to outline a fourth – the transformative function. 'Transformative work takes reflective practice to a place of observable action whereby the change that occurs results in a shift of behaviour and thinking moving a person in a new direction' (Weld 2012). However the emphasis on transformation does not lead this author into dismissing the normative function: 'Within supervision there will still be obligations on behalf of the supervisor to notice if standards of practice are met and possible harm prevented'. Here we are in touch with the newer thinking on supervision. See also Shohet (2011), in which Fiona Adamson (2011) says:

> Transformational supervision can support us to explore both our thinking and our social-emotional selves. We can learn to hold this wide agenda with heart as well as mind and will. As we begin to do this kind of learning we can develop insight and compassion for ourselves. In turn we then develop a good sense of the challenges many of our clients face daily and facilitate those aspects of their development that they need in order to be effective at work.
>
> (p.94)

There is also the question of ethics, which often comes up in supervision. The classic book on this is Sperry (2007), which makes the basic point that there are two great approaches to ethics: in Perspective 1, ethics and professional practice are not usually considered linked or integrated. Attention is primarily on rule-based ethics, standards and statutes. In Perspective 2, ethics and professional practice are integrally connected. Attention is primarily on virtue and relational or care ethics, while mindful of standards and statutes. Professional ethics is integrated with organizational and personal ethics. This is a very important distinction, which is always to be observed in therapy.

Mary Creaner writes about supervision practice, training and research. Christina Breene has an interesting chapter all about resistance. She speaks of 'the paradox that the most resistant person can often be the most open, the level of resistance an indicator of the openness hiding underneath, perhaps protecting some deep sensitivity, requiring even more to keep safe, conceal and cover'. She also speaks about the relationship in supervision. 'Neither the superior nor the inferior position feels comfortable to me. In supervision I believe we are best operating as partners exploring together. Most supervisors do this'. Well, maybe.

The seven-eyed approach to supervision

One of the best approaches to supervision comes from Hawkins and Shapiro (2012). The normal situation in supervision is that one session with one client is brought in and looked at. But the focus of the supervision can change depending on what is relevant for the particular event. There are basically seven areas that can be focused on.

1   The client. Attention can be paid to what is going on in the client. This is often valuable, but it is not all.

2   The interventions of the therapist. What does the therapist actually do? What techniques are used? What is the range of interventions used? Are they appropriate?

3   The relationship between the therapist and the client. This includes all the five different kinds of relationship outlined by Petruska Clarkson: The basic alliance, the transferential, the person-to-person, the developmentally needed and the transpersonal.

4   The therapist. What is going on in the therapist? This may often be the prime focus, and it will include countertransferential material.

5   The relationship between the therapist and the supervisor. It is sometimes necessary to make this the focus, as it can either help or hinder the process of supervision. Questions of parallel process may come in here.

6   The supervisor. What is going on in the supervisor? This is harder to focus on, but it is sometimes necessary, particularly if there is any issue concerning the supervisor's countertransference.

7   The organizational and social context. This will include professional codes and ethics, organizational constraints and expectations, economic realities and pressures, family issues and general social norms and pressures.

Any of these areas may become the focus of the supervision session, and it is important not to neglect any of them, or pretend that they are not present. It may be quite a strain at first to keep them all in mind, but ultimately it is necessary.

So much for the general question of what the supervisor is up to, and the style in which supervision is carried out. Now let us go on to the more specific question of how the supervisee is actually to present the client.

The media of supervision

There are five main ways in which the supervisor can obtain knowledge of the therapist–client interactions. They are: direct observation through one-way mirrors; direct observation through joint interviews (the apprenticeship model); mechanical recording devices, such as audio or video recordings; process notes taken during or after the session; written reports which are given to the supervisor and later discussed.

The one-way mirror is used in settings with a high degree of organization and technical expertise. The interview room in such settings tends to be rather bare and impersonal, and not the usual room in which therapy is conducted. It is therefore more suitable for one-off meetings, where for example a whole family is brought in for a session, or for a brief series of meetings, all of which can be followed up in the same way. It is normally easy to record such sessions for later playback. It is even possible to provide the therapist with an earpiece so that suggestions can be given at the time, instead of later.

Joint interviews where the supervisor is present in the same room are more rare except in certain forms of social work. We shall not consider them here.

Recording devices are much more common. Obviously audio recording is easier than video recording, because video is more expensive and also needs a technician to handle it in most cases, particularly in humanistic therapy, where both therapist and client may move about a good deal. Audio recording is much more easy to arrange, because modern microphones of the omnidirectional type can pick up what is said all over the room, even in a fair-sized room. The effect is particularly good in a soundproofed room, such as many humanistic therapists need for regression work.

The strange thing is that many therapists and supervisors resist the obvious advantages of recordings. The reasons for this may be phrased in high-flown ways, such as – 'It interferes with the existential flow between therapist and client' – 'the emotional matrix is disturbed' – 'a third party has intruded into a two-person event' – 'we must be human and not mechanistic . . .' But in reality the reasons may be more simple, as Korchin (1976) suggests:

> Seeing the microphone itself seems not to have any direct effect on patients. Indeed, it is the interviewer rather than the patient who is more likely to be disturbed by the matter of recording. The patient usually accepts it matter-of-factly as part of a generally strange procedure. By contrast, the interviewer is threatened by having his work preserved and open to later criticism by himself and colleagues.

So let us suppose that we want to use recordings in supervision – how do we do it? It is best to use short segments of interviews, about 7 minutes at a time works quite well. It is best to have the therapist start the recording at a point where some specific bit of action is starting, and to tell the supervisor and the group what they want listened for and what they want special help with.

When we listen to recordings, what are we looking for? Obviously we are looking for obvious mistakes, things that were missed, points not followed through sufficiently, not listening, over-use of one kind of intervention, and so forth. But many more subtle things can be looked for, as Rice (1980) says:

> There is a kind of voice quality that seems to indicate an inner focus on something that is being seen or felt freshly. Sometimes in the midst

of a long client discussion expressed in a highly external voice quality one hears just a small blip of focussed voice. The voice slows, softens without losing energy, pauses, and loses the 'premonitored' quality of the externalizing voice. This should be an indicator to the therapist that this part must be heard and responded to. There is a liveliness here that might flower into a whole new moment of experiencing. . . . Another indicator of liveliness is the presence of highly sensory or idiosyncratic words, or combinations of words. For instance, the client is talking about approaching situations with trepidation, and reports feeling 'cringy', or talks about a 'stretched' smile on his face.

(p.143)

These are the sort of things that come out on a recording which are very hard to pin down in any other way. Voice tones are very hard to describe, but they affect us emotionally below the level of conscious awareness.

My experience is that students often approach the idea of tape recordings with some fear, as adding yet one more difficulty to their relationship with a client, which is difficult enough already; but that when they see how useful they can be, they come round to using them regularly. As Marshall and Confer (1980) put it:

Some of the most profitable (for us) interventions by our supervisors were those which permitted us to experience the pitfalls of our efforts. An example of this strategy is 'therapeutic alter ego' whereby the supervisor wears out his fingertips on the 'stop' button of the tape recorder to inquire 'why did you say this?', 'what are you leading to?' and 'how do you think the patient received that?'

(p.99)

It is important, of course, to avoid any suggestion of punitiveness in the supervision session. Some therapists seem to be punitive towards themselves, blaming themselves for their clients' failure to progress or change. But the constructive use of recordings can help to establish an impunitive focus. The therapist and the supervisor can join in listening for clues to process, letting the recording speak for itself. As Rice (1980) says: 'The optimal climate for the therapist's growth is a great deal of moment-to-moment feedback based on listening to tapes, and a minimum of evaluation as a person'.

Much the same considerations apply to videotape. Console (1978) has a good discussion of the value of videotape as a teaching medium. As an experienced practitioner, he found it valuable to make tapes of his initial interviews with clients, and to play these over for teaching purposes, stopping the tape often to make comments and allow the group to comment in turn.

And he found that it was the little things – apparent mistakes, hesitations, slips of the tongue – which were the most revealing and helpful: just the things that would tend to get eliminated in any presentation based upon notes. After one such incident, he said:

> I mention this episode in some detail because if it were not for the videotape technique, it would be extremely unlikely, in my trying to reproduce the session verbally and present it to the residents, that I would have included this interchange in my account, because it was so simple and natural a thing for me to have said. . . . And I would therefore have missed the opportunity of making clear to the residents in the most vivid fashion, that the psychotherapeutic stance which we encourage – that of relative anonymity, of avoiding a social relationship and so on – does not preclude being human.
>
> (pp. 29–30)

From all this we can see that recordings can be a very useful adjunct to the supervisory process. For a full discussion, bringing in much research evidence, see Gill *et al.* (1954). And for an up-to-date account of the whole question of using technology to enhance supervision, see the chapter by Tony Rousmaniere (2014). He says, for example, that past techniques were always rather obvious:

> It was clear when they were on, and what they were doing. Now, most technology runs on microprocessors and software. While this greatly increases the functionality of these devices, it can also make it challenging to know when the devices are on, and what they are doing.
>
> (p.206)

Process notes are the most common method of bringing in material to the therapy session. These should always be as full as possible, using actual quotations whenever this is practicable. But they should neither be attempts to label the client, nor attempts to theorize the interaction; they should simply be a record of the interaction itself. What went on between therapist and client, and what stages did this go through? Therapy sessions quite often divide themselves up quite naturally into sections, and to treat each section separately is usually a helpful move.

Process notes are normally written up after the session, not during it. (Verbatim notes taken during the session tend to get in the way of the personal interaction, and in any case do not lend themselves to the more active type of intervention used by the humanistic practitioner.) They tend to be rather bare and scrappy (or overloaded with unnecessary detail) in the early days of supervision, but gradually improve, so that in the end they are in the personal style of the individual therapist, while containing all the relevant information.

What information is relevant? This is partly a matter of what the therapist needs, and partly a matter of the institution within which the work is taking place. Some places require a certain sort of record to be kept, and of course these rules have to be adhered to. But it is always wise for a therapist to keep a record of what is going on; this becomes particularly important if the client suddenly does something unexpected, and the therapist wants to go over the previous sessions that led up to it, looking for explanations and insights. Much the same considerations apply to written reports. Normally the supervisor will make it quite clear as to what form these reports should take.

Of course, supervision can and should be creative. Other methods that may be used are well described by Steve Page and Val Wosket:

> Approaches such as sculpting, where small objects such as coins, pebbles or Russian dolls are assembled to represent aspects of, or individuals involved in, an issue, or the drawing of an image or metaphor relating to a client may prove particularly useful where the supervisee is uncertain about the specific issue.
>
> (Page and Wosket 1994, pp.80–1)

Role-playing can also be used in various ways, one of the most powerful being where the supervisee role-plays the client. This very often gives new insights into how the client's mind works. If there is a group, a more elaborate role-play can be used, where other people in the group take up the roles of the others who may be involved in the problem.

Summing up, then, on the media of supervision, we have seen that those media which offer direct feedback and self-confrontation are the most suitable for humanistic psychotherapy, counselling or personal growth.

Humanistic education

This fits with the whole approach of humanistic education, with its emphasis on experiential work and personal feedback, and the production of self-actualizing people. I have written about this elsewhere (Rowan 2001) and this is not the place to go into it in detail, but there is a good account of it in Rogers and Freiberg (1994).

The essence of it is that in humanistic education we have a tradition of treating the student as a complete human being, with total responsibility for what he or she does. To apply this to supervision is to say that the supervisor must at no time take that responsibility away from the student.

One of the ways of applying that approach in practice is to introduce a system of self- and peer-assessment. This means that it is the student who decides what he or she is ready to work on at a given time, and lays down the criteria according to which this is to be assessed. John Heron (1979) has argued powerfully and persuasively that this is the only way of translating humanistic values into educational practice. So the supervisor, on this model, would be a facilitator for the student's own self-assessment process.

What humanistic educators tend to find when they carry out this sort of approach (Rogers and Freiberg 1994) is that students initially resist. They want to be told what to do and how to do it. But if this initial resistance is worked with and negotiated about and generally worked through, it is usually possible to work out some way of achieving a relationship that is genuinely democratic and participatory.

One of the best simple summaries of what humanistic education is all about is to be found in a paper by Stewart Shapiro. He has devised a test of orientations to learning, which can be given to students, teachers and others (see Table 12.1). It can be seen how well it summarizes the values we have been emphasizing all the way through this book. If taken seriously, it could be a very helpful instrument for training courses of all kinds.

But what we are also saying is that if this is good for the beginning student, it is also good for the experienced supervisor. Every humanistic practitioner, no matter how experienced, needs some continuing system of self-education, possibly along the lines of self- and peer-assessment, or possibly along the lines of the peer supervision group as described by Aponte and Lyons (1980). There is no point where a good therapist has finally 'got there' and needs to do no more self-development. As even Ekstein and Wallerstein (1972) say:

> Supervision is not only an integral part of the training in social work school but remains a permanent pattern in most agencies. It is often maintained even for those who supervise, who then in turn become dependent on case-work consultants employed by the agency, or on outside psychiatric and psychoanalytic consultants.

For Ekstein and Wallerstein this is a peculiarity of social work, which is of dubious value, but for me it is of very central value. The point is that anyone who works with people is either keeping up and keeping on with self-knowledge and self-development and self-education, or is stagnating in some mould which was laid down long ago, perhaps in the worst cases by someone else entirely.

As far as we in this book are concerned, humanistic education means that the therapist goes on learning throughout life. This is because the process

Table 12.1 Orientation to learning test: sixteen humanistic values

1 **Process-oriented**
'How' is more important than 'what' or 'why'. This orientation emphasizes 'processing', talking over how an activity is being conducted and how it is being experienced.

2 **Self-determination**
Includes autonomy, self-direction and self-evaluation. In this approach, students assume initiative, responsibility and accountability whenever feasible and possible.

3 **Connectedness**
Encourages empathy, pluralism and good relationships. This approach is sometimes contrasted to individualism. Involves mutual caring and understanding.

4 **Relevance**
Stresses the students' personal meanings and readiness to learn. Instruction is related to underlying concerns and needs of the students as well as to society's interests.

5 **Integration**
Affect is combined with cognition and living is combined with learning. Stresses educating the whole person including the values, feelings and attitudes, body, mind and spirit.

6 **Context**
This includes awareness of the environment, culture, history, political and economic climate in which the learning takes place. Awareness of oppression and prejudice.

7 **Affective bias**
Preference for the use of feelings and concrete experience in learning. Also includes sensory awareness and the expression of emotions as a central part of learning.

8 **Innovation**
An anti-authoritarian, social and educational orientation toward change. Concern with something new intended to benefit those involved, both teachers and students.

9 **Democratic participation**
Emphasizes social equity, consensus and collaboration in learning. Co-creation with students, teachers, administrators and the community.

10 **Personal growth**
Stresses both methods and outcomes of learning as self-actualization through self-awareness. Persons take precedence over hardware and software in education.

11 **People-oriented**
People have intrinsic or ultimate value, not merely instrumental value. The educational process has to trust in the learner's capacity to work hard and care for others.

12 **Individualism**
The person who is the learner is unique, self-determining and self-aware. There must be freedom of expression and room for authentic selfhood in education.

continued . . .

Table 12.1 Continued

---

13 **Reality**
We can only know true reality by direct, primary feelings and experiences, not by fantasy or mental constructions. It is in the present, not in the past or the future.

14 **Evaluation**
Formative evaluation is favoured over summative evaluation. The process is emphasized and quality is preferred to measures of quantity.

15 **Variety and creativity**
Valuing of spontaneity, originality and diversity. Not conformity, standardization and preset goals. Flexibility is encouraged in the instructional approach.

16 **Transpersonal**
The development of the whole human being includes spiritual potential, and mystical, intuitive and receptive modes as well as rational and active modes of consciousness.

Source: Shapiro (1997) 'The UCSB confluent education program: its essence and demise', *Journal of Humanistic Psychology*, 37(3), 80–105 (slightly abbreviated).

of self-actualization, which we start on in therapy, never ends. Eventually it goes beyond therapy, if we let it continue, into spiritual territory. But if we carry on being therapists, so long as we do so, some process of supervision is necessary. There is no spiritual being who can be so useful as a good human supervisor.

Useful websites

BACP is the biggest counsellor organization in the UK: www.bacp.co.uk
Another good website for counselling supervision: http://counsellingresource.com/lib/therapy/aboutcouns/supervision

13 Ethics

In recent years much more attention has been paid to the ethics of therapy. One of the strongest influences in making this happen was the revelation of Alice Miller (1985) that not only was there such a thing as child abuse, but that the therapist in the session could often be abusing the client all over again. This created an enormous impression, not only on the psychoanalysts who were Miller's main targets, but also on therapists of all persuasions who suddenly saw many of their interventions in quite a different light.

In the 1970s it was quite common for group leaders to fly in, run a weekend group and fly out again. On the Saturday night they would often sleep with one of the more attractive women in the group. In fact, in some cases the women would jostle for position as to who was going to be favoured in this way. Nowadays this does not happen, and it would be seen as abusive, because of the extra power position of the leader, used in an unaware way. More books have come along after Alice Miller, making it clear that sexual abuse in the therapy hour is all too common, and that many therapists have still not taken on board the message.

Private practice

One of the issues which is sometimes raised as an ethical issue is the question of private practice. Is it ethical to make money out of someone else's misery? People such as David Pilgrim (1990) have certainly raised this as a serious question, saying – 'To say the least, the edge is taken off the humanitarian advantages of psychotherapy if these are selectively awarded to richer and lesser disturbed members of society'. Let us look, then, at the case for private practice.

Counselling grew up in institutions, often educational institutions, and later other institutions such as churches, hospitals, prisons and commercial organizations. It also flourished in social work settings of one kind and another. It was only later that it became something offered on the market on an individual basis, and later still that it became something obtainable through insurance. Today it is widespread and daily growing more so. There is no way of containing it between narrow boundaries and insisting that it only be offered within institutions, even if one wanted to do so.

The trouble with institutions is that they impose their own values upon what is done in them. It is hard for them to realize that they do not have the right to control something that goes on within them. Social workers are sometimes called by working-class people the 'soft cops' because they serve the system rather than the person. This is why there has been a persistent confusion between counselling in the BACP sense of the word (which is really about personal growth), and counselling in the older sense of guidance and advice-giving. It is even true that the major journal in this country in this area is called the *British Journal of Guidance and Therapy*: the confusion is perpetuated in that very title.

In private practice it is easier for therapy to be therapy, because we do not have the institution looking over our shoulders. Confidentiality, which I believe to be crucially important, can really be confidentiality. In an institution there is always the suspicion that juicy information will somehow leak out. There is often a whole list of people who are entitled to look at case notes and hear case reports. In private practice this is not so. A supervisor may hear the information, but in the best practice the supervisor never hears the client's real name. (More about this later on).

In private practice there is no ambiguity as to whom the therapist is working for. The therapist is working exclusively for the client: hence it is a secure relationship. And most of us believe that a secure relationship is very important, particularly when it turns out that a long-term stint is needed. In an institution, it is quite common for a client to find that suddenly he or she is faced with a new counsellor or therapist, because the old one has left, or been transferred, or it is just more administratively convenient.

The question of choice seems extremely important to me. The relationship between a client and a practitioner is a personal one. It is not a service that can just as well be done by one person as another. There is a delicate matching that needs to take place, which ideally works out by the client choosing the therapist. Unless there is genuine choice, the relationship can be dogged by mismatch, and a mismatch which cannot be questioned or changed. It is often hard enough to change therapists in private practice, because of feelings of inferiority and self-blame, but it can be made doubly and trebly hard by institutional rigidities and resistances.

If we value the autonomy and empowerment of the client, and aim at increasing these things through the therapy process, we have to be consistent about it. We must not take away the client's power of choice by allocating a therapist arbitrarily. All the research seems to indicate that it is a genuine two-person relationship that is most effective and valuable in therapy. But it is only the choice that can make it genuine. Take that away and you have a constrained relationship in which other values dominate. Therapy is not a medical matter. If I have a broken leg, it is a matter of complete indifference to me which surgeon operates on it: I assume that one surgeon is as good as another for this purpose. But if I have a personal problem to talk about and explore more deeply, it matters a lot to me that I trust the person I am talking to, and have a choice as to who that is. If I get the wrong person, I may not be able to do it at all.

Therapy can become a form of social control. It can be a way of keeping tabs on people for the benefit of the institution and its smooth running. I am not saying this always happens or is bound to happen: for all I know it is rare. But if it is rare this is due only to the decency of the people operating the system. The system itself allows it. But in private practice the safety of the client from social control is built in and assured.

There is of course the question of cost. In an institutional setting, the costs tend to be hidden, but of course they are still there. Somebody somewhere pays for the service. In private therapy this is out in the open. But there are several stages of removal from the most expensive services that are offered. Therapists charge different amounts, and a little searching can often find people with reasonable charges. Even the most expensive therapists may operate a sliding scale: many of them are conscientious about seeing a certain proportion of clients at a reduced rate, so that people without much money do not have to be turned away. So there is no ethical problem about cost – Carl Rogers never avoided private practice, and helped to train many people for private practice.

Then there is the network of trainees: most training centres have a system by which people in training – most of whom are mature, and all of whom are working under professional supervision – see people on a low-cost basis.

In a slightly different way, there is also the system of co-counselling, by which people go on a brief course to learn how to engage in reciprocal therapy with another person: some of these courses are quite expensive, but others are put on by local authorities with the customary concessions, and in the final analysis there is the book *The barefoot psychoanalyst* (Southgate and Randall 1989) where you can learn the system from a book of cartoons, which can be borrowed from the public library or bought on Amazon. I used this method for several years, and taught it too, and got a great deal of benefit from it. All these methods honour the basic requirement of a relationship which is chosen and secure and personal.

To me there is something sacred about the therapy relationship. It sets up a space within which true openness is permissible and often possible. And this entails the setting up of a framework which is reliable and genuinely agreed to by both parties. Within this safe frame the process can continue as long as it needs to. To interfere with this, or to make it impossible, destroys therapy as I understand it.

Ethical perspectives

Len Sperry (2007) has laid down a useful distinction between two basic perspectives in the study of ethics. He says:

Perspective I – In this perspective, ethics and professional practice are not usually considered linked or integrated. The focus of ethical thinking is limited to ethical codes, ethical standards, and legal statutes with an emphasis on enforceable rules and standards. Furthermore, risk management is the goal of ethical behavior. For the most part, personal and professional ethics are separated. This perspective is developmentally consistent with the needs of trainees, and beginning therapists and counselors look to codes and statutes for guidance in specific situations and circumstances. However, it also reflects the practice of some experienced counselors. In its most unadulterated form this perspective reflects a defensive, or negative, ethics. I personally do not think much of this perspective, as it does not appear to match with the values of the HEART therapist.

Perspective II – This perspective provides a comprehensive focus wherein it is possible to integrate professional codes, as well as other ethical traditions, with one's personal ethics. Here, virtues and values are considered as important as ethical codes, standards, and rules. The focus is on positive behavior and virtues, ethical ideals, character development, and integrating one's personal philosophy of life with one's professional goals and career aspirations. Self-care is valued and considered essential in this perspective, because it is believed that as professionals take care of themselves, they are better able to care for others. In this perspective, which values prevention, risk management is integrated with personal and professional development. Ethical decision making involves the professional, contextual, and ethical domains as well as the personal, relational, and organizational considerations. Ethical sensitivity is essential in this perspective, as is an integration of personal and professional ethical principles. Needless to say, this perspective reflects a positive ethics. It also represents the actualization and realization of the emerging trend in the ethical and professional practice of counseling and psychotherapy. My own view is that this is the best approach for the HEART therapist to adopt. Val Wosket (2009) seems to agree with this when she says: 'It now seems to me that relational ethics at its best can and must allow for creative, spontaneous and even unorthodox practice that privileges the needs of individual clients and supervisees over the limits and constraints of externally imposed professional protocols'.

(p.56)

Accreditation

Another question which has been raised as an ethical issue is as to whether accreditation is an ethical activity. The argument in the book by Richard Mowbray (1995) is that all forms of accreditation or registration are opposed to the public interest in that they favour the professional against the general public.

In 1980 I helped to found the Association for Humanistic Psychology Practitioners, because I wanted to grasp the nettle of accreditation. A couple of years earlier I had resigned from the Psychology and Psychotherapy Association because it had (after several inconclusive meetings) failed to do this.

The point of accreditation, as we spelled it out at that time, was to put some structure into a disorganized field which had become quite messy. We felt we wanted to put our own house in order, so that we could say to all and sundry that there were some decent standards of practice, and that some of us cared enough about that to make sure that they were upheld, at least within the bounds of the organization we were setting up. And so we set out some guidelines for how people could assess themselves and their practice, and submit themselves to the judgement of their peers. We also set out some ethical standards, and a complaints procedure so that clients or others who felt offended against by one of our members could find redress.

Inward and outward

We were clear that there were two sides to the issue of accreditation: an inward side, where we became clearer about what we were doing ourselves and the kind of values we wanted to uphold for ourselves; and an outward side, where we said to the world – 'We take collective responsibility for our practice, and are prepared to have it examined for its adequacy by anyone who wants or needs to do so'. We were also clear that there were many different kinds of humanistic practitioners, and that we wanted to cater for all of them – therapists of various persuasions, group facilitators, counsellors, organization consultants, educators, researchers and so on.

Then came, gradually and bit by bit, the United Kingdom Standing Conference for Psychotherapy, which later became the UK Council for

Psychotherapy. This consists of some eighty organizations representing all the main schools of psychotherapy in Britain. I'd like some acknowledgement that the people involved with it have done a tremendous job under enormously difficult conditions. To hold together in one regular meeting all the various tendencies within psychotherapy, to enable dialogue and mutual understanding to take place, and to find a growing mutual respect emerging, is no mean achievement. The reason why this has been possible is that it is not agreement on theory that is being attempted, but agreement on staying together so that the UKCP can be recognized as the only competent authority in the UK that can speak for psychotherapists of all schools: hopefully thus preventing the atrocious oppression that has taken place in most countries of Europe, where only such psychotherapy as is approved and controlled by the psychiatric establishment is allowed to take place. Those countries where strict control is also exercised by the psychological establishment are regarded on the Continent as liberal. The UKCP stands for a system by which free organizations freely combine into groupings with explicit criteria of membership, which can be scrutinized and modified by mutual criticism. It is unfortunate that some of the narrower schools of psychoanalysis eventually split off and formed their own exclusive organization, the British Confederation of Psychotherapists.

Now because of the UKCP's existence, and the pressure from Europe to produce some kind of rationale for what we were doing in this country, the Association of Humanistic Psychology Practitioners had to devote special attention to psychotherapy. Our work on accreditation in this particular area was not only under scrutiny from our peers in the Humanistic and Integrative Psychotherapy Section (HIPS) of the UKCP, but also under scrutiny from other sections, and from the Board of that organization. In the event, AHPP members took a leading role in drawing up criteria for membership of the Section which took into account many of the lessons we had learned in the AHPP.

But what this meant was that the *outward* aspect of the accreditation process now became much more important. We had to satisfy not only our own consciences, but also the critical gaze of outsiders. So our requirements, and our procedures, had to be tight enough to stand up to this. One of the things we took on board was the necessity to have an External Moderator – someone senior and sympathetic, but not connected with the organization, who could scrutinize what we were doing, and tell us whether we were living up to our own self-description, or if we were kidding ourselves in some way. We also took to heart the formal assessment by two other organizations in the same Section, which could reveal any weaknesses and holes in our procedures. So now the accreditors were getting, so to speak, accredited by peers. Just the same as what they were doing for others, and just as valuable.

Criticisms

In the light of all this history, consider the articles in *Self & Society* by Shohet and others (1991), House and Hall (1991), Postle and Anderson (1990), Brown and Mowbray (1990), Kalisch (1990a and b) and Heron (1990). Incidentally, the publishers Routledge, having taken over *Self & Society*, are now providing access to all the back issues of that journal, so they are available to all.

In the Shohet *et al.* article, five people got together to experiment with accrediting each other, and discovered many interesting things. But it seems to me that they concentrated on the *inward* aspects of accreditation, and ignored all of the *outward* aspects.

Similarly with the House and Hall article – here thirteen people got together, and discovered a great deal of value for themselves. Again it seems to me that they ignored the outward aspects of the matter.

Postle and Anderson quarrel with many of the details of AHPP accreditation, and eventually suggest their own substitute for that, which in my view really amounts to much the same thing as the proposals just mentioned – and similar to them refers much more to the inward than to the outward requirements of any viable accreditation process.

Brown and Mowbray want to argue that psychotherapy should not adopt a medical model. Here they are pushing at an open door, because all of us in the HIPC group agree on that, and will argue it to the door of hell if necessary. We don't want to abandon psychotherapy to the psychiatrists, or even the psychologists: we want it to be recognized as a diverse activity with many different expressions, all legitimate. It is the strength of the UKCP (and its weakness in the eyes of those who want narrower definitions favouring their own approach) that it has insisted on the legitimacy of this diversity.

The Kalisch articles both say that bureaucratization is a bad thing, and that instead we should adopt the myth of rebellion, in which endeavour the figure of Hermes might help us. This seems to me a kind of either/or which is not helpful. To argue against bureaucracy is similar to arguing against traffic lights: at a certain stage in the development of an organization it has to become more bureaucratic, just as at a certain stage in the development of traffic it becomes appropriate and helpful to introduce traffic lights. This doesn't mean that we have to abandon Hermes, who I find personally a very helpful figure, particularly in relation to psychotherapy, with his ability to go back and forth between the underworld and the overworld carrying messages. The whole essence of the Greek pantheon is that we need many gods and goddesses, not just one. Not the either/or, but the both/and.

The Heron piece is marred by a determination to use the word 'transference' as often as possible, but seems to be basically trying to say that psychotherapy creates its own clients, or at any rate 'exacerbates and reinforces the very processes' which create them. I don't think this can be seriously maintained: of all the forces creating the kind of distress which brings clients into therapy, I would have thought the existence of psychotherapy itself was one of the weakest. He also seems to be saying – though I find it hard to see how he can – that the fact that we are involved in psychotherapy and the UKCP makes it impossible, or less likely, that we will be involved in personal growth through workshops, therapy, groupwork, education of various kinds, organizational work, community work and so forth. These are activities that are very central and important to the whole humanistic approach, and will in my view continue to be so (Rowan 2001). This kind of work in the area of what Heron calls 'emotional competence' is something that humanistic practitioners have always done and will presumably continue to do. Again there is the appearance of this either/or which I find so hurtful and damaging.

The thoughtful articles of Hawkins (1990a and b) and of Young (1990) seem very useful to me in correcting some of the misinformation still being carried around, but even they do not mention some things which are well known to those of us who have been involved in all this stuff since the beginning. For example, the way the UKCP is often referred to makes me think that many people have an idea of it as a very formal and hierarchical set-up, such that it would surprise them to find out that informal clothes are worn even in formal sessions of the organization. One of the best articles I have seen on accreditation is the one by Alan Frankland (1996), and this should be seen by anyone involved in these issues.

To me it seems obvious that accreditation is here to stay, and that it has to take a form that does justice both to the outward face and to the inward face of our work as practitioners. I am sure we can do this better as time goes on, but not if the criticism comes out in the virulent form that it sometimes seems to.

Boundaries

One of the most important ethical issues that arises in all forms of therapy is the question of boundaries. It is the job of the therapist to hold the ring, to maintain the frame, to secure the *temenos* (the sacred space), to keep the *vas* (the alchemical vessel) closed. We need to keep the energy in, on the one hand, and to keep distractions out, on the other.

It is within the boundary that the relationship takes place. As Petruska Clarkson (2003) has told us so brilliantly, there are at least five relationships all going on at the same time in therapy.

The **therapeutic alliance** is where we make a contract with the client, make sure that time, place and money are taken care of, that the client is motivated and responsible – all the practical things that have to be secured if the process is to be protected.

The **transferential relationship** is where we pay attention to the unconscious part of the transaction, where both the client and the therapist may be subject to influences from the past which provoke reactions not under conscious control.

The **reparative relationship** is where the therapist has to be willing to be what the client's fantasy needs. The therapist may turn into a mother, a father, a sibling, a teacher or other authority figure, and the client may regress into a much earlier age state.

The **real relationship** is where the therapist is authentic, relating to the client in an I/You way, not in an I/It fashion. This is particularly important in humanistic work, where authenticity is a prime value, and must be actually available in the session.

The **transpersonal relationship** is where the therapist is paying attention to the spiritual dimension of the work, and where the client's spiritual aspirations and spiritual problems are taken seriously for what they are, and not reduced to something else.

More details about all of these are of course to be found in the book mentioned: here we are simply admitting that they exist and can only be ignored at our peril. In all of them the question of boundaries is important.

As mentioned earlier, we have become more aware since about 1985 of the boundaries of sex and anger. It has become crystal clear that sexual relations between therapist and client are always harmful, because they are always based on a difference in power, such that the therapist is the abuser even when they feel as if they are the seduced. There is a good discussion of this issue in Russell (1993).

This does not mean that the therapist has to be cold – indeed, Rogers has told us that non-possessive warmth is an essential quality for any therapist. But it does mean taking care of the difference between acceptance and approval. Acceptance is fine – taking clients as they are, not as they should be. But approval is a kind of warmth that goes too far. We do not tell clients that they are OK, that they are good-looking, that they are well-dressed, that they are intelligent – none of these things or others of the same kind. That is reassurance, that is our judgement, that is manifesting our superiority. And we take care not to let our private opinions about the client become a part of the therapy, unless there is clearly some therapeutic gain to be achieved by doing so. There is a good discussion of this point in Chapter 2 of Windy Dryden's book (1985).

This leads to the whole question of dual relationships. In a 1997 issue of *Self & Society* the dilemma is raised by Moira, someone who runs a small psychotherapy training. Among the applicants for training this year is someone who is currently a client of Moira. Should this person be accepted for training, and should this person change therapists? In other words, can the same person be a therapist and a trainer to the same individual at the same time? The general rule for this is that such a dual relationship is to be avoided. One of the main reasons for this is that people often find therapy training very stressful, one of the sources of stress being the relationship with the trainers. If a student is having problems with a trainer, such as thinking the trainer is no good, and the trainer is also the therapist, this is not going to work. Another problem that can arise in such situations is that other members of a seminar group may get jealous or rivalrous when it becomes known that one individual has the seminar leader for a therapist. Also the individual may come to feel that their therapy is continuing in the seminar, and is becoming inescapable, particularly if the degree of transference is high. It used to be quite common in psychoanalysis and in Jungian circles for the training analyst also to be one of the trainers, and even one of the people responsible for passing the candidate as accredited, but this has now changed a great deal.

Other dual relationships are therapist and supervisor. Can the same person be my therapist and my supervisor? Again the answer is no, for the same sort of reason. If my relationship with my supervisor got into difficulties, such as feeling dissatisfied with the service I am getting, I would normally go to my therapist in the first instance, to explore my feelings about this and trying to decide whether the problem is in me or out there – but if it is the same person how can I? This can be a very difficult problem in rural areas, where there is a shortage both of therapists and of supervisors. I even came across the case, in one such area, where the therapist, and the supervisor, and the wife, were all the same person!

On the other hand, humanistic training centres see no problem in the trainee having several therapists one after the other. It is quite common for people to move from a male to a female, or from a female to a male, in order to get the benefit of a different gender perspective. The ideal of one central relationship which continues indefinitely, is not held by the humanistic schools. What has to be watched, however, is the question of why the client is transferring NOW at this precise moment. Is it out of health – a readiness to end with one and begin with another – or is it out of sickness – to avoid resolving problems with the first therapist? The boundary question is this: am I really ready to end with this therapist, or not?

Probably the most important boundary issue is confidentiality. This is something that few people outside the world of therapy understand. Social workers don't understand it, nurses don't understand it, teachers don't understand it. It means that the words of the client are sacred. They are not to be repeated or quoted to anyone else. The obvious exception to this is the supervisor, but in the best practice even the supervisor does not know the client's name or address. In supervision it is best to give the client a pseudonym or a letter or a number. So the therapist does not gossip about the client, the supervisor does not gossip about either the client or the supervisee. I use the word gossip to describe any conversation about someone when that person is not present.

Still further, the therapist attempts to ensure that the client does not talk about what happens in their therapy to a third party. This is particularly important when that third party is involved in the therapy, often being mentioned or referred to – partners and parents are the obvious examples. It is all too easy for someone to refer to their therapy in terms which bring forth a defensive reaction from the hearer. Also there are times in therapy when strong negative feelings are expressed towards someone, and if the client then meets that someone and reveals that, the hearer may take the message much too strongly and finally, as if it were the last word on the subject. If the client, later in the therapy, discovers that some of those negative feelings were exaggerated or unwarranted, it is hard, and may be impossible, to undo the damage. People go through phases in therapy, and even the most definite conclusions may turn out to be not the final conclusions after all. So confidentiality is important in this way too.

Finally there is the issue of competence. It is wrong to take on a client if there are clear indications that such a client is beyond the expertise of the therapist. The most obvious example is that of a therapist who takes on a child in therapy when they have had no training in child psychotherapy. This kind of training is very rigorous, particularly in the area of ethics, and it deals with the vexed question of who the client is, which may otherwise be very confusing. Another example would be the case of someone who wanted to work through material pertaining to their birth and the perinatal period, if the therapist had no training in or experience of this kind of work. Another would be to take on a client experiencing a spiritual emergency, when the therapist had not worked through their own material in this area. There are plenty of examples of where an over-optimistic therapist has taken on the wrong client, and both of them have ultimately had a bad experience.

Telling the client

The question sometimes arises about the therapist leaving town or moving house, or going in for major redecorations. When to tell the clients about this? In my opinion the best time is as soon as the date is known and the full story can be given. If the therapist tries to anticipate trouble by telling the clients too far in advance, it merely gives them anxiety unconnected with any other real benefit. This also applies to the question as to whether the therapist should take on new clients during the period of uncertainty, and what to tell them. Again I think the therapist had better carry on as normal, and as if nothing were happening, until the actual date is known. Then is the time to break it to all concerned. In these days of much greater mobility, this is quite likely to arise at some time or another.

Dual relationships

This is an area which has come under a lot of scrutiny in recent years, and a new understanding has emerged. Can a client also be used as a carpenter? Can a client be chatted to in the swimming pool? Can a client be paid for secretarial work? Can a client invite his or her therapist to a wedding? It used to be thought that all these things were forbidden. But subsequent to the publication of books such as Lazarus and Zur (2002) and Gabriel (2005) it has been possible to see more clearly that all of these, and many such others are usually all right, and not to be dismissed out of hand. The essential distinction is between boundary crossing, which all the examples above exemplify, and boundary violation, which is strictly forbidden. The difference is that boundary violation always involves exploitation of the client for the therapist's benefit. This exploitation may be financial, or sexual, or work-related, but it always involves the therapist using the client in some way, for gain.

There are still therapists, of course, who have stricter rules, but this seems now to be the general consensus, and it represents a great relief to most of us that this clarification has taken place. Obviously there are some tricky areas which deserve special scrutiny: 'Several of the contributors to this book have explicitly emphasized the importance of *not* pursuing dual relationships with highly dependent, borderline, histrionic, antisocial, and other seriously disturbed individuals' (Scheflin, p.267, in Lazarus and Zur 2002).

Ethics is an area which has come under more scrutiny lately, and it may be confidently predicted that it will become more and more complex and hard to handle.

Useful websites

UKCP is the umbrella organization in Britain for all forms of psychotherapy, and worth consulting on any difficult questions of ethics: www.psychotherapy. org.uk

BACP has actually issued recommended standards for ethics in counselling, and keeps on revising them in the light of current thinking: www.bacp.co.uk

AHPP is the humanistic organization for therapy in Britain, and their views on ethics are perhaps more advanced than those of other organizations: http://ahpp.org.uk

14 The transpersonal

This is a new chapter, not found in the last edition. There has been much more interest and development in this field in the past few years, and in 2013 there appeared *The Wiley-Blackwell handbook of transpersonal psychology*, an ambitious affair of some 700 pages, showing how much the field has developed recently.

It can be said that transpersonal psychotherapy has been known from ancient times: there is an Egyptian document of approximately 2200 BCE which contains a dialogue of a suicidal man with his soul. This is quoted in full and explained at length by the Jungian Barbara Hannah (1981), who makes some very interesting comments on it. In the twentieth century, the classic psychologist William James had a great deal of value to say about spiritual experiences of one kind and another, though he never applied this to psychotherapy.

But so far as anything actually named transpersonal psychotherapy is concerned, we can only go back as far as Jung and Assagioli, and the discussions which led to the founding of the *Journal of Transpersonal Psychology* in 1967–69. So this is a recent speciality, in so far as it has an identity of its own. It was Abraham Maslow who inspired the modern movement: Roberto Assagioli says that the term *transpersonal* was introduced:

> by Maslow and by those of his school to refer to what is commonly called spiritual. Scientifically speaking, it is a better word: it is more precise and, in a certain sense, neutral in that it points to that which is beyond or above ordinary personality. Furthermore it avoids confusion with many things which are now called spiritual but which are actually pseudo-spiritual or parapsychological.
>
> (Assagioli 1991, p.16)

It was taken up in various countries in the years after 1969, and now five of the members of the United Kingdom Council for Psychotherapy have that label. In Europe, thirty national associations of transpersonal psychology are united under the banner of EUROTAS, the umbrella organization for Europe. One of the great schools of transpersonal work is psychosynthesis, founded by Assagioli, and this is now represented worldwide.

One of the pioneers of transpersonal research was Stanislav Grof, who conducted many studies in the 1950s and early 1960s using LSD. He made some very interesting discoveries about the effects of the birth experience on later psychopathology, and in his later research, using holotropic breathing instead of LSD, explored the whole range of transpersonal states of consciousness, particularly in his 1988 book.

In more recent years there has been an explosion of transpersonal research that explicitly deals with the question of spirituality. Well-known exponents of this approach are William Braud and Rosemarie Anderson (1998), whose book is a classic.

In 1993 was formed the Association for Accredited Psychospiritual Psychotherapists in the UK, as a body serving the Institute of Psychosynthesis, the Psychosynthesis & Education Trust, the Karuna Institute, ReVision and the Centre for Transpersonal Psychology. They choose to call themselves psychospiritual rather than transpersonal.

This all illustrates one of the most important facts about the transpersonal: it has no centre, no founder, no basic texts, just a number of people who are all trying, in their various ways, to make sense of what Maslow called 'the farther reaches of human nature'.

It also needs to be said that the primary interest of many organizations is in transpersonal psychology generally, not just in psychotherapy: in fact, some of them are not very interested in psychotherapy at all. The transpersonal field includes psychiatry, anthropology, sociology, ecology and altered states of consciousness – particularly as attained through meditation, as described by Roger Walsh and Frances Vaughan (Walsh and Vaughan 1993). One of the most important developments in the field of the transpersonal was the publication in 1980 of *The Atman Project* by Ken Wilber. This was later followed up by the book *No boundary* (1981) which applies the same thinking to psychotherapy in particular. This puts the transpersonal on a much better theoretical footing, showing how it represents a particular stage in psychospiritual development, linking psychology with spirituality in a convincing manner. Wilber has since published a detailed study (Wilber *et al.* 1986) of how different forms of therapy relate to problems which emerge at different stages on the psychospiritual journey. And I myself have tried to relate all this to actual practice in the field (Rowan 2005a).

Recent work in the field by Len Sperry (2012) has shown just how widely the new ideas have spread and the excellent book by David Matteson (2008) demonstrates that the new thinking is politically savvy as well. One of the issues, of course, in this area, is that of religion, and most of the transpersonal writers tend to steer clear of saying anything at all about religion. The reason for this is that the great religions of the world have a terrible, terrible record when it comes to prejudice. The two main prejudices, of course, shared by all the main religious practices, are those against women and against homosexuality. Books such as Blyth and Landau (2009) document the extent and severity of this problem. We shall say no more in this book, because that is not what we are most interested it, but it has to be said.

So what does all this imply for practice? As we said earlier, there is a whole broad field here, but the essential step is to admit that we are spiritual beings. In other words, as well as having a body, feelings and an intellect, we also have a soul. This is a huge step to make in our present culture, which has no place for such things. But unless we take this step, we cannot reap the benefits of the new thinking that we have just been describing.

So what exactly do we mean by saying we have a soul? Many people have been put off such talk by memories of their religious upbringing. But the notion of the soul being urged now is much more generous than that. In fact, there are now a number of synonyms of the soul which are much more appealing to many people. Here is an incomplete list of words we can use if we do not like the word 'soul':

Higher Self
Inner Teacher
Deep Self
Heart
Transpersonal Self (1)
Genius
Daimon
Guidance Self
Higher Intuitive Self
Archetype of the Self
Guardian Angel
Wise Being
Bliss
Savikalpa
Luminosity
Psychic centre
Antaratman

The idea of all these names is that we have within us a level of consciousness which goes beyond what we have been calling the mental ego, and also beyond what we have been calling the centaur, or the existential self, or the authentic self, and so forth.

One of the most accessible and attractive of the approaches to these matters is that of psychosynthesis. Psychosynthesis says that we have a lower unconscious (much like the Freudian unconscious), a middle unconscious (what the analysts call the Preconscious) and a higher unconscious, or Superconscious. This latter is the home of our creativity, our intuition, our ability to enter trance states and so forth.

Wilber (2000) calls this the Subtle level of consciousness. One of the best ways of accessing it is through guided fantasy, and psychosynthesis is one of the best sources for finding guided fantasies. Those who wish to really enter and occupy this **stage** of consciousness development will have to go through an initiation involving ritual and ceremony, but anyone can experience this **state** of consciousness at any time they wish. This distinction between state and stage is very important, and makes it clear that the ability to use the Subtle realm is open to any therapist who wants or needs to use it.

One of the great pioneers of the Subtle realm is Jung, and his work is a constant source of inspiration in this area. His idea of an archetype is a very powerful one, and useful in practice – the Anima, the Daimon, the Trickster are just three of many. Caroline Myss has a list of eighty. Other Jungians who have made huge contributions include James Hillman (very good on polytheism), Barbara Hannah, Marie-Louise von Franz (particularly on dreams) and many others.

From quite a different angle, Stanislav Grof has made a huge contribution, and his collection of art works from the Subtle realm are quite remarkable and challenging. Another wide-ranging contributor to our understanding of this realm is Joseph Campbell (1990), who has written book after book expanding our knowledge of the whole world of the Subtle.

Women who have contributed to our understanding of the Subtle realm include Jocelyn Chaplin, Jean Houston (1996), Marion Woodman, Marie-Louise von Franz (the greatest writer on dreams and fairy tales), Barbara Sullivan (1989) and others. The first two of these come from the humanistic camp, and the other three from the Jungian camp.

A word of warning is justified here. It is possible to enter the Subtle realm too suddenly and unprepared. This is particularly likely if artificial means are used to enter that state, such as ayahuasca or LSD. For many years LSD was forbidden, even for research purposes, but since 2006 it has been approved again, and some of the results are detailed in Fadiman and Kornfeld (2013). If the Subtle realm is entered too quickly, a person may get the feeling that they are going mad. This in fact happened to Jung, with the results detailed in his magnificent *Red book* (Jung 2009). However, it is also true that artificial means can yield valid results in the form of genuine mystical experiences (Smith 2000).

In Appendix 1 I have outlined all these levels with the names of the people associated with them, and this may form a useful summary and aide-memoire to show how the various approaches to therapy are linked and divided.

Practice

We could go on. But let us stop here and ask the question – what do we actually do that is any different? One simple answer is that we can use guided fantasy with our clients, as the psychosynthesis people do. Another answer is that we can encourage our clients to enter the Subtle realm with us, and experience what has been called 'working at relational depth' (Knox *et al*. 2013) or 'linking' (Rowan 1998). Here the mind of the client and the mind of the therapist enter the same space at the same time. This is something unknown at lower levels. Another feature of this level is intuition. All therapists use their intuition, but at this level there is a particular way of doing this, which is – 'Go to a place of not knowing, and wait'. This way of working has been called 'negative capability' and is easier than it sounds. One of the most striking accounts of the use of intuition is to be found in the book by Peter Heinl (2001).

One interesting feature of the Subtle is that there is a different logic in this realm. Here we cannot ask the question – 'Is it true?' Instead, we have to ask the question – 'And what effect did that have on you?' This means that it is a very personal level of consciousness, where what is true for me may not be true for you. This induces a much greater respect for the experiences of others, and makes it virtually impossible to put anybody down.

At the level of the Subtle a new kind of compassion appears, which I have called 'juicy compassion'. And in general a new appreciation of love appears – a love which is infinite rather than having to be rationed out. Basically, the soul is unlimited, and offers a huge resource when it is tapped.

Once we open up to the Subtle realm, we find ourselves in a place where it is possible to take seriously all manner of Subtle phenomena, as William Bloom (1998) has shown us. Instead of rejecting all talk of angels, fairies, nature spirits and previous lives (Woolger 1990), we start to take them seriously as possibilities. It is actually quite easy to learn the technique of accessing previous lives, although it is wise to have the experience for one-self before introducing it to other people. This is true of everything in psychotherapy, of course (Rowan 2014).

The subtle and the dialogical self

One of the most exciting possibilities opened up by access to the Subtle realm is that we can use the theory of the Dialogical Self (which we met in

Chapter 7) to bring to life the many entities proposed as existing in the Subtle realm. My own favourites include Erishkigal, Tiamat, Kali-Ma, Aphrodite, Kwanyin, Bride, Sophia, Isis and Kamala, and on the male side (for the Subtle is very gender-oriented) Shiva, Cernunnos, Pan, Eros, Avalokitesvara, Hermes, Dionysos, Osiris and Ganesh. But of course we are not restricted to these, and others may invoke Obatala, Muhammed, the Guardian Angel, the Mahatma, Meister Eckhart, Socrates and so forth.

On those occasions when we need advice or help, it is companions such as these we can call upon. This is the level of prayer and supplication covered in Bhakti Yoga, the companion and equal of Jnana Yoga, which we shall meet in the next section. You may remember that in Dialogical Self work we go back and forth between two chairs, speaking from both in dialogue form. This may remind us of the extensive work of Donald Walsch in his 'Conversations with God' series (e.g., Walsch 1997). He was furiously writing out all his complaints about his life, addressing them to God as responsible for it all. When he finally slackened down and paused, his pen started to move on its own, and he found himself writing – 'Do you really want an answer to all these questions, or are you just venting?' He allowed the conversation to continue, and the result was a book which sold millions of copies.

In every form of therapy, it sometimes happens that we feel the need to get advice from someone we respect. The identity of that person seems to matter less than the basic idea of asking. Now the problem with orthodox religion is that we never (or very rarely) get an answer to our prayers. But in our approach here we address our concerns to an empty chair, and then, when we are ready, we change chairs and speak from the other one. Of course this is not the only way, and we have already seen how Walsch found another – there may be many others.

In my experience this can often be a very powerful move, and the advice given is often miraculously apposite and helpful. Of course the choice of who to talk to is very individual, and the client has to be asked to choose carefully – not to use the ideas of the therapist, but to seek within themselves the appropriate character. In my own experience, one client chose a charismatic football manager, another chose Sherlock Holmes, another the Wise Woman, and so forth. Sometimes it works to ask a tree for the answer. In Dialogical Self work there are no limits to the entities who can be contacted (Rowan 2010).

The upper level of the transpersonal

It is worth pointing out that there is another level of the transpersonal that can be accessed, which Wilber calls the Causal (no connection with determinism, by the way). It is a stage which can only be accessed through the use of meditation, though glimpses can be had much earlier, in the usual way. At this level there are no angels, no fairies, no nature spirits – there is only the One. There are various ways of naming this One, as we also found with the soul, and here is an incomplete list:

Spirit
Divine Spark
Void
'O'
Essence
Transpersonal Self (2)
God within
No-Self
The Ineffable
The Absolute
The One without a Second
Neti-Neti (not this, not that)
Universal Mind
Overmind
Kether
Emptiness
Gnosis
Nirvikalpa
One Mind
Cosmic Consciousness
All-Self
Big Mind, Big Heart

It can be seen that we have quite a wide choice as to what to call this level, but the essence of it is that everything is seen as One. It may be the One, the All, the Nothing, the Absolute, and so forth – some call it the God experience. It is usually seen as the ultimate, though some say that beyond that is the Nondual (Rowan 2010).

The point is that at this level there are no problems. This is because there are no words, no distinctions, no perceptions, no descriptions of any kind. Because of this, there is no empathy at this level – just a very accurate unblinkered perception. There is no particular reason why psychotherapists should be very interested in this, but it is good to know that it is there – that there are more mystical states beyond the Subtle.

Levels of consciousness

The key idea of levels of consciousness was pioneered by Jean Piaget, but the most important steps were taken by Abraham Maslow, whose work is so popular now in management circles. His work was at first dismissed by academia, because it was not research-based, but in recent years a great deal of research by other people has been published, all backing up Maslow's basic insights. (See Appendix 3).

I have myself tried to apply this idea to all the different schools of therapy, with the results detailed in Appendix 1. It can be seen from this that the idea of levels of consciousness applies not only to clients and to therapists, but to whole schools of therapy. This now makes it possible to take the client where he or she actually is, and not assume that all clients are the same.

It should perhaps be said that most clients are living at the Mental Ego level, and that one of the main things they might be trying to do in their therapy is to move upward and onward to what Wilber calls the Centaur level. This is, after all, the main level of consciousness for understanding people in all their complexity. I have pointed out elsewhere (Rowan 2005b) that most students studying counselling, psychotherapy and coaching are in fact led by their involvement in groupwork and practice with clients from the Mental Ego to the Centaur almost without realizing it.

Trauma and the transpersonal

A client who has suffered some trauma very often comes to therapy wanting to return to the state they were in before it happened, but of course this is impossible. In transpersonal therapy we more often take the view that trauma has a purpose, and that purpose is to wake us up. Of course this is not always the case, and each person is unique, but one of the great themes in transpersonal work is that the negative can lead to the positive. Ralph Metzner wrote a whole book on different images of spiritual transformation to be found in the literature, and death and rebirth is one of them:

> Self-knowledge is the ultimate favour and reward given to those who confront their own death. In such an experience, the self that I thought I was dies, and my true Self is revealed and recognized. Such an experience may be devastating, but is certainly humbling, and potentially ecstatic and liberating.
>
> (Metzner 1986, p.144)

An old Indian story seems very telling here. The tale goes that a woman's first child had died on its first birthday. She was incapacitated by grief, and wandered around incapable of any activity other than asking everyone for some solution. Her terrible feelings were unstoppable, no matter what she tried, and rendered her incapable of any action. Finally someone suggested that she went to the Great Teacher, famed far and wide for his wisdom and compassion. She explained her suffering and he said that he had just the right solution. However, he needed a potato to make it, and it had to be a potato from a house where no one had ever died. There were no new houses to be found, so she had to go to the existing houses, all quite old. She went from house to house, but after a long time she had to go back to the Great Teacher to report her failure. However he had died himself in the interim. She had discovered herself that she was not alone, that she was just one of many who had lost a son, or a mother, or an aunt – the list went on. She had discovered the law of impermanence – that everyone dies, that nothing lasts for ever, that we just have to survive, to go on, to go on going on.

The mention of death makes it clear that we are talking about quite extreme experiences, and Kate Maguire has spent many years dealing with these extremes, and has much to say that is really valuable about such matters:

> In my early work with survivors of torture and witnesses of violent events, I came to realise that all of them without exception had developed their own private, sometimes secretive, ways of trying to make meaning of what had happened to them and those ways were mostly through poetry and imagery which is also an integral part of my way of communicating.
>
> (Maguire 2001, p.130)

She makes the point that in talking about such matters, metaphors have a large part to play, and that death and rebirth is certainly one of them. We are talking here not about the small traumas of everyday life, or even injury or ill health, but about trauma that is so severe as to bring the possibility or even reality of death seriously into the picture. Zandvoort writes movingly about this when he says:

> My own experience and my work with clients have led me to accept that feelings such as anxiety, guilt and grief are not destructive or pathological but provide the traumatically bereaved individual with opportunities for growth and creativity.
>
> (Zandvoort 2012, p.41)

He makes it clear that the negative, which trauma inevitably is, can have a salutary function in opening up the spaces that are often referred to in the literature as the Shadow. A trauma can lead us into the deeper feelings which we often ignore, play down or deny, and many workers in the field say the same thing: 'When terrible things do happen, they can also be occasions for positive transformation' (Lawlis 2013, p.645).

This is true not only in the adult field, but also with children. Children, too, may have to face serious trauma, particularly in times of war, but also at times in many families. There have been some examples in the papers recently of families where the parents have killed the children, or the children have killed the parents, or both have been killed in fires or other accidents, often leaving just one child alive. Doing therapy with such children may be testing indeed for the therapist, as Crenshaw and Garbarino discovered in their research:

> At many points, there may be the temptation to turn back and return to shore by both child and healer; but reaching the other side and discovering that such troubled waters can be crossed and survived leads to not only a fuller access to human potential in the child but also a validation of all that draws us to this work and greater confidence in our clinical skills.
>
> (Crenshaw and Garbarino 2007, p.192)

All our work in this difficult field tells us that the transpersonal view can be very helpful. Just because we do not believe that death is the end, but rather a transition into another level of being, we can welcome and use it in our work, and not be fazed by such extreme experiences and happenings. Example after example of the actual work tells us again and again that extreme experiences can be eye-opening and very positive if treated in a transpersonal way: 'All these examples suggest that mind is independent of the brain and free to roam through unlimited space beyond the brain or affect matter' (Berger 2010, p.54).

It is therefore quite distressing to us when we meet the dogmatism of some in the field who sternly tell us that death is the end, and that to avoid this hard fact betrays our wishy-washiness. Often this dogmatism is not recognized, but rather extolled as the highest wisdom. But perhaps having a more open attitude towards death is actually more realistic, and more helpful, than the stark alternative? Maybe trauma can be our great teacher, rather than the end of everything?

Useful websites

International Transpersonal Association: www.transpersonalassociation.com
Association for Transpersonal Psychology: http://atpweb.org
EUROTAS – The European umbrella organization for transpersonal psychology:
    http://eurotas.org

Appendix 1

A comparison of four positions in personal development

A comparison of four positions in personal development

	1	2	3	4
WILBER LEVEL	*MENTAL EGO*	*CENTAUR*	*SUBTLE*	*CAUSAL*
Wilber colours	Orange	Green-teal-turquoise	Indigo Violet	Ultraviolet-Clear light
ROWAN POSITION	Instrumental Self	Authentic Self	Transpersonal Self 1 (Soul)	Transpersonal Self 2 (Spirit)
WADE LEVEL	Egocentric Conformist	Authentic	Transcendent	Unity
Definition	I am defined by others	I define who I am	I am defined by the Other(s)	I am not defined
Motivation	Need	Choice	Allowing	Surrender
Personal Goal	Adjustment	Self-Actualization	Contacting	Union
Social Goal	Socialization	Liberation	Extending	Salvation
Process	Healing – Ego-building	Development – Ego-extending	Opening – Ego-reduction	Enlightenment
Buddhism	Nirmanakaya	No Buddhism	Sambhogakaya	Dharmakaya
Yoga	Dharma Yoga	No Yoga	Bhakti Yoga	Jnana Yoga
Great Exemplar	Albert Ellis	James Bugental	Roberto Assagioli	Shankara

continued . . .

Continued

	1	*2*	*3*	*4*
WILBER LEVEL	*MENTAL EGO*	*CENTAUR*	*SUBTLE*	*CAUSAL*
Story Example	Erickson	May or Wheelis	Naropa	George Fox
Traditional role of Helper	Physician Analyst	Growth Facilitator	Advanced Guide	Priest(ess) Sage
Representative approaches	Hospital treatment Chemotherapy Some psy-ana ACT Behaviour mod Cognitive-behavioural DBT Crisis work REBT Brief therapy Solution-based cognitive	Primal integration Gestalt therapy Some psy-ana Psychodrama POP Bodywork therapies Some TA Person-centred Co-counselling Regression Experiential Existential	Psycho-synthesis Some Jungians Some pagans Transpersonal Voice Dialogue Some Wicca or Magic Kabbalah Some astrology Some Tantra Shamanism Core process Holotropic	Mystical Buddhism Raja Yoga Taoism Monasticism Da Avabhasa Christian mysticism Sufi Goddess mystics Some Judaism Advaita Impersonal Buddha

	1	*2*	*3*	*4*
WILBER LEVEL	*MENTAL EGO*	*CENTAUR*	*SUBTLE*	*CAUSAL*
ROWAN POSITION	Instrumental Self	Authentic Self	Transpersonal Self 1 (Soul)	Transpersonal Self 2 (Spirit)
WADE LEVEL	Egocentric Achievement Affiliative	Authentic	Transcendent	Unity
Focus	Individual and Group	Group and Individual	Supportive Community	Ideal Community
Representative names	Freud Ellis LeBon	Maslow Rogers Mahrer	Jung Hillman Starhawk	Prendergast Peter Fenner Adyashanti

continued . . .

Continued

	1	2	3	4
WILBER LEVEL	*MENTAL EGO*	*CENTAUR*	*SUBTLE*	*CAUSAL*
	Beck	Perls	Assagioli	Mark Epstein
	Eysenck	Searles	Gordon-Brown	Rosenbaum
	Skinner	Laing	Mary Watkins	Ram Dass
	Lazarus	Moreno	Jean Houston	A H Almaas
	Watzlawick	Winnicott	Bolen	Sylvia Krystal
	Marinoff	Lomas	Grof	Welwood
	Haley	Bugental	Boorstein	David Brazier
	Erickson	Hycner	Whitmore	Dorothy Hunt
	Linehan	Bohart	Nathan Field	Amy Mindell
	Ivey	Satir	Fukuyama	Berkow
	Egan	Bozarth	Maguire	Wittine
	NLP	Spinelli	Milner	Bradford
	Dryden	van Deurzen	Eigen	Michael Eigen
	Rangell	May	Corbin	Puhakka
Intuition	Chancy	Reliable	Constant	Not needed
Compassion	Subject to fatigue	Reliable Cool	Juicy Warm	Constant Steady
Research methods	Qualitative Quantitative	Collaborative Action research	Transformative Mindful	None
Questions	What is the best method?	What is the best relationship?	How far can we go together?	Dare you face the loss of all your words?
Questions	Dare you face the challenge of change?	Dare you face the challenge of freedom?	Dare you face the loss of your boundaries?	Dare you face the loss of all your symbols?
Key issues	Acceptability Respect	Autonomy Authenticity	Openness Vision	Devotion Commitment

Appendix 2
Ground rules for groups

(Taken from the work of Will Schutz, James Elliott and Elizabeth Mintz)
Revised 2008.

1 **Awareness of the body**
   Your body is you. It expresses your feelings, if you will let it. If you suppress your own body, you may be willing to suppress other people. In groups such as this we often get rid of chairs and tables so that interaction may take place physically as well as verbally (See also No.9).

2 **The here and now**
   Talk about what you are aware of in this group at this moment. If you want to talk about the past, or about events outside the group, find ways of making them present to the group members. This can often be done by action or role-playing.

3 **Feelings**
   Let reality have an emotional impact on you, especially the reality of the other group members. Let yourself feel various emotions – but if they are blocked, be aware of that too. Feel what it is like to experience whatever is happening at an emotional level.

4 **Self-disclosure**
   Be open about your feelings or lack of them. Let people into your world. If you are anxious, let people know about it; if you are bored, it is OK to say so. Be as honest as you can bear to.

5 **Confidentiality**
   Don't talk about what is said or done in the group outside it.

6 **Taking responsibility**
   Take responsibility for yourself – do what you want and need to do, not what you think the group wants you to do. If the leader suggests something, it is still your decision whether to go along with it. Be aware of what you are doing to other people by what you say and do: take responsibility for that. Be aware of the 'I and thou' in each statement. You are not an impartial observer.

7 **Risk-taking**

If you are torn between expressing something and not expressing it, try taking a risk. Doing the thing you are most afraid of is usually a good idea in this group. You can reduce the danger of hostile statements by saying them non-evaluatively: instead of saying 'You are a cold person', say 'I feel frozen when you talk like that'. This is more likely to be true, and it makes you more real to the others. In a good group, people support risk-takers.

8 **Safety**

If at any point you are in danger of going beyond the limits of what you can take, use the code phrase STOP! I MEAN IT! and everything will stop immediately. No physical violence in the group. No physical sex.

9 **Listening**

Listening to others lets us in to their worlds. But listening is not just about words – it means being aware of expressions, gestures, body positions, breathing. Allow your intuition and compassion to work. Really be there with the other people in the group.

10 **Bridging distances**

As relationships in the group become clearer, there may be one or two members you feel very distant from, or want to be distant from. By expressing this, a new kind of relationship may begin to appear. Opposition and distance are just as likely to lead to growth as closeness and support, as long as the feelings are owned.

11 **Distress**

When someone in the group is distressed, encourage them to stay with that feeling until the distress is fully worked through, or turns into some other emotion. There is a 'Red Cross nurse' in all of us who wants to stop people feeling distressed, and jumps in too soon. A person learns most by staying with the feeling, and going with it to its natural end, which is often a very good place.

12 **Support and confrontation**

It is good to support someone who is doing some self-disclosure, some risk-taking, some bridging of distances. It is good to confront someone who is not being honest, who is avoiding all risk-taking, who is diverting energy away from the group's real work. It is possible to do both these things with love and care. A good group is full of mutual support.

13 **Avoidance**

Don't ask questions – make the statement which lies behind the question. Address people directly, saying 'I' rather than 'it' or 'you'. Don't say – 'I feel' when you mean – 'I think'. Ask yourself – 'What am I avoiding at this moment?'

14 The saver
Don't take any of these rules *too* seriously. Any set of rules can be used to put someone down – perhaps yourself. In a good group, you can be who you are, say what you mean, and not have to be some particular way.

SOURCE: John Rowan (2005) *A guide to humanistic psychology*, London: AHPP

Appendix 3 (1)

Maslow's hierarchy of needs and some collateral research

Level	Maslow	Kohlberg	Loevinger

6	Self-actualization
	Being that self
	  which I truly am
	Being all I have it
	  in me to be
	Fully functioning
	  person
	Authentic
	Creative
		Individual principles
		True personal
		  conscience
		Universal principles
		  fully internalized
		Genuinely
		  autonomous
		Selfishness B
			Autonomous:
			  Integrated
			Flexible and creative
			Internal conflicts
			  are faced and
			  recognized
			Tolerance for
			  ambiguity
			Respect for autonomy

5	Esteem 2
	Goals founded on
	  self-evaluated
	  standards
	Self-confidence
		Social contract
		Utilitarian law-
		  making
		Principles of
		  general welfare
		Long-term goals
			Conscientious
			Bound by self-
			  imposed rules
			Differentiated
			  thinking
			Self-aware

THE GREAT GAP

Level	Maslow	Kohlberg	Loevinger

4	Esteem 1
	Respect from
	  others
	Social status
	Recognition
		Law and order
		Authority
		  maintenance
		Fixed social rules
		Find duty and do it
			Conformist 2
			Seeking general
			  rules of social
			  conformity
			Justifying conformity

3	Love and
	  belongingness
	Wish for affection
	Need for acceptance
	Need for tenderness
		Personal
		  concordance
		Good-boy morality
		Seeking social
		  approval
		Liking to be liked
			Conformist 1
			Going along with
			  the crowd
			Anxiety about
			  rejection
			Need for support

continued . . .

Continued

Level	Maslow	Kohlberg	Loevinger

2	Effectance
	Mastery
	Imposed control
	Blame and
	   retaliation
	Domination
		Instrumental
		   hedonism
		Naive egocentrism
		Horse-trading
		   approach
		Profit-and-loss
		   calculation
		Selfishness A
			Self-protective
			Wary and exploitative
			People are means
			   to ends
			Competitive stance
			Fear of being caught

1	Safety
	Defence against
	   danger
	Fight or flight
	Fear: world is a
	   scary place
		Obedience/
		   Punishment
		Deference to
		   superior power
		Rules are external
		   and eternal
		Musts and shoulds
			Impulsive
			Domination by
			   immediate cue,
			   body feelings
			No reflection

Sources

After David Wright (1973), omitting lowest level of Maslow (physiological) and Loevinger (Pre-social, symbiotic).

Kohlberg, L. (1984) *Essays on moral development* (Vol.2 – The psychology of moral development), San Francisco, CA: Harper & Row.

Loevinger, J. (ed.)(1998) *Technical foundations for measuring ego development*, Mahwah, NJ: Lawrence Erlbaum.

Maslow, A. H. (1987) *Motivation and personality* (3rd edn), San Francisco, CA: Harper & Row.

Wright, D. (1973) 'Images of human nature underlying sociological theory: A review and synthesis', Annual Meeting of the American Sociological Association.

Appendix 3 (2)

Maslow's hierarchy of needs and some collateral research

Level	Piaget	Spiral dynamics	Wilber
6	Dialectical operations (Klaus Riegel 1984) Beyond formal logic Integration of contradictions	Yellow	Centaur 2 Vision-logic Bodymind integration Peak experiences Existential self
5	Formal operations Substage 2: Thinking about thinking Forethought, speculation	Green	Centaur 1 Ecological imagination Awareness of awareness Relative autonomy
		THE GREAT GAP	
4	Formal operations Substage 1: Capacity for hypothetico-deductive thinking	Orange	Mental ego Full rationality Syllogistic logic Science/mathematics
3	Concrete operations Ability to take role of other	Blue	Mythic-membership Dependent on roles Norm-dominated
2	Preoperational Mastery Incapable of seriation	Purple/Red	Magical Primary process thinking High credulity

continued . . .

Continued

Level	Piaget	Spiral dynamics	Wilber
1	Sensoriphysical	Beige	Body ego Archaic level of thought

Sources

Beck, D. E. and Cowan, C. C. (1996) *Spiral dynamics: Mastering values, leadership and change*, Oxford: Blackwell.

Piaget, J. (1954) *The construction of reality in the child*, New York: Basic Books.

Riegel, K. F. (1984) Chapter in M. L. Commons, F. A. Richards and C. Armon (eds) *Beyond formal operations: late adolescence and adult cognitive development*, New York: Praeger.

Wilber, K. (2000) *Integral psychology*, Boston, MA: Shambhala.

See also Wilber's novel *Boomeritis* for a spirited, readable, and informal description of Spiral Dynamics.

Appendix 3 (3)
Maslow's hierarchy of needs and some collateral research

Level	Cook-Greuter	Torbert	Kegan
6	Autonomous	Strategist	5
5	Pluralist Individualist	Individualist	4

THE GREAT GAP

Level	Cook-Greuter	Torbert	Kegan
4	Conscientious	Achiever	3/4
3	Conformist Self-aware	Diplomat Expert	3
2	Opportunist	Opportunist	2/3
1	Impulsive	Impulsive	1

Sources

Cook-Greuter, S. R. (1999) *Postautonomous ego development: a study of its nature and measurement*, Boston: Integral Publishers.

Kegan, R. (1994) *In over our heads: the demands of modern life*, Cambridge, MA: Harvard University Press.

Miller, M. and Cook-Greuter, S. (eds)(1994) *Transcendence and mature thought in adulthood: the further reaches of adult development*, Lanham, MD: Rowman and Littlefield.

Torbert, W. (1991) *The power of balance: transforming self, society and scientific inquiry*, Thousand Oaks, CA: Sage.

Appendix 4

Should I take on this client?

A practitioner should not expect to be able to take on everyone who applies. Very often in training there is a preliminary interview by a staff member before a client is referred, but even at this stage there may be some people who are taken on in other ways. Some considerations:

1 *The nature and severity of the client's symptoms*
   For example, prolonged delusional thinking may be a sign of psychosis, and people suffering in this way usually need residential facilities, rather than once or twice a week therapy. Or outbursts of uncontrolled anxiety or hostility again require quite secure environmental situations before a practitioner should be asked to deal with them.

2 *Length and persistence of symptoms*
   The longer something has been going on the longer it is going to take to deal with it. 'Am I ready to take on a client who may require constant attention for 5 years?' There is a responsibility not to bite off more than one can chew. One of the terrible things about some institutional set-ups is that personnel are transferred without any consideration of the possible effects on clients.

3 *The nature of the predisposing and precipitating experiences*
   If a client has had a series of severe traumas over a short period there may be a need for sessions much more frequently than you can in practice offer. It may be better to refer the client to someone who can offer this. Do not be panicked into fire-fighting if you have not been trained as a firefighter.

4 *Past stability and defensive functioning*
   Has the person shown the ability to handle deep feelings in the past, or is there a history of breakdown, self-mutilation, attempted suicide or similar? You are going to be asking the person to explore their inner life, and you want to be reasonably sure that this is not simply asking for trouble. Again residential facilities may be required.

5   *Resistance to therapy*

If in the first interview there is a lot of blocking of your attempts to open up significant areas, this may be because they are generally resistant to therapy, or it may be that they are resistant to you and your approach. Either way, it is not a good bet. It may also be that they are not ready to do therapy at the moment, but would be later.

6   *The person's network*

Does the person have friends, relatives, colleagues, etc. around and available? It is more acceptable to take on a difficult client who has such things than one who does not.

7   *Extent and adequacy of the practitioner's training*

Generally speaking, although there can be exceptions to this, it is unwise to take on someone who has had more experience of therapy than you. There are games that can be played in therapy; if the client knows more of them than you do, the therapy may go off the rails. You can refer such a client to someone more experienced.

8   *The problems of the practitioner*

Often the practitioner is unable to handle feelings because the client's feelings touch upon sore spots of his or her own. If this is so, it may be better to refer the client on. Empathy can turn into sympathy, and sympathy into collusion to avoid what needs to be faced.

9   *The amount of time available*

It is better not to take on long-term clients if you know you will be leaving the country or the neighbourhood, or retiring, etc. within a relatively short period of time (see also 2 above).

10   *Institutional policy*

If you are working for an agency or other organization, they may have rules as to which clients you may take on, or how deep you are to go with them. These have to be observed, and you should think about whether you are willing to abide by such rules when you take on such a job.

Appendix 5
Doing good therapy

The following criteria were developed out of a number of meetings of the AHPP Self and Peer Assessment Group. They are all things which can actually be monitored in training.

1   *Awareness of client*
    Listening and hearing, seeing and sensing, responding at various levels:

    •   body level;
    •   sexual level;
    •   emotional level;
    •   conscious level;
    •   imaginative level;
    •   spiritual level;
    •   political level.

    Openness, empathy, resonance, phenomenal experiencing, telepathic leaps, intuition. Ability to pick up cues the client is offering. Ability to at least see the obvious.

2   *Awareness of self*
    Congruence, genuineness, authenticity. Openness to own responses at various levels, and ability to make use of own countertransference, restimulation, reintegration, etc. Appropriately self-disclosing.

3   *Encouragement of client's autonomy*
    Non-judgemental attention and acceptance. Appreciation of client's uniqueness. Concern for client's self-direction. Giving space to client to move in own direction. Respect for client's energy. Hence at the very least:

    •   not putting the client down;
    •   not competing with the client;
    •   not knowing better than the client;

- not taking out one's own shit on the client;
- not keeping distance – hostile or scared – from the client;
- not seducing the client; and
- not smothering the client with warmth.

Some if these things can be used awarely at times, but appropriateness is all.

4   *Keeping track of the client*

Not ignoring signs or marks of success. Building upon good rapport. Keeping movement going, keeping interaction alive. Not changing direction before the vein has been exhausted. Not taking client away from important material. Not taking client to less appropriate level of working. Staying with the client, and encouraging the client to stay with the client.

5   *Making good interventions*

Appropriate to client and situation and timed well. Having a sufficient repertoire of skills. Ability to take risks when appropriate. Balance between important opposites, such as:

- circling round and homing in;
- active and passive (doing and not doing);
- hard and soft;
- support and confrontation;
- raising anxiety and inducing calm;
- warmth and coolness;
- facilitation and teaching; and
- present time and past distress.

6   *Long-term considerations*

Regularity of practitioner's own personal growth work. Regularity of practitioner's own supervision, whether traditional or by peer review. Awareness of when the practitioner needs extra help, nourishment, deeper work, etc. and ability to get it. Ability to handle transference, resistance, etc. Ability to grit one's teeth and hang on where necessary. Having a coherent theoretical rationale, and being able to modify this when appropriate.

Note – it is important that these are all means rather than ends. It is tempting to put in things such as:

- produce a breakthrough in client;
- cure client;
- enlighten client;
- get client to go from adjustment to ecstasy;
- ability to facilitate client change of self-direction; and

- ability to get client catharsis/insight/body change/pivotal attitude change.

But these are all, ultimately, things the client does, rather than things the therapist or counsellor does. What I think works on a list such as this is to stick to things that the therapist does.

Appendix 6
Dangers and traps

There are a number of traps it is easy to fall into when working with the body.

- *The destroy-the-defence game*
  Always keep in touch with what the client is really ready for, and don't push on at a pace which is fine for you but too much for the client. Don't pull green apples.
- *The flying chair*
  Be careful that you only use techniques you are really familiar with yourself. Otherwise you may release much more energy than you expect, frightening yourself and the client.
- *Flying high without ground control*
  It is important to be grounded when working with high-energy techniques. One good rule, for example, is to keep eye contact at all times, and not to let the client go off into unknown spaces.
- *Liberated soul for a day*
  Pushing for peak experiences without working through all the problems and impasses of ordinary therapy can produce experiences, all right, but they do not last. It is better to work gradually through, arriving at peak experiences in their natural order.
- *The laying on of the trip*
  Don't get too enthusiastic about a method which works well with one person. It is not necessarily the best thing for the next person. Take your cue from the client, not from the last workshop you went to.
- *My guru is better than your guru*
  Don't be intolerant of other systems than the one you learned first or best. Every approach is good for some people and not for others.

Bibliography

Adamson, F. (2011) 'The tapestry of my approach to transformational learning in supervision', in R. Shohet (ed.) *Supervision as transformation: a passion for learning*, London: Jessica Kingsley.

Allen, M. H. (1982) 'Transilience – a new name for a reality experience', *Association for Transpersonal Psychology Newsletter*, Spring issue.

Anthony, D., Ecker, B. and Wilber, K. (1987) *Spiritual choices*, New York: Paragon House.

Aponte, J. F. and Lyons, M. J. (1980) 'Supervision in community settings: concepts, methods and issues', in A. K. Hess (ed.) *Psychotherapy supervision*, New York: John Wiley & Sons.

Argyle, M. (1967) *The psychology of interpersonal behaviour*, Harmondsworth: Penguin.

Argyris, C. (1971) *Intervention theory and method*, Reading: Addison-Wesley.

Assagioli, R. (1975) *Psychosynthesis: a manual of principles and techniques*, London: Turnstone Books.

Assagioli, R. (1991) *Transpersonal development*, London: Crucible.

Bakhtin, M. M. (1981) *The dialogic imagination: four essays*, Austin, TX: University of Texas Press.

Balint, M. (1968) *The basic fault*, London: Tavistock.

Bambling, M. (2014) 'Creating positive outcomes in clinical supervision', in C. E. Watkins and D. L. Milne (eds) *The Wiley international handbook of clinical supervision*, Chichester: Wiley-Blackwell.

Bandler, R. and Grinder, J. (1975) *The structure of magic* (Vol. 1), Palo Alto, CA: Science and Behaviour Books.

Bandler, R. and Grinder, J. (1979) *Frogs into princes: neuro linguistic programming*, Moab, UT: Real People Press.

Barnett, L. and Madison, G. (2012) *Existential therapy: legacy, vibrancy and dialogue*, Hove: Routledge.

Bartholomew, K. (1997) 'Adult attachment processes: individual and couple perspectives', *British Journal of Medical Psychology*, 70(3), 249–63.

Bateson, G. (1972) *Steps to an ecology of mind*, New York: Ballantine.

Beahrs, J. O. (1982) *Unity and multiplicity*, New York: Brunner/Mazel.

Beck, A. T. (1979) *Cognitive therapy and the emotional disorders*, New York: Meridian.

Beckwith, L. (1972) 'Relationship between infants' social behaviour and their mothers' behaviour', *Child Development*, 43(2); 397–411.

Beisser, A. (1972) 'The paradoxical theory of change', in J. Fagan and I. L. Shepherd (eds) *Gestalt therapy now*, New York: Harper.

Belson, W. (1975) *Juvenile theft: the causal factors*, New York: Harper & Row.

Benson, L. (1974) *Images, heroes and self-perception: the struggle for identity – from mask-wearing to authenticity*, Englewood Cliffs, NJ: Prentice Hall.

Bentz, V. M. and Shapiro, J. J. (1998) *Mindful inquiry in social research*, London: Sage.

Berger, A. S. (2010) 'Practising death: alternate views', *The Journal of Transpersonal Psychology*, 42(1), 48–60.

Berke, J. H. (1979) *I haven't had to go mad here*, Harmondsworth: Penguin.

Berman, J. S. and Norton, N. C. (1985) 'Does professional training make a therapist more effective?', *Psychological Bulletin*, 98(2) 401–7.

Berne, E. (1961) *Transactional analysis in psychotherapy*, New York: Grove Press.

Berne, E. (1972) *What do you say after you say hello?*, New York: Grove Press.

Bloom, W. (1998) *Working with angels, fairies and nature spirits*, London: BCA.

Bloomgarden, A. and Mennuti, R. B. (eds)(2009) *Psychotherapist revealed: therapists speak about self-disclosure in psychotherapy*, Hove: Routledge.

Blyth, E. and Landau, R. (2009) *Faith and fertility: attitudes towards reproductive practices in different religions from ancient to modern times*, London: Jessica Kingsley.

Boadella, D. (1988) *Biosynthesis*, Milton Keynes: Open University Press.

Bogart, V. (2007) *Explore the undiscovered you*, Walnut Creek, CA: Baskin Publishing.

Boorstein, S. (ed.)(1996) *Transpersonal psychotherapy* (2nd edn), Albany, NY: State University of New York Press.

Bott, D. and Howard, P. (2014) 'The drama of the therapeutic encounter: a cross-modality approach', in D. Charura and S. Paul (eds) *The therapeutic relationship handbook: theory and practice*, Maidenhead: Open University Press.

Boyesen, G. (1970) 'Experiences with dynamic relaxation', *Energy & Character*, 1(1), 21–30.

Boyle, M. (1996) 'Schizophrenia: the fallacy of diagnosis', *Changes*, 14(1), 5–13.

Boyle, M. (2002) *Schizophrenia: a scientific delusion?* (2nd edn), Hove: Routledge.

Brammer, L. M., Shostrom, E. L. and Abrego, P. J. (1989) *Therapeutic psychology: fundamentals of counseling and psychotherapy* (5th edn), Englewood Cliffs, NJ: Prentice Hall.

Braud, W. and Anderson, R. (1998) *Transpersonal research methods for the social sciences: honoring human experience*, London: Sage.

Brazier, D. (1991) *A guide to psychodrama*, London: AHP(B).

Bromberg, P. M. (2004) 'Standing in the spaces: the multiplicity of self and the psychoanalytic relationship', in H. J. M. Hermans and G. Dimaggio (eds) *The dialogical self in therapy*, London: Brunner-Routledge.

Broughton, J. (1975) 'The development of natural epistemology in adolescence and early adulthood', Harvard: unpublished doctoral dissertation.

Brown, J. and Mowbray, R. (1990) 'Whither the human potential movement', *Self & Society*, 18(4), 32–5.

Brown, J. and Mowbray, R. (1994) 'Primal integration', in D. Jones (ed.) *Innovative therapy: a handbook*, Buckingham: Open University Press.

Brown, P. (1974) *Toward a Marxist psychology*, New York: Harper Colophon.

Buber, M. (1961) *Tales of the Hasidim: the early masters*, New York: Schocken.

Buber, M. (1963) *Pointing the way*, New York: Harper Torchbooks.

Buber, M. (1965) 'Dialogue between Martin Buber and Carl Rogers', in M. Friedman (ed.) *Man and the knowledge of man*, New York: Harper & Row.

Bugental, J. F. T. (1978) *Psychotherapy and process: the fundamentals of an existential-humanistic approach*, Reading: Addison-Wesley.

Bugental, J. F. T. (1981) *The search for authenticity* (Enlarged edition), New York: Irvington.

Bugental, J. F. T. (1987) *The art of the psychotherapist*, New York: W. W. Norton.

Bugental, J. F. T. (1999) *Psychotherapy isn't what you think*, Phoenix, AZ: Zeig, Tucker & Co.

Cain, D. J. (2002) 'Defining characteristics, history, and evolution of humanistic psychotherapies', in D. J. Cain (ed.) *Humanistic psychotherapies: handbook of research and practice*, Washington, DC: APA.

Campbell, J. (1990) *Transformations of myth through time*, New York: Harper & Row.

Chamberlain, D. (1998) *The mind of your newborn baby*, Berkeley, CA: North Atlantic Books.

Cherniss, C. (1980) *Staff burnout: job stress in the human services*, Beverley Hills, CA: Sage.

Cherniss, C. and Egnatios, E. (1978) 'Clinical supervision in community mental health', *Social Work*, 23, 219–23.

Chesler, P. (1972) *Women and madness*, New York: Avon.

Clarkson, P. (1989) *Gestalt counselling in action*, London: Sage.

Clarkson, P. (1992) *Transactional analysis therapy: an integrated approach*, London: Routledge.

Clarkson, P. (1996) *The bystander*, London: Whurr.

Clarkson, P. (2003) *The therapeutic relationship* (2nd edn), London: Whurr.

Clements, J., Ettling, D., Jenett, D. and Shields, L. (1998) 'Organic research: feminine spirituality meets personal research', in W. Braud and R. Anderson (eds) *Transpersonal research methods for the social sciences: honoring human experience*, Thousand Oaks, CA: Sage.

Cohen, J. M. and Phipps, J-F. (1979) *The common experience*, London: Rider & Co.

Cohen, R. J. and DeBetz, B. (1977) 'Responsive supervision of the psychiatric resident and clinical psychology intern', *American Journal of Psychoanalysis*, 37(1), 51–64.

Cohn, H. W. (1997) *Existential thought and therapeutic practice*, London: Sage.

Connell, R. W. (1987) *Gender and power*, Cambridge: Polity Press.

Console, W. A., Simons, R. C. and Rubinstein, M. (1978) *The first encounter: the beginnings in psychotherapy*, New York: Jason Aronson.

Cook-Greuter, S. R. (1999) *Postautonomous ego development: a study of its nature and measurement*, Harvard, MA: Integral Publishers.

Cooper, M. (2003) *Existential therapies*, London: Sage.

Corriere, R. and Hart, J. (1978) *The dream makers*, New York: Bantam.

Corsini, R. (ed.)(1981) *Handbook of innovative psychotherapies*, Chichester: John Wiley.

Costello, T. W., Costello, J. T. and Holmes, D. A. (1995) *Abnormal psychology*, London: Harper Collins.

Crabtree, A. (1988) *Multiple man*, London: Grafton Books.

Cranmer, D. (1994) 'Core energetics', in D. Jones (ed.) *Innovative therapy: a handbook*, Buckingham: Open University Press.

Crenshaw, D. A. and Garbarino, J. (2007) 'The hidden dimensions: profound sorrow and buried potential in violent youth', *Journal of Humanistic Psychology*, 47(2), 160–74.

Cunningham, I. (1988) 'Interactive holistic research: researching self-managed learning', in P. Reason (ed.) *Human inquiry in action: developments in new paradigm research*, London: Sage.

Daniels, A. K. (1970) 'The social construction of military psychiatric diagnoses', in H. P. Dreitzel (ed.) *Recent sociology No. 2*, London: Collier-Macmillan.

Dansky, S., Knoebel, A. and Pitchford, K. (1977) 'The effeminist manifesto', in J. Snodgrass (ed.) *A book of readings for men against sexism*, New York: Times Change Press.

Davies, D. and Neal, C. (2000) *Pink therapy Vol. 2: therapeutic perspectives on working with lesbian, gay and bisexual clients*, Buckingham: Open University Press.

DeCarvalho, R. J. (1991) *The founders of humanistic psychology*, New York: Praeger.

Deida, D. (2004) *Way of the superior man*, Boulder, CO: Sounds True.

Denzin, N. K. (1987) 'A phenomenology of the emotionally divided self', in K. Yardley and T. Honess (eds) *Self and identity*, Chichester: John Wiley.

Dobson, D. and Dobson, K. S. (2009) *Evidence-based practice of cognitive-behavioural therapy*, New York: The Guilford Press.

Dreyfuss, A. and Feinstein, A. D. (1977) 'My body is me: body-based approaches to personal enrichment', in B. McWaters (ed.) *Humanistic perspectives: current trends in psychology*, Monterey, CA: Brooks/Cole.

Dryden, W. (ed.)(1985) *Therapists' dilemmas*, London: Harper & Row.

Dryden, W. (1991) *Dryden on counselling Vol. 3: training and supervision (Chapter 6)*, London: Whurr.

Durlack, J. A. (1979) 'Comparative effectiveness of paraprofessional and professional helpers', *Psychological Bulletin*, 86(1), 80–92.

Duval, S. and Wicklund, R. A. (1972) *A theory of objective self-awareness*, New York: Academic Press.

Edinger, E. (1960) 'The ego-self paradox', *The Journal of Analytic Psychology*, 5(1), 3–18.

Egan, G. (2009) *The skilled helper* (International edition), Monterey, CA: Wadsworth.

Eisler, R. (1995) *Sacred pleasure: sex, myth and the politics of the body*, Shaftesbury: Element.

Ekstein, R. (1969) 'Concerning the teaching and learning of psychoanalysis', *Journal of the American Psychoanalytic Association*, 17(3), 312–332.

Ekstein, R. and Wallerstein, R. S. (1972) *The teaching and learning of psychotherapy* (2nd edn), New York: International Universities Press.

Ellis, A. (1970) *The essence of rational psychotherapy*, New York: Institute for Rational Living.

Ellis, A. (1995) 'Fundamentals of rational-emotive behaviour therapy for the 1990s', in W. Dryden (ed.) *Rational-emotive behavioral therapy: a reader*, London: Sage.

Enright, J. (1972) 'Awareness training in the mental health professions', in J. Fagan and I. L. Shepherd (eds) *Gestalt therapy now*, Harmondsworth: Penguin.

Epstein, M. (1999) *Going to pieces without falling apart: a Buddhist perspective on wholeness*, London: Harper Collins.

Erickson, B. (1993) *Helping men change: the role of the female therapist*, Newbury Park, CA: Sage.

Erikson, E. (1965) *Childhood and society*, Harmondsworth: Penguin.

Ernst Jr, F. H. (1971) 'The OK Corral: the grid for get-on-with', *Transactional Analysis Journal*, 1(4), 33–42.

Ernst, S. and Goodison, L. (1981) *In our own hands*, London: The Womens Press.

Esterson, A. (1972) *The leaves of spring: a study in the dialectics of madness*, Harmondsworth: Penguin.

Fadiman, J. and Kornfeld, A. (2013) 'Psychedelic-induced experiences', in H. L. Friedman and G. Hartelius (eds) *The Wiley-Blackwell handbook of transpersonal psychology*, Chichester: Wiley-Blackwell.

Fairbairn, W. R. D. (1952) *Psychoanalytic studies of the personality*, London: Tavistock.

Farber, B. A. (2006) *Self-disclosure in psychotherapy*, New York: The Guilford Press.

Farrelly, F. and Brandsma, J. (1989) *Provocative therapy*, Capitola, CA: Meta Publications.

Federn, P. (1952) *Ego psychology and the psychoses*, New York: Basic Books.

Feher, L. (1980) *The psychology of birth*, London: Souvenir Press.

Ferrucci, P. (1982) *What we may be: the visions and techniques of psychosynthesis*, Wellingborough: Turnstone Press.

Firestone, S. (1972) *The dialectic of sex*, New York: Bantam.

Firman, J. and Gila, A. (1997) *The primal wound: a transpersonal view of trauma, addiction and growth*, Albany, NY: SUNY Press.

Firman, J. and Gila, A. (2002) *Psychosynthesis: a psychology of the spirit*, Albany, NY: SUNY Press.

Fisch, R., Weakland, J. and Segal, L. (1982) *The tactics of change*, San Francisco, CA: Jossey-Bass.

Fiske, D. W. and Maddi, S. R. (eds)(1961) *Functions of varied experience*, Homewood, IL: The Dorsey Press.

Forman, M. D. (2010) *A guide to integral psychotherapy: complexity, integration and spirituality in practice*, Albany, NY: SUNY Press.

Frankland, A. (1981) 'Mistaken seduction', *New Forum*, 7(4).

Frankland, A. (1996) 'Exploring accreditation', in S. Palmer, S. Dainow and P. Milner (eds) *Counselling: the BAC counselling reader*, London: Sage, pp. 412–25.

Fransella, F. (1972) *Personal change and reconstruction*, London: Academic Press.

Freedman, J. and Combs, G. (1996) *Narrative therapy: the social construction of preferred realities*, New York: W. W. Norton.

Freeman, H. E. and Giovannoni, J. M. (1969) 'Social psychology of mental health', in G. Lindzey and E. Aronson (eds) *The handbook of social psychology* (2nd edn) Vol. 5, Reading: Addison-Wesley.

Freud, S. (1923) *The Ego and the Id and other works* (CW19), London: Hogarth Press.

Freudenberger, H. J. (1975) 'The staff burnout syndrome in alternative institutions', *Psychotherapy: Theory, Research and Practice*, 12(1), 35–45.

Friedenberg, E. Z. (1973) *Laing*, London: Fontana/Collins.

Friedman, H. L. and Hartelius, G. (2013) *The Wiley-Blackwell handbook of transpersonal psychology*, Chichester: Wiley-Blackwell.

Friedman, M. (1991) *The worlds of existentialism: a critical reader*, New York: Prometheus Books.

Fromm, E. (1941) *Escape from freedom*, New York: Farrar, Strauss & Giroux.

Fromm-Reichmann, F. (1950) *Principles of intensive psychotherapy*, Chicago: University of Chicago Press.

Gabriel, L. (2005) *Speaking the unspeakable: the ethics of dual relationships in counselling and psychotherapy*, Hove: Routledge.

Gabriel, L. and Casemore, R. (eds)(2009) *Relational ethics in practice: narratives from counselling and psychotherapy*, Hove: Routledge.

Gallagher, S. (1997) 'Mutual enlightenment: recent phenomenology in cognitive science', *Journal of Consciousness Studies*, 4(3), 195–214.

Gardner, L. H. (1971) 'The therapeutic relationship under varying conditions of race', *Psychotherapy: Theory, Research and Practice*, 8(1), 78–87.

Garfield, P. L. (1976) *Creative dreaming*, London: Futura Publications.

Garfield, S. L. (1978) 'Research on client variables in psychotherapy', in S. L. Garfield and A. E. Bergin (eds) *Handbook of psychotherapy and behaviour change* (2nd edn), New York: John Wiley & Sons.

Garfield, S. L. (1979) *Training and outcome in psychotherapy*, New York: BMA Audio Cassettes.

Garfield, S. L. and Bergin, A. A. (eds)(1978) *Handbook of psychotherapy and behaviour change: an empirical analysis* (2nd edn), New York: John Wiley & Sons.

Gazzaniga, M. (1985) *The social brain*, New York: Basic Books.

Gelb, L. (1973) 'Masculinity-femininity: a study in imposed inequality', in J. B. Miller (ed.) *Psychoanalysis and women*, Harmondsworth: Penguin.

Gendlin, E. (1969) 'Focussing', *Psychotherapy: Theory, Research and Practice*, 6(1), 4–15.

Gendlin, E. T. (1996) *Focusing-oriented psychotherapy: a manual of the experiential method*, New York: The Guilford Press.

Gergen, K. J. (1972) 'Multiple identity', *Psychology Today*, 5(12), 31–5.

Gill, M. M., Newman, R., Redlich, F. C. and Sommers, M. (1954) *The initial interview in psychiatric practice*, New York: International Universities Press.

Giorgi, A. (ed.)(1975) *Duquesne studies in phenomenological psychology* (Vol. 2), Pittsburgh, PA: Duquesne University Press.

Glauber, I. P. (1953) 'The nature of stuttering and the treatment of stuttering', *Social Casework*, 34.

Goffman, E. (1974) *Frame analysis*, New York: Harper & Row.

Goldberg, C. (1995) 'The daimonic development of the malevolent personality', *Journal of Humanistic Psychology*, 35(3), 7–36.

Goleman, D. (1978) *The varieties of the meditative experience*, London: Rider & Co.

Gove, W. R. (1975) *The labelling of deviance*, Beverly Hills, CA: Sage.

Greenberg, L. S., Watson, J. C. and Lietaer, G. (eds)(1998) *Handbook of experiential psychotherapy*, New York: The Guilford Press.

Greenley, J. R. (1975) 'Alternate views of the psychiatrist's role', in T. J. Scheff (ed.) *Labelling madness*, Englewood Cliffs, NJ: Prentice Hall.

Greenwald, H. (1974) *Direct decision therapy*, San Diego, CA: Edits.

Gregg, G. S. (1991) *Self-representation: life narrative in identity and ideology*, New York: Greenwood Press.

Grinder, J. and Bandler, R. (1981) *Trance-formations*, Moab, UT: Real People Press.

Grof, S. (1975) *Realms of the human unconscious*, New York: The Viking Press.

Grof, S. (1980) *LSD psychotherapy*, Pomona, CA: Hunter House.

Grof, S. (1988) *The adventure of self-discovery*, Albany, NY: SUNY Press.

Grof, S. (1992) *The holotropic mind: the three levels of human consciousness and how they shape our lives*, San Francisco, CA: HarperOne.

Grove, D. J. and Panzer, B. I. (1989) *Resolving traumatic memories: metaphors and symbols in psychotherapy*, New York: Irvington.

Guntrip, H. (1971) *Psychoanalytic theory, therapy and the self*, New York: Basic Books.

Gurdjieff, G. (1950) *Meetings with remarkable men*, London: Routledge.

Hall, B. L. (1975) 'Participatory research: an approach for change', *Convergence: An International Journal of Adult Education*, 8(2), 24–31.

Hall, J. (1977) *Clinical uses of dreams: Jungian interpretations and enactments*, New York: Grune & Stratton.

Hampden-Turner, C. (1977) *Sane asylum*, New York: William Morrow & Co.

Hannah, B. (1981) *Encounters with the soul: active imagination*, Boston, MA: Sigo Press.

Harding, E. (1965) *The I and the Not-I*, Princeton, NJ: Princeton University Press.

Hardy, G. E., Aldridge, J., Davidson, C., Rowe, C. and Reilly, S. (2004) 'Assessing and formulating attachment issues and styles in psychotherapy', *British Journal of Psychotherapy*, 20(4), 493–512.

Harré, R. (1979) *Social being*, Oxford: Blackwell.

Harris, T. A. (1973) *I'm OK, you're OK*, London: Pan Books.

Hart, T. (2000) 'Deep empathy', in T. Hart, K. Puhakka and P. Nelson (eds) *Transpersonal knowing: exploring the horizon of consciousness*, Albany, NY: SUNY Press.

Hartley, L. (ed.)(2009) *Contemporary body psychotherapy: the Chiron approach*, Hove: Routledge.

Hattie, J. A., Sharpley, C. F. and Rogers, H. J. (1984) 'Comparative effectiveness of professional and paraprofessional helpers', *Psychological Bulletin*, 95, 534–41.

Haugh, S. and Merry, T. (eds)(2001) *Empathy (Rogers' therapeutic conditions: evolution, theory & practice)* (Vol. 2), Ross-on-Wye: PCCS Books.

Hawkins, P. (1990a) 'Registration of psychotherapists – whither, why and how', *Self & Society*, 18(1), 10–12.

Hawkins, P. (1990b) 'A response to John Heron, David Kalisch and Roger Horrocks', *Self & Society*, 18(4), 30–31.

Hawkins, P. and Shapiro, R. (2012) *Supervision in the helping professions* (4th edn), Maidenhead: Open University Press.

Heinl, P. (2001) *Splintered innocence*, Hove: Brunner-Routledge.

Hendricks, M. (2002) 'Focusing-oriented/experiential psychotherapy', in D. J. Cain and J. Seeman (eds) *Humanistic psychotherapies: handbook of research and practice*, Washington, DC: APA.

Hermans, H. J. M. (1999) 'The polyphony of the mind: a multi–voiced and dialogical self', in J. Rowan and M. Cooper (eds*) The plural self: multiplicity in everyday life*, London: Sage.

Hermans, H. J. M. (2004) 'The dialogical self: between exchange and power', in H. J. M. Hermans and G. Dimaggio (eds) *The dialogical self in psychotherapy*, Hove: Brunner-Routledge.

Hermans, H. J. M. and Gieser, T. (eds) (2012) *Handbook of dialogical self theory*, Cambridge, UK: Cambridge University Press.

Heron, J. (1979) *Assessment revisited*, Guildford: HPRP, University of Surrey.

Heron, J. (1981) 'Experiential research methodology', in P. Reason and J. Rowan (eds) *Human inquiry: a sourcebook of new paradigm research*, Chichester: John Wiley.

Heron, J. (1990) 'The politics of transference', *Self & Society*, 18(1), 17–23.

Heron, J. (1996) *Co-operative inquiry*, London: Sage.

Hilgard, E. R. (1986) *Divided consciousness*, New York: John Wiley.

Hill, C. E. (1989) *Therapist techniques and client outcomes*, Newbury Park, CA: Sage.

Hillman, J. (1979) *The dream and the under-world*, New York: Harper Colophon.

Hillman, J. (1989) *The essential James Hillman: a blue fire*, London: Routledge.

Hobson, B. (1985) *Forms of feeling: the heart of psychotherapy*, London: Tavistock.

Hogan, D. (1979) *The regulation of psychotherapists* (4 vols), Cambridge, MA: Ballinger.

Holmes, J. (2001) *The search for the secure base: attachment theory and psychoanalysis*, Hove: Brunner-Routledge.

House, R. and Hall, J. (1991) 'Peer accreditation: within a humanistic framework?', *Self & Society*, 19(2), 33–6.

Houston, J. (1996) *A mythic life: learning to live our greater story*, San Francisco, CA: HarperSanFrancisco.

Howard, A. (1996) *Challenges to counselling and psychotherapy*, Basingstoke: Macmillan.

Hycner, R. (1993, 1991) *Between person and person: toward a dialogical psychotherapy*, Highland, NY: Gestalt Journal Press.

Ingersoll, R. E. and Zeitler, D. M. (2010) *Integral psychotherapy: inside out/outside in*, Albany, NY: SUNY Press.

Ingram, B. L. (2012) *Clinical case formulations: matching the integrative treatment plan to the client* (2nd edn), Hoboken, NJ: Wiley.

Jackins, H. (1965) *The human side of human beings*, Seattle, WA: Rational Island.

Janov, A. (1973) *The primal scream*, London: Abacus.

Janov, A. and Holden, M. (1977) *Primal man*, London: Abacus.

Jaspers, K. (1931) Quoted in Maurice Friedman (ed.) *The worlds of existentialism: a critical reader*, Chicago, IL: University of Chicago Press.

Jennings, J. L. (1992) 'Husserl revisited: the forgotten distinction between psychology and phenomenology', in R. B. Miller (ed.) *The restoration of dialogue: readings in the philosophy of clinical psychology*, Washington, DC: APA.

Joffe, J. M. (1969) *Prenatal determinants of behaviour*, Oxford: Pergamon Press.

Johnstone, L. and Dallos, R. (2014) *Formulation in psychology and psychotherapy: making sense of people's problems* (2nd edn), Hove: Routledge.

Jung, C. G. (1928) 'The structure of the psyche', in *CW8*, London: Routledge.

Jung, C. G. (2009) *The red book*, London: W. W. Norton.

Kalisch, D. (1990a) 'Professionalisation – a rebel view', *Self & Society*, 18(1), 24–9.

Kalisch, D. (1990b) 'The living tradition and the division of the spoils', *Self & Society*, 18(4), 36–7.

Kapelovitz, L. H. (1976) *To love and to work: a demonstration and discussion of psychotherapy*, New York: Grune & Stratton.

Karp, M., Holmes, P. and Tauvon, K. B. (1998) *The handbook of psychodrama*, London: Routledge.

Kauffman, K. and New, C. (2004) *Co-counselling: the theory and practice of re-evaluation counselling*, Hove: Routledge.

Kelly, G. (1955) *The psychology of personal constructs*, New York: Norton.

Kihlstrom, J. F. and Cantor, N. (1984) 'Mental representations of the self', in L. Berkowitz (ed.) *Advances in experimental social psychology* (Vol. 17), New York: Academic Press.

Kirschenbaum, H. and Henderson, V. L. (eds)(1990) *Carl Rogers dialogues*, London: Constable.

Klein, M. (1948) *Contributions to psychoanalysis*, London: Hogarth Press.

Knox, R., Murphy, D., Wiggins, S. and Cooper, M. (eds)(2013) *Relational depth: new perspectives and developments*, Basingstoke: Palgrave Macmillan.

Knutson, J. K. (ed.)(1973) *Handbook of political psychology*, San Francisco, CA: Jossey-Bass.

Kohlberg, L. (1969) 'Stage and sequence: the cognitive-developmental approach to socialization', in D. Goslin (ed.) *Handbook of socialization theory and research*, Chicago, IL: Rand McNally.

Korchin, S. J. (1976) *Modern clinical psychology*, New York: Basic Books.

Krim, S. (1960) 'The insanity bit', in S. Krim (ed.) *The beats*, New York: Gold Medal.

Kupers, T. A. (1993) *Revisioning men's lives: gender, intimacy and power*, New York: The Guilford Press.

Labov, W. (1972) 'The logic of nonstandard English', in P. P. Giglioli (ed.) *Language and social context*, Harmondsworth: Penguin.

Laing, R. D. (1965) *The divided self*, Harmondsworth: Penguin.

Laing, R. D. (1967) *The politics of experience*, Harmondsworth: Penguin.

Laing, R. D. (1976) *The facts of life*, Harmondsworth: Penguin.

Laing, R. D. (1982) *The voice of experience*, Harmondsworth: Penguin.

Laing, R. D. and Esterson, A. (1970) *Sanity, madness and the family*, Harmondsworth: Penguin.

Lake, F. (1966) *Clinical theology*, London: Darton, Longman & Todd.

Lake, F. (1980) *Studies in constricted confusion: exploration of a pre- and perinatal paradigm*, Nottingham: Clinical Theology Association.

Lawley, J. and Tompkins, P. (2000) *Metaphors in mind*, London: The Developing Company Press.

Lawlis, G. F. (2013) 'Modern miracles from ancient medicine: transpersonal medicine approaches', in H. L. Friedman and G. Hartelius (eds) *The Wiley-Blackwell handbook of transpersonal psychology*, Chichester: Wiley-Blackwell, pp. 640–51.

Lazarus, A. A. and Zur, O. (eds)(2002) *Dual relationships and psychotherapy*, New York: Springer.

Lester, D. (1995) *Theories of personality: a systems approach*, Washington, DC: Taylor & Francis.

Levant, R. F. and Pollack, W. S. (eds)(1995) *A new psychology of men*, New York: Basic Books.

Lewin, K. (1936) *Topological psychology*, New York: McGraw-Hill.

Linington, M. (2003) 'Book Review', *British Journal of Psychotherapy*, 19(4), 531–4.

Loevinger, J. (1976) *Ego development*, San Francisco, CA: Jossey-Bass.

Loewenthal, D. and Samuels, A. (eds)(2014) *Relational psychotherapy, psychoanalysis and counselling: appraisals and reappraisals*, Hove: Routledge.

Lowen, A. (1967) *The betrayal of the body*, New York: Macmillan.

Lowen, A. (1976) *Bioenergetics*, London: Coventure.

Luria, A. R. (1969) 'The origin and cerebral organization of man's conscious action', An evening lecture to the XIX International Congress of Psychology.

McAdams, D. P. (1985) 'The "Imago": A key narrative component of identity', in P. Shaver (ed.) *Self, situations and social behaviour*, Beverly Hills, CA: Sage.

McCurdy, A. (1985) 'Establishing and maintaining the analytical structure', in M. Stein (ed.) *Jungian analysis*, Boston, MA: Shambhala.

Macecevic, J. P. (2008) *Embodied transcendental empathy: a phenomenological study of psychotherapists' transpersonal embodied experiences in therapeutic relationship*, Institute of Transpersonal Psychology dissertation. http://pqdt open.proquest.com (225 pages).

MacLean, P. D. (1973) *A triune concept of the brain and behaviour*, Toronto: University of Toronto Press.

McLellan, B. (1995) *Beyond psychoppression: a feminist alternative therapy*, North Melbourne: Spinifex Press.

McNeilly, C. L. and Howard, K. I. (1991) 'The effects of psychotherapy: A reevaluation based on dosage', *Psychotherapy Research*, 1(1), 74–8.

Madison, P. (1969) *Personality development in college*, Reading, MA: Addison-Wesley.

Maguire, K. (2001) 'Working with survivors of torture and extreme experiences', in S. King-Spooner and C. Newnes (eds) *Spirituality and psychotherapy*, Ross-on-Wye: PCCS Books, pp. 122–36.

Mahler, M. S., Pine, F. and Bergman, A. (1975) *The psychological birth of the human infant*, London: Hutchinson.

Mahrer, A. R. (1985) *Psychotherapeutic change: an alternative approach to meaning and measurement*, New York: W. W. Norton.

Mahrer, A. R. (1986) *Therapeutic experiencing*, New York: W. W. Norton.

Mahrer, A. R. (1989) *Experiencing*, Ottawa: University of Ottawa Press.

Mahrer, A. R. (1996) *The complete guide to experiential psychotherapy*, New York: John Wiley & Sons.

Mahrer, A. R., Dessaules, A., Nadler, W. P., Gervaize, P. A. and Stirner, I. (1987) 'Good and very good moments in psychotherapy: content, distribution and facilitation', *Psychotherapy*, 24, 7–14.

Mair, M. (1977) 'The community of self', in D. Bannister (ed.) *New perspectives in personal construct theory*, London: Academic Press.

Malan, D. H. (1979) *Individual psychotherapy and the science of psychodynamics*, London: Butterworth.

Marina, N. (1982) 'Restructuring of cognitive-affective structure: a central point of change after psychotherapy', Brunel: Unpublished doctoral dissertation.

Markus, H. (1977) 'Self-schemata and processing information about the self', *Journal of Personality and Social Psychology*, 35(2), 63–78.

Markus, H. and Nurius, P. (1987) 'Possible selves: the interface between motivation and the self-concept', in K. Yardley and T. Honess (eds) *Self and identity: psychosocial perspectives*, Chichester: John Wiley.

Marlan, S. (1981) 'Depth consciousness', in R. S. Valle and R. von Eckartsberg (eds) *The metaphors of consciousness*, New York: Plenum Press.

Marshall, W. R. and Confer, W. N. (1980) 'Psychotherapy supervision: super-visees' perspective', in A. K. Hess (ed.) *Psychotherapy supervision*, New York: John Wiley & Sons.

Martin, D. (2014) 'Hakomi in my life', in C. Eigen (ed.) *Inner dialogue in everyday life*, London: Jessica Kingsley.

Martindale, C. (1980) 'Subselves: the internal representation of situational and personal dispositions', in L. Wheeler (ed.) *Review of personality and social psychology* (Vol. 1), Beverly Hills, CA: Sage.

Maruyama, M. (1978) 'Endogenous research and polyocular anthropology', in R. E. Holloman and S. Arutionov (eds) *Perspectives on ethnicity*, The Hague: Mouton.

Maslow, A. H. (1968) *Toward a psychology of being*, New York: Van Nostrand Reinhold.

Maslow, A. H. (1973) *The farther reaches of human nature*, Harmondsworth: Penguin.

Maslow, A. H. (1987) *Motivation and personality* (3rd edn), New York: Harper & Row.

Masson, J. (1989) *Against therapy*, London: Collins.

Masters, R. and Houston, J. (1978) *Listening to the body*, New York: Delacorte Press.

Matteson, D. R. (2008) *Exploring the spiritual: paths for counsellors and psychotherapists*, Abingdon: Routledge.

May, R. (1969) *Love and will*, New York: W. W. Norton.

May, R. (1983) *The discovery of being*, New York: W. W. Norton.

Meade, M. (1993) *Men and the water of life*, San Francisco, CA: HarperSanFrancisco.

Mearns, D. and Dryden, W. (1990) *Experiences of counselling in action*, London: Sage.

Mearns, D. and Thorne, B. (2000) *Person-centred therapy today*, London: Sage.

Metzner, R. (1986) *Opening to inner light: the transformation of human nature and consciousness*, Los Angeles, CA: Tarcher.

Middlebrook, P. N. (1974) *Social psychology and modern life*, New York: Knopf.

Miller, A. (1985) *Thou shalt not be aware*, London: Pluto Press.

Miller, J. B. (ed.)(1974) *Psychoanalysis and women*, Harmondsworth: Penguin.

Miller, J. B. (1978) *Toward a new psychology of women*, Harmondsworth: Penguin.

Miller, N. (1973) 'Letter to her psychiatrist', in P. Brown (ed.) *Radical psychology*, London: Tavistock.

Miller, S. D., Duncan, B. L. and Hubble, M. A. (1997) *Escape from Babel: toward a unifying language for psychotherapy practice*, New York: W. W. Norton.

Mindell, A. (1985) *Working with the dreaming body*, London: RKP.

Minsky, M. (1988) *The society of mind*, London: Picador.

Mitchell, J. (1975) *Psychoanalysis and feminism*, Harmondsworth: Penguin.

Miyuki, M. (1979) 'A Jungian approach to the pure land practice of Nien-fo', Paper presented to the Sixth Annual Conference of Jungian Analysts, Asilomar.

Montagu, A. (1978) *Touching* (2nd edn), New York: Harper & Row.

Moreno, J. L. (1974) 'The Viennese origins of the encounter movement, paving the way for existentialism, group psychotherapy and psychodrama', in I. A. Greenberg (ed.) *Psychodrama: theory and therapy*, London: Souvenir Press.

Moss, L. E. (1981) *A woman's way: a feminist approach to body psychotherapy*, Ann Arbor, MI: University Microfilms International.

Mott, F. J. (1969) *The nature of the self*, London: The Integration Publishing Co.

Mowbray, R. (1995) *The case against psychotherapy registration*, London: Transmarginal Press.

Natterson, J. M. and Friedman, R. J. (1995) *A primer of clinical intersubjectivity*, London: Jason Aronson.

Neimeyer, R. (2009) *Constructivist psychotherapy*, Hove: Routledge.

Neugarten, B. L., Crotty, W. F. and Tobin, S. S. (1964) *Personality in middle and later life*, New York: Atherton.

Neumann, E. (1963) *The great mother: an analysis of the archetype*, Princeton, NJ: Princeton University Press.

Nichols, M. P. and Zax, M. (1977) *Catharsis in psychotherapy*, New York: Gardner Press.

Noble, E. (1993) *Primal connections*, New York: Simon & Schuster.

O'Connor, E. (1971) *Our many selves*, New York: Harper & Row.

Ornstein, R. (1986) *MultiMinds: a new way to look at human behaviour*, Boston, MA: Houghton Mifflin.

Osherson, S. (1986) *Finding our fathers*, New York: Fawcett Columbine.

Page, R. C., Weiss, J. F. and Lietaer, G. (2002) 'Humanistic group psychotherapy', in D. J. Cain and J. Seeman (eds) *Humanistic psychotherapies: handbook of research and practice*, Washington, DC: APA.

Page, S. and Wosket, V. (1994) *Supervising the counsellor: a cyclical model*, London: Routledge.

Painter, J. W. (1986) *Deep bodywork and personal development*, Mill Valley, CA: Bodymind Books.

Palmer, B. (1979) 'Learning and the group experience', in W. G. Lawrence (ed.) *Exploring individual and organizational boundaries*, Chichester: John Wiley.

Palmer, B. (1992) 'Ambiguity and paradox in group relations conferences', in M. Pines (ed.) *Bion and group psychotherapy*, London: Routledge.

Parfitt, W. (2003) *Psychosynthesis: the elements and beyond*, Glastonbury: PSAvalon.

Parloff, M. B., Waskow, I. E. and Wolfe, B. E. (1978) 'Research on therapist variables in relation to process and outcome', in S. L. Garfield and A. E. Bergin (eds) *Handbook of psychotherapy and behaviour change* (2nd edn), New York: John Wiley & Sons.

Paul, S. and Charura, D. (2015) *An introduction to the therapeutic relationship in counselling and psychotherapy*, London: Sage.

Peebles, M. J. (2012) *Beginnings: the art and science of planning psychotherapy* (2nd edn), Hove: Routledge.

Peerbolte, L. (1975) *Psychic energy in prenatal dynamics*, Wassenaar, The Netherlands: Service.

Pennington, D. (2003) *Essential personality*, London: Arnold.

Perls, F. S. (1969) *Gestalt therapy verbatim*, Moab, UT: Real People Press.

Perls, F. S. (1976) *The Gestalt approach and eyewitness to therapy*, New York: Bantam.

Perls, F. S., Hefferline, R. and Goodman, P. (1951) *Gestalt therapy*, New York: Dell.

Phillips, E. L. (1977) *Counselling and psychotherapy: a behavioural approach*, New York: John Wiley & Sons.

Pilgrim, D. (1990) 'British psychotherapy in context', in W. Dryden (ed.) *Individual therapy: a handbook*, Buckingham: Open University Press.

Polsky, N. (1969) *Hustlers, beats and others*, New York: Doubleday Anchor.

Postle, D. and Anderson, J. (1990) 'Stealing the flame', *Self & Society*, 18(1), 13–15.

Rawson, P. and Legeza, L. (1973) *Tao: the Chinese philosophy of time and change*, London: Thames & Hudson.

Reason, P. (ed.)(1988) *Human inquiry in action*, London: Sage.

Reason, P. (ed.)(1994) *Participation in human inquiry*, London: Sage.

Reason, P. and Rowan, J. (eds)(1981) *Human inquiry: a sourcebook of new paradigm research*, Chichester: John Wiley.

Redfearn, J. W. T. (1985) *My self, my many selves*, London: Academic Press.

Reeves, A. (2014) 'Research in individual therapy', in W. Dryden and A. Reeves (eds) *The handbook of individual therapy* (6th edn), London: Sage.

Reich, W. (1950) *Character analysis*, London: Vision Press.

Reik, T. (1948) *Listening with the third ear: the inner experience of a psychoanalyst*, New York: Farrar, Strauss & Giroux.

Rice, L. N. (1980) 'A client-centred approach to the supervision of psychotherapy', in A. K. Hess (ed.) *Psychotherapy supervision*, New York: John Wiley & Sons.

Riesman, D. (1954) *The lonely crowd*, New York: Doubleday.

Rioch, M. J., Coulter, W. R. and Weinberger, D. M. (1976) *Dialogues for therapists*, San Francisco, CA: Jossey-Bass.

Roberts, T. B. and Winkelman, M. J. (2013) 'Psychedelic induced transpersonal experiences, therapies, and their implications for transpersonal psychology', in H. L. Friedman and G. Hartelius (eds) *The Wiley-Blackwell handbook of transpersonal psychology*, Chichester: Wiley.

Rogers, C. R. (1961) *On becoming a person*, London: Constable.

Rogers, C. R. (1968) 'Some thoughts concerning the presuppositions of the behavioural sciences', in W. R. Coulson and C. R. Rogers (eds) *Man and the science of man*, Columbus, OH: Charles E. Merrill.

Rogers, C. R. (1978) *On personal power*, London: Constable.

Rogers, C. and Freiberg, H. J. (1994) *Freedom to learn* (3rd edn), New York: Merrill.

Rogers, T. B. (1981) 'A model of the self as an aspect of the human information processing system', in N. Cantor and J. F. Kihlstrom (eds) *Personality, cognition and social interaction*, Hillsdale, NJ: Lawrence Erlbaum.

Rolf, I. (1978) *Structural integration*, New York: Viking/Esalen.

Rosenhan, D. L. (1975) 'On being sane in insane places', in T. J. Scheff (ed.) *Labelling madness*, Englewood Cliffs, NJ: Prentice Hall.

Ross, P. (1996) 'Paperless client records', in S. Palmer, S. Dainow and P. Milner (eds) *Counselling*, London: Sage.

Rousmaniere, T. (2014) 'Using technology to enhance clinical supervision and training', in C. E. Watkins and D. L. Milne (eds) *The Wiley international handbook of clinical supervision*, Chichester: Wiley-Blackwell.

Rowan, J. (1974) 'Research as intervention', in N. Armistead (ed.) *Reconstructing social psychology*, Harmondsworth: Penguin.

Rowan, J. (1976) *The power of the group*, London: Davis-Poynter.

Rowan, J. (1978) *The structured crowd*, London: Davis-Poynter.

Rowan, J. (1990) *Subpersonalities: the people within you*, London: Routledge.

Rowan, J. (1992a) 'Integrative encounter', in W. Dryden (ed.) *Integrative and eclectic therapy: a handbook*, Buckingham: Open University Press.

Rowan, J. (1992b) 'Holistic listening', in J. Rowan (ed.) *Breakthroughs and integration in psychotherapy*, London: Whurr.

Rowan, J. (1996) 'The psychology of furniture', in S. Palmer, S. Dainow and P. Milner (eds) *Counselling: the BAC counselling reader*, London: Sage.

Rowan, J. (1997a) *Healing the male psyche: therapy as initiation*, London: Routledge.

Rowan, J. (1997b) 'Transformational research', in P. Clarkson (ed.) *Textbook of counselling psychology*, London: Sage.

Rowan, J. (1998) 'Linking: its place in therapy', *International Journal of Psychotherapy*, 3(3), 245–54.

Rowan, J. (2001) *Ordinary ecstasy: the dialectics of humanistic psychology* (3rd edn), Hove: Routledge.

Rowan, J. (2005a) *The transpersonal: spirituality in counselling and psychotherapy* (2nd edn), Hove: Routledge.

Rowan, J. (2005b) *The future of training in psychotherapy and counselling: instrumental, relational and transpersonal perspectives*, Hove: Routledge.

Rowan, J. (2008) 'The politics of psychotherapy: a gender issue', *Psychotherapy and Politics International*, 6(2), 133–42.

Rowan, J. (2010) *Personification: using the dialogical self in psychotherapy and counselling*, Hove: Routledge.

Rowan, J. (2012) 'Levels of consciousness and the Great Gap', *The British Journal of Psychotherapy Integration*, 9, 131–40.

Rowan, J. (2014) 'The transpersonal in individual therapy', in W. Dryden and A. Reeves (eds) *The handbook of individual therapy* (6th edn), London: Sage.

Rowan, J. and Jacobs, M. (2003) *The therapist's use of self*, Buckingham: Open University Press.

Rowe, D. (1978) *The experience of depression*, Chichester: John Wiley.

Russell, J. (1993) *Out of bounds: sexual exploitation in counselling and therapy*, London: Sage.

Russell, R. (1981) *Report on effective psychotherapy: legislative testimony*, New York: R. R. Latin Associates.

Sadger, I. (1941) 'Preliminary study of the psychic life of the foetus and the primary germ', *Psychoanalytic Review*, 28(3), 327–58.

Salvatore, S. and Venuleo, C. (2008) 'Understanding the role of emotion in sense-making', *Journal of Integrative Psychological and Behavioral Science*. Special Issue: Consciousness within communication: the stream of thought reconsidered, 42(1), 32–46.

Samuels, A. (1993) *The political psyche*, London: Routledge.

Samuels, A. (2001) *Politics on the couch: citizenship and the internal life*, London: Profile Books.

Sanford, N. (1981) 'A model for action research', in P. Reason and J. Rowan (eds) *Human inquiry: a sourcebook of new paradigm research*, Chichester: John Wiley.

Satir, V. (1988) *The new peoplemaking*, Mountain View, CA: Science & Behavior Books.

Schneider, K. (2015) 'An existential-integrative approach to experiential liberation', in K. J. Schneider, J. F. Pierson and J. F. T. Bugental (eds) *The handbook of humanistic psychology: theory, research and practice* (2nd edn), London: Sage.

Schneider, K. J. and Krug, O. T. (2010) *Existential-humanistic therapy*, Washington, DC: APA.

Schneider, K. J., Pierson, J. F. and Bugental, J. F. T. (eds)(2015) *The handbook of humanistic psychology* (2nd edn), London: Sage.

Schuster, R. (1979) 'Empathy and mindfulness', *Journal of Humanistic Psychology*, 19(1), 72–77.

Schutz, W. C. (1971) *Here comes everybody*, New York: Harper & Row.

Schutz, W. C. (1983) *Professional manual for Schutz Measures*, Palo Alto, CA: Consulting Psychologists Press.

Schutz, W. (1988) *Profound simplicity* (3rd edn), Muir Beach, CA: WSA.

Segal, H. (1979) *Klein*, London: Fontana.

Seidenberg, R. (1974) 'The trauma of eventlessness', in J. B. Miller (ed.) *Psychoanalysis and women*, Harmondsworth: Penguin.

Self & Society (2014) Spring 2014 Special Issue on Maurice Merleau-Ponty, *Self & Society*, 41(3).

Shaffer, J. and Galinsky, M. D. (1989) *Models of group therapy* (2nd edn), Englewood Cliffs, NJ: Prentice Hall.

Shapiro, D. A. and Shapiro, D. (1982) 'Meta-analysis of comparative therapy outcome studies: a replication and refinement', *Psychological Bulletin*, 92(3), 581–604.

Shapiro, S. B. (1976) *The selves inside you*, Berkeley, CA: Explorations Institute.

Shapiro, S. B. (1997) 'The UCSB confluent education program: its essence and demise', *Journal of Humanistic Psychology*, 37(3), 80–105.

Shohet, R. (1991) 'Peer group accreditation of psychotherapists', *Self & Society*, 19(22), 31–2.

Shohet, R. (2011) *Supervision as transformation: a passion for learning*, London: Jessica Kingsley.

Shorr, J. E. (1972) *Psycho-imagination therapy*, New York: Intercontinental Medical Corporation.

Shotter, J. (1999) 'Life inside dialogically structured mentalities: Bakhtin's and Voloshinov's account of our mental activities as out in the world between us', in J. Rowan and M. Cooper (eds) *The plural self: multiplicity in everyday life*, London: Sage.

Sliker, G. (1992) *Multiple mind*, Boston, MA: Shambhala.

Smail, D. (1996) 'Psychotherapy and tragedy', *BPS Psychotherapy Section Newsletter* No. 20.

Smith, E. W. L., Clance, P. R. and Imes, S. (1998) *Touch in psychotherapy: theory, research and practice*, New York: The Guilford Press.

Smith, H. (2000) *Cleansing the doors of perception: the religious significance of entheogenic plants and chemicals*, New York: Tarcher.

Smith, P. B. (1973) *Groups within organizations*, London: Harper & Row.

Snell, R. (2013) *Uncertainties, mysteries, doubts: romanticism and the analytic attitude*, Hove: Routledge.

Southgate, J. and Randall, R. (1989) *The barefoot psychoanalyst* (3rd edn), Loughton: The Gale Centre.

Sparks, E. (2009) 'Learning to be authentic with clients', in A. Bloomgarten and R. B. Mennuti (eds) *Psychotherapist revealed: therapists speak about self-disclosure in psychotherapy*, Hove: Routledge.

Sperry, L. (2007) *The ethical and professional practice of counselling and psychotherapy*, Boston, MA: Allyn & Bacon.

Sperry, L. (2012) *Spirituality in clinical practice: theory and practice of spiritually oriented psychotherapy* (2nd edn), Hove: Routledge.

Spinelli, E. (1989) *The interpreted world*, London: Sage.

Spinelli, E. (2015) *Practising existential therapy: the relational world* (2nd edn), London: Sage.

Staemmler, F-M. (1997) 'Towards a theory of regressive processes in Gestalt therapy', *The Gestalt Journal*, 20(1), 49–120.

Starhawk (1982) *Dreaming the dark: magic, sex and politics*, Boston, MA: Beacon Press.

Starhawk (1989) *The spiral dance*, New York: Harper & Row.

Stein, H., Koontz, A. D., Fonagy, P., Allen, J. G., Fultz, J., Brethour, J. R., Allen, D. and Evans, R. B. (2002) 'Adult attachment: what are the underlying dimensions?', *Psychology and Psychotherapy: Theory, Research and Practice*, 75(1), 77–91.

Stevens, B. (1975) 'Body work', in J. O. Stevens (ed.) *Gestalt is*, Moab, UT: Real People Press.

Stevens, B. and Rogers, C. R. (eds)(1967) *Person to person*, Moab, UT: Real People Press.

Stevens, J. O. (1971) *Awareness: exploring, experimenting, experiencing*, Moab, UT: Real People Press.

Stiles, W. B., Osatuke, K., Glick, M. J. and Mackay, H. C. (2004) 'Encounters between internal voices generate emotion: an elaboration of the assimilation model', in H. J. M. Hermans and G. Dimaggio (eds) *The dialogical self in psychotherapy*, Hove: Brunner-Routledge.

Stone, H. and Winkelman, S. (1985) *Embracing our selves*, Marina del Ray, CA: Devorss & Co.

Sullivan, B. S. (1989) *Psychotherapy grounded in the feminine principle*, Wilmette, IL: Chiron.

Sullivan, C., Grant, M. Q. and Grant, J. D. (1957) 'The development of interpersonal maturity', *Psychiatry*, 20(4), 373–85.

Tart, C. (1986) *Waking up: overcoming the obstacles to human potential*, Boston, MA: New Science Library.

Temerlin, M. K. (1975) 'Suggestion effects in psychiatric diagnosis', in T. Scheff (ed.) *Labelling madness*, Englewood Cliffs, NJ: Prentice Hall.

Thera, N. (1972) *The power of mindfulness*, San Francisco, CA: Unity Press.

Tompkins, P. and Lawley, J. (1997) *Principles of Grovian Metaphor Therapy*, London: The Developing Company.

Torbert, W. (1972) *Learning from experience: toward consciousness*, New York: Columbia University Press.

Treleaven, L. (1994) 'Making a space: a collaborative inquiry with women as staff development', in P. Reason (ed.) *Participation in human inquity*, London: Sage.

Truax, C. B. and Carkhuff, R. R. (1967) *Toward effective counselling and psychotherapy*, Chicago, IL: Aldine.

Truax, C. B. and Mitchell, K. M. (1971) 'Research in certain therapist interpersonal skills in relation to process and outcome', in S. L. Garfield and A. E. Bergin (eds) *Handbook of psychotherapy and behavior change*, New York: John Wiley & Sons.

Turner, R. (ed.)(1974) *Ethnomethodology: selected readings*, Harmondsworth: Penguin.

Ullman, C. (2014) 'Commentary on relational psychoanalysis in Europe', in D. Loewenthal and A. Samuels (eds) *Relational psychotherapy, psychoanalysis and counselling: appraisals and reappraisals*, Hove: Routledge.

van Deurzen-Smith, E. (1997) *Everyday mysteries: existential dimensions of psychotherapy*, London: Routledge.

van Rijn, B. (2014) *Assessment and case formulation in counselling and psychotherapy*, London: Sage.

Varela, F. (1997) 'The specious present: a neurophenomenology of time consciousness', in J. Petitot, F. J. Varela, J-M. Roy and B. Pachoud (eds) *Naturalizing phenomenology: issues in contemporary phenomenology and cognitive science*, Stanford, CA: Stanford University Press.

Verny, T. (1982) *The secret life of the unborn child*, London: Sphere.

Voloshinov, V. N. (1986) *Marxism and the philosophy of language*, Cambridge, MA: Harvard University Press.

Wade, J. (1996) *Changes of mind: a holonomic theory of the evolution of consciousness*, Albany, NY: SUNY Press.

Walkenstein, E. (1975) *Shrunk to fit*, London: Coventure.

Walsch, N. D. (1997) *Conversations with God, Book 1: an uncommon dialogue*, London: Hodder & Stoughton.

Walsh, R. and Vaughan, F. (eds)(1993) *Paths beyond ego*, Los Angeles, CA: Tarcher.

Wampold, B. E. (2001) *The great psychotherapy debate: models, methods and findings*, Mahwah, NJ: Lawrence Erlbaum.

Watkins, J. G. (1978) *The therapeutic self*, New York: Human Sciences Press.

Watkins, M. (1986) *Invisible guests*, Hillsdale, NJ: The Analytic Press.

Watson, J. C. and Bohart, A. C. (2015) 'Humanistic-experiential therapies in the era of managed care', in K. J. Schneider, J. F. Pierson and J. F. T. Bugental (eds) *The handbook of humanistic psychology* (2nd edn), London: Sage.

Watson, J. C., Greenberg, L. S. and Lietaer, G. (1998) 'The experiential paradigm unfolding: relationship and experiencing in therapy', in L. S. Greenberg, J. C. Watson and G. Lietaer (eds) *Handbook of experiential psychotherapy*, New York: The Guilford Press.

Weld, V. (2012) *A practical guide to transformative supervision for the helping professions*, London: Jessica Kingsley.

Wessler, R. L. and Ellis, A. (1980) 'Supervision in rational-emotive therapy', in A. K. Hess (ed.) *Psychotherapy supervision*, New York: John Wiley & Sons.

West, W. (1994) 'Post-Reichian therapy', in D. Jones (ed.) *Innovative therapy: a handbook*, Buckingham: Open University Press.

Wheelis, A. (1975) *How people change*, London: Harper.

Wilber, K. (1980) *The Atman Project: a transpersonal view of human development*, Wheaton, IL: The Theosophical Publishing House.

Wilber, K. (1981) *No boundary*, London: Routledge.

Wilber, K. (1991) *Grace and grit: spirituality and healing in the life and death of Treya Killam Wilber*, Boston, MA: Shambhala.

Wilber, K. (2000) *Integral psychology*, Boston, MA: Shambhala.

Wilber, K., Engler, J. and Brown, D. P. (eds)(1986) *Transformations of consciousness: conventional and contemplative perspectives on development*, Boston, MA: New Science Library.

Wilson, J. E. (1996) *Time-conscious psychological therapy*, London: Routledge.

Winnicott, D. W. (1965) *The maturational processes and the facilitating environment*, London: Hogarth Press.

Winnicott, D. W. (1975) *Through paediatrics to psychoanalysis*, London: Hogarth Press.

Wolberg, L. R. (1977) *The technique of psychotherapy* (3rd edn)(Vol. 1), New York: Grune & Stratton.

Woolger, R. (1990) *Other lives, other selves*, Wellingborough: Crucible.

Wosket, V. (2009) 'Relational ethics in supervision', in L. Gabriel and R. Casemore (eds) *Relational ethics in practice: narratives from counselling and psychotherapy*, Hove: Routledge.

Wyckoff, H. (1975) 'Problem-solving groups for women', in C. Steiner, H. Wyckoff, D. Golstine, P. Lariviere, R. Schwebel, J. Marcus and Members of the Radical Psychiatry Center (eds) *Readings in radical psychiatry*, New York: Grove Press.

Yalom, I. (1980) *Existential psychotherapy*, New York: Basic Books.

Young, C. (1990) '1992 and all that', *Self & Society*, 18(1), 4–9.

Young, J. E., Klosko, J. S. and Weishaar, M. E. (2003) *Schema therapy: a practitioner's guide*, New York: The Guilford Press.

Zandvoort, A. (2012) 'Living and laughing in the shadow of death: complicated grief, trauma and resilience', *The British Journal of Psychotherapy Integration*, 9(2), 33–44.

Author index

Subject index